A Match Made in Heaven

Volume Two

A Match Made in

HEAVEN

Volume Two

More Inspirational

Love Stories

SUSAN WALES & ANN PLATZ

Multnomah Publishers® *Sisters, Oregon*

This is a work of fiction. The characters, incidents, and dialogues are products of the authors' imaginations and are not to be construed as real.
Any resemblance to actual events or persons, living or dead, is entirely coincidental.

A MATCH MADE IN HEAVEN, VOLUME II
published by Multnomah Publishers, Inc.
© 1999 by Susan Huey-Wales and Ann Williams-Platz
International Standard Book Number: 1-57673-658-X

Cover photograph by Victoria Yee/Tony Stone Images
Cover design by Kirk DouPonce

Scripture quotations are from:
The Holy Bible, New International Version
© 1973, 1984 by International Bible Society,
used by permission of Zondervan Publishing House

Also quoted:
The Holy Bible, King James Version (KJV)

Multnomah is a trademark of Multnomah Publishers, Inc.,
and is registered in the U.S. Patent and Trademark Office.
The colophon is a trademark of Multnomah Publishers, Inc.

Printed in the United States of America

For information:
MULTNOMAH PUBLISHERS, INC.•P.O. BOX 1720•SISTERS, OR 97759

Library of Congress Cataloging-in-Publication Data:
Match made in heaven–volume two. / [compiled] by Ann Platz and Susan Wales.
   p. cm.
   ISBN 1-57673-658-X (alk. paper)
   1. Love—Religious aspects—Christianity. 2. Love—Anecdotes.
   3. Marriage—Religious aspects—Christianity. 4. Marriage—Anecdotes.
   I. Platz, Ann.   II. Wales, Susan.
   BV4639.M334 1999
   242'.644—dc21   98-46112
                                    CIP

99 00 01 02 03 04 05 — 10 9 8 7 6 5 4 3 2 1 0

To the joys of our lives, the wind beneath our sails, and the colors in our rainbows, we lovingly dedicate this book to you, our darling daughters,

MEGAN CHRANE (SUSAN),

COURTNEY NORTON (ANN),

AND MARGO CLOER (ANN)

To Megan and Margo
we pray that God will bring you a Match Made in Heaven.
To Courtney, we thank God for your Match Made in Heaven,
Dr. Michael Norton.
We thank you for embracing our beloved husbands,
Ken Wales and John Platz, as your stepfathers,
with the joys, and sometimes tears, of having daughters.

CONTENTS

With This Ring

I Thee Wed

To Have and to Hold

From This Day Forward

To Love, Honor, and Cherish

For Better, for Worse

ACKNOWLEDGMENTS
To love what you do and feel that it matters—
how could anything be more fun?
KATHARINE GRAHAM

To Don Jacobson and our Multnomah family,
thank you for your monumental efforts and for believing in us!
A special thank-you to our editor Tracy Sumner, for his guidance.
To Penny Whipps, Cliff Boersma, Ken Ruettgers, Kirk DouPonce,
Jennifer and Steven Curley, Judith St. Pierre, Jeff Gerke,
Heather Kopp, and Holly Halverson, thank you.

Ken Wales and John Platz for your love, patience,
and support throughout this project.
To Dorothy Altman and Fran Beaver,
thank you from Ann Platz. You are great!
To Pam Zelek, thank you from Susan Wales.

For the gift of storytelling:
Susan's parents,
Mr. and Mrs. Arthur J. Huey Jr.,
and Ann's parents,
Mrs. Margaret Williams and
the late Senator Marshall Williams.

Dear Readers, Family, and Friends:

What joy God has blessed us with by entrusting this collection of inspirational love stories to present to you! Do you believe that marriages are made in heaven? We do, wholeheartedly! As the pages of this book unfold you will see how God miraculously reaches down into our lives when we allow him to direct us. He will not only make your paths straight, but he will lead you to the road of love and romance. Along the way we can guarantee that you will encounter storms, rocky roads, and thorns, but we can promise you that the trip will make your journey worthwhile as you encounter the joys along the way to where only God can take you.

As we've walked through the joys and sorrows of our own marriages; the pain, rejection, and loss of divorce; and, at last, discovering the blessing of finding love again; we have not been alone. The difficulties of life have taught us to trust God with all our hearts and not to lean on our own understanding. He has been with us every step along the way in both our joy and in our pain. It was through stories much like these in our book *A Match Made In Heaven, Volume II,* that God gave us encouragement, instruction, comfort, laughter, and hope.

We present this book with our love to offer encouragement to single men and women everywhere who desire to have someone special with whom to share their lives. God is waiting for you to relinquish your hopes, dreams, and desires to him so he can bring his best to you.

We present this book with joy to invite married couples to take their own walk down memory lane to rekindle the love, sense of humor, and romance in your marriage as the stories in this book remind you of those glorious days when you first fell in love.

We present this book with comfort to offer hope for those men and women who have loved and lost as a gentle reminder that one day you will meet again for all eternity.

We present this book to our husbands, Ken and John...*if we never met again in our lives I should feel that somehow the whole adventure of existence was justified by my having met you* (Lewis Mumford).

And most of all we thank the lovers in our book who have shared their hearts and their love with us and our readers. And once again, we thank God for a friendship that endures while celebrating the delights and tribulations of birthing yet another book of love!

When love finds you, send us the miracle of your love story to share with others so that we can continue to spread God's love, joy, hope, and comfort to the hearts that need it the most.

The minute I heard my first love story
I started looking for you,
not knowing how blind that was.
Lovers don't finally meet somewhere.
They're in each other all along.

RUMI

Divine Appointment

The Lord God said,
"It is not good for man to be alone.
I will make a helper suitable for him."

GENESIS 2:18

IMAGINE WHAT IT MUST HAVE BEEN LIKE FOR ADAM IN THE GARDEN OF EDEN.

THERE WAS ADAM, THE FIRST HUMAN, AS GOD BROUGHT THE BEASTS AND BIRDS IN A PARADE BEFORE HIM. ADAM GAVE THEM NAMES AND MARVELED AT THE ENDLESS VARIETY OF CREATURES GOD HAD MADE. BUT AT THE END OF THAT DAY ADAM MUST HAVE BEEN TIRED AND LONELY. HE WATCHED THE LION SAUNTER OFF TO ITS CAVE WITH HIS LIONESS. THE WHITE DOVE PERCHED IN AN OLIVE TREE WITH ITS MATE. THE STALLION THUNDERED ACROSS THE MEADOW WITH A MARE.

FOR ADAM, NO SUITABLE HELPER WAS FOUND (GENESIS 2:20).

PERHAPS ADAM LOOKED AROUND, FEELING THAT SOMETHING WAS MISSING BUT NOT KNOWING WHAT IT WAS. BEFORE DRIFTING OFF TO AN EXHAUSTED SLEEP, HE MAY HAVE DARED TO ASK GOD, "HAVEN'T YOU FORGOTTEN SOMETHING?"

WAS GOD WAITING FOR ADAM TO EXPERIENCE A SENSE OF SUBTLE LONGING BEFORE HE FINISHED HIS WORK? WE DON'T KNOW, BUT WE DO KNOW GOD WAS NOT FINISHED YET. IN THAT DEEP AND QUIET NIGHT, GOD CREATED WOMAN FOR MAN. SHE WAS EVERYTHING ADAM NEEDED, AND WOULD BECOME HIS INSPIRATION.

AT DAWN, AS ADAM AWOKE TO THE SLEEPING FORM BESIDE HIM, SO DIFFERENT YET THE SAME, WHAT THOUGHTS MUST HAVE RACED THROUGH HIS MIND? HOW SURPRISED HE MUST HAVE BEEN. HOW SWEET THE ENCOUNTER. BUT IT WOULD TAKE A LIFETIME TO DISCOVER ALL THE WAYS WOMAN WAS THE COMPLETION OF GOD'S DIVINE DESIGN. "THEREFORE A MAN SHALL...BE JOINED TO HIS WIFE" (GENESIS 2:24).

AND GOD HAS BEEN DESIGNING SURPRISE ENCOUNTERS EVER SINCE.

THE MAN IN CHARGE

"For I know the plans I have for you,"
declares the Lord.
"Plans to prosper you, and not to harm you,
plans to give you a hope and a future."
JEREMIAH 29:11

s a young man I had big plans for my life. The war was raging
in Europe, and, wanting to serve my country, I enlisted in the
Navy Air Corp. As a young cadet, with dreams of flying military aircraft,
I found the competition among the men was fierce. When the grades were
posted, I was relieved to discover that I had made a high B, until a men-
toring officer pulled me aside and gave me a dose of reality.

"Ray, you're a good soldier," he said, "but there's so much competition in the navy that you most likely won't make the cut with a B." Sensing
my disappointment, the officer suggested, "Why don't you go back home
and apply for Army Air Corp? You'd make an excellent pilot, and there's
not as much competition in that branch. They'll be lucky to get you."

Those words were music to my ears. With renewed hope, I headed
back home. Fortunately, I knew the lady who ran the draft board in my
hometown of Columbus, Ohio. After I explained my situation, she
promised me that she would put a hold on my papers until the next crop
of recruits was admitted into the Army Air Corp. It would only delay my
plans for a matter of weeks. I was flying high on hope.

I was shocked a few days later when I went to the mailbox and found
the letter with the news: I was about to be drafted into the army. My entry

into the Army Air Corp was only days away. *How could this have happened?* I wondered. I figured a trip down to the draft board was all I needed to straighten this mess out. I found out that while my friend at the draft board was away on vacation another woman in the office had processed my papers. Now there was nothing that could be done. I was drafted.

My hopes and dreams of becoming a pilot were permanently dashed when I was assigned to the Infantry Division of the United States Army. "Why, Lord?" I questioned. Despair flooded my being. And yet I was strengthened knowing that God had a plan for me. Maybe it wasn't the plan I had in mind, but I knew without a doubt that I had to trust him. My family rallied around me lending their support and prayers.

After basic training, I was shipped off to Europe just after D-Day. I arrived on French soil and was immediately placed on the front lines, where we faced combat every day. Through all that, my faith in God sustained me. I prayed often and kept the New Testament the Army had issued me in my pocket, close to my heart, often seeking it for words of comfort and faith.

My days on the front line were filled with the horrors of war. Death was all around me. Each time I watched the American planes overhead from my foxhole, my heart broke a little more. I wondered if God realized I was supposed to be up there and not down here on the front line. *Did God forget me?* I wondered.

Our division was assigned to General Patton and we fought through Normandy and the Saint Lo breakthrough. During the siege, my hands were wounded with shrapnel and I was taken away to have them bandaged. This injury probably saved my life, because when I returned to the outfit, I was horrified to discover that only three men—including me—were left in my platoon.

From Saint Lo we marched into Paris and liberated the city. It was obvious to me that God had intervened to spare my life. I was then assigned to another platoon. Next we headed for the Hurtegn Forest in Germany. We dug foxholes and put covers over them because artillery shells were hitting the treetops and crashing down on us. Again, as I looked up at the planes fighting in the sky above me, I cried out, "Lord, don't you know that I'm supposed to be up there and not down here? Why didn't you give me my dream of flying?"

I went on out to check on my men, when suddenly, an 80 shell, a weapon used by the Germans, came close and barreled me over. I felt a sting. The shrapnel had gone through the front of my right thigh. I was treated in the field by my platoon sergeant. As he walked me back to the aid station, I had to step over the dead soldiers lying in the forest. I was thankful to be alive.

The medics transported me to a hospital in Belgium for surgery, but before I could undergo the procedure, the hospital was bombed. My fate again was suddenly changed when all the patients had to be transported to Paris, where we were scheduled on a flight to England. When we arrived in Paris, a thick, heavy fog hung over the airport and our plane couldn't take off.

Once again, I found out how God had intervened. While we waited for a train to the hospital in Cherbourg, France, I saw one of the fellows from my platoon and asked, "How did we do on our attack of the village?"

"There's nobody left but you and me, Sarge," he told me.

Our entire platoon was wiped out. I was awestruck that God had spared me.

The first morning I awoke in the Cherbourg hospital, an attractive American Red Cross nurse with a beautiful smile and a pen and paper in her hand greeted me with a smile. I rubbed my eyes, wondering if she was a figment of my imagination. But then she spoke.

"Write to your wife," she instructed me, "and tell her you're alive and safe and sound in a hospital in France."

"I don't have a wife," I confessed.

"Well, write to your girlfriend, then," she prodded.

There was a girl back home, but I quickly forgot her as I gazed into the beautiful hazel eyes of the nurse before me. I was sure I wasn't the first soldier to look wistfully into those eyes, but I wanted to be the last. The nurse, whose name I learned was Betty, was very professional and a bit standoffish. But she was simply obeying orders. All the nurses had been warned not to fraternize with enlisted men. Their major had sternly warned them, "You'll be sent to the hospital in the Philippines." While the pretty nurse's mannerisms said no, her eyes told me that she had an interest in me. I was not about to give up easily.

Betty and I became better acquainted each day as she nursed me back to health. One day when she appeared she noticed that I was reading my New Testament. We were both delighted to discover that we shared the Christian faith, and we began talking about the Lord. I relayed to her how God had miraculously spared me time and time again in the battlefield. Our Christian fellowship strengthened our relationship, and I then knew without a doubt that God had orchestrated all those circumstances to bring me to this place to meet this special woman.

The hospital at Cherbourg was only allowed to keep a patient for thirty days, and as I watched the pages on the calendar change each day, I knew I had to work quickly to win the pretty nurse's heart. I was being sent to England to recuperate and would be sent back to battle as soon as I regained my strength.

When the time came for me to go to Oxford to recuperate, I was saddened to tell Betty good-bye. I presented her with a gold wedding band that I had found on the battlefield, and she promised to wear it around her neck on a dog tag chain in remembrance of me. I managed to get a promise from her that she would write to me in Oxford.

Our letters crossed the English Channel with speed and regularity. We were becoming better acquainted through the mail. With each letter we were falling more and more deeply in love.

I knew what I felt for this woman, and I knew it was real. But it was going to take a miracle of God to keep us together.

When I recovered from my injury, I was sent back into the battlefield in Germany. One night when we were advancing, I became disoriented and separated from my group. Because of the shadows in the German forest, I thought the trees were my men. I suddenly found myself in a small German village. Praying all the while that God would protect me, I finally made my way to a home of a farmer about three miles behind our line. I'll never forget the look on his face when an American soldier appeared at his door. In broken German I tried to explain to the farmer and his terrified family that I was there in peace, that I was lost and exhausted and needed a place to sleep. Eventually, the farmer led me to his barn where I prayed for a safe night of sleep. It was not to be.

I was later awakened by a group of German soldiers the farmer had led to me. I was terrified as I cradled my New Testament close to my heart. *There will be no more letters to Betty now*, I thought.

The Germans didn't know quite what to do with me, so I traveled with them. All the time I was with them, American forces were attacking them—and me—from all sides. *How ironic!* I thought. *I'll be killed by my own men.* When we reached the POW camp in Munich, they handed me over as an escaped prisoner. When I embraced the other prisoners, both French and American, they took care of some minor wounds I had incurred along the way. That night, the camp was bombed so we had to be transported to the dreaded Stalag VII A in Munich.

I was aware that Munich was one of the targets that American forces had planned to bomb, so I expressed some concern for our lives.

"What are you worried about?" a fellow prisoner asked. "You're listed as an escaped prisoner. You're scheduled to be shot at dawn with a group of us."

"Were these the plans you had for me all along, Lord?" I prayed. "Is this how my life is going to end?"

With the stark realization that I was about to meet my Maker, my thoughts traveled to home, family, and Betty, the pretty nurse who, unbeknownst to her, I'd planned to make my wife. I knew I would never see her again. I spent the night on my knees praying and seeking solace from my battered New Testament. I prayed that God would somehow intervene in this hopeless situation. The men surrounding me were encouraged to have a Christian among them. I was their *ray* of hope.

Back in France, Betty had been devastated when one of her letters to me was returned marked "killed in action." At that moment she realized just how much she loved me. She was numb with grief as she went through the motions of caring for her patients. The news of losing me was more than she could bear.

But Betty's spirits soared when the next morning another letter arrived marked "missing in action." Hope flooded her as she prayed every moment for my safety. She was very much in love with me…as I was with her.

Perhaps it was Betty's prayers that night, but the Americans chose on the eve of my death watch to bomb Munich. Amid the rubble and confusion I was spared, and in a matter of days American soldiers marching through Munich liberated us. The war was over.

I was sent to France to recover and then sent home. When I returned home my mother received a letter from Betty asking if she had heard from me. I answered the letter myself but somehow it had the wrong APO (post office) box. But as Betty was leaving for home, someone ran up to her and handed her my letter just as she boarded the ship. She has since said she was surprised that I hadn't heard her scream all the way to America.

Betty and I were reunited back in the States, where we finished out our duties after brief furloughs. We finally rendezvoused in New Orleans, where I was stationed. That is where we became man and wife.

The bride didn't wear a white gown but her uniform. I also wore mine. We were proud to wear our military dress, and it was also our tribute to the armed forces, which God used to bring us together.

As I look back over my wartime service, I realize that God was in charge all along. Without God's divine appointment, my path would never have crossed with Betty's. If I hadn't been wounded, I would have never met her.

God had led me into the battles through the long and winding path that led me to the woman he had for me. My disappointments were transformed into joy through these difficult circumstances. I am still in awe at how God had his hand on me and carried out his plans for my life through some bitter disappointments.

He had a plan all along. Little did I realize when I was so devastated over not realizing my dream of flying that God had something better in store for me.

Since the day I left the service, the Lord has been in charge of my life. I have learned to remember that when the going gets rough during the courses of our lives, he still has a plan.

He is the man in charge!

BETTY AND RAY WHIPPS, AS TOLD TO SUSAN WALES

THE FEAST OF ST. STEPHEN

✍

I live with those who love me
whose hearts are kind and true

GEORGE LINNAEUS BANKS

hat do you want for Christmas?" my mother asked. So many answers swelled in my throat, but none of those were possible.

With a lopsided smile, I replied, "I'd really like a man on my Christmas tree."

In July of that year, my husband had drowned while lobster fishing off our small village in a remote corner of Maine. A young fisherman on his way home had discovered the wreckage of the boat, and divers had searched for three days before finding my husband's body.

My husband had just finished college and I had been teaching for three years. We were anticipating the day we would move from the parsonage we rented from the church to a home of our own. Our dream was to buy and restore an old cape cod house and raise children in the nurturing intimacy of small-town life. Now at twenty-five, I felt cheated of the future we had planned. My husband's self-confidence and ambition had made him the decision maker in our marriage. Alone, I felt adrift on an ocean of uncertainty.

The house we rented had an old piano, and I decided that music lessons would take me outside myself and demand my total concentration.

Though I had no ear for music and an appalling lack of rhythm, I doggedly practiced scales and simple songs. By Christmas I could labor through my favorite carol, "Good King Wenceslas." I liked the medieval imagery of Wenceslas the Holy looking out upon the Feast of Stephen. The tune replayed itself in my head as I tied ribbons, baked cookies, and tried not to examine how I felt about the approaching holiday.

I spent Christmas Day at my parents' house. Their attempts to give me a generous Christmas must have stretched their meager resources. Among their gifts to me was a cloth ornament my mother had stitched— a little white doughboy wearing a chef's hat and a smile. It appeared that my wish for a man on my Christmas tree had been answered.

On December 26, aching to escape the post-holiday slump, I settled into my easy chair for a nap. When I heard a knock at the door, I did not feel at all hospitable. *Probably the chairman of the parsonage committee, here to take more measurements for the furnace,* I thought. "Come in," I called out.

The chairman's son stood in the doorway with a package in his hand. He was about my age, but I had seldom had occasion to speak with him. I knew that he was a lobster fisherman and that his passion was baseball. My grandfather, an avid baseball fan, often praised this young man's pitching ability. In a fleeting flashback to the previous summer, I saw him drive past my house, wearing his red and white uniform and a smile on his face after winning his game. At that time I had thought idly, *I wonder what he lives for besides baseball?* He never dated, and I couldn't imagine a life of just baseball and lobstering.

"I've brought you some scallops," he said, while I stared at him as if he were a genie who had materialized from a bottle. My cousin was visiting me, and since her father and his mother were cousins, I assumed that he was bringing the scallops to her. He continued to stand. I continued to stare. At last it occurred to me that he expected me to ask him in. I croaked a feeble invitation, offered him some Christmas cookies, and strained to make my knowledge of baseball last for a twenty-minute conversation. When the door finally closed behind him, I thought I had figured out the reason for his visit. Everyone in our small town had been particularly thoughtful to me, and no doubt his family had dispatched him on this kind errand.

The following evening, he phoned to tell my cousin and me that he had a surprise for us, and he soon arrived with a pail of lobsters. This time the conversation was easier, and we talked of our love for our town and its way of life, our extended families, and the pristine beauty of our harbor.

We saw each other every day for two weeks, then he said, "I would ask you to marry me if I thought you were ready."

Offhandedly, I replied, "If I thought I was ready, I would say yes."

That August, the church next door to the parsonage overflowing with our extended families, we began a marriage that is now in its twenty-fifth year.

Every Christmas the doughboy occupies a place of honor on the tree, and on the day after Christmas, our thoughts turn to our first awkward visit. We later discovered that, according to the church calendar, December 26 marks the Feast of St. Stephen, and we remark on the fact that he shares his name with the feast day. We seldom dwell on the fact that Stephen was the fisherman who discovered the wreckage of my first husband's boat some twenty-seven years ago.

Stephen and I built a traditional Cape overlooking the harbor. There we raised two children who grew up surrounded by loving aunts, uncles, cousins, great-aunts, great-uncles, and grandparents.

The life that I had thought lost to me returned with an abundance I never could have imagined.

PAULINE CATES

MOM'S LAST LAUGH

Oh happy living things! no tongue
Their beauty might declare:
A spring of love gushed from my heart,
And I blessed them unaware.

SAMUEL TAYLOR COLERIDGE

Consumed by my loss, I didn't notice the hardness of the pew where I sat. I was at the funeral of my dearest friend—my mother. She finally had lost her long battle with cancer. The hurt was so intense, I found it heard to breathe at times.

Always supportive, Mother clapped loudest at my school plays, held a box of tissues while listening to my first heartbreak, comforted me at my father's death, encouraged me in college, and prayed for me my entire life.

When Mother's illness was diagnosed, my sister had a new baby and my brother had recently married his childhood sweetheart, so it fell to me, the twenty-seven-year-old middle child without entanglements, to take care of her. I counted it an honor.

"What now, Lord?" I asked, sitting in church. My life stretched out before me as an empty abyss.

My brother sat stoically with his face toward the cross while clutching his wife's hand. My sister sat slumped against her husband's shoulder, his arms around her as she cradled their child. All so deeply grieving, no one noticed I sat alone.

My place had been with our mother, preparing her meals, helping her walk, taking her to the doctor, seeing to her medication, reading the Bible together. Now she was with the Lord.

My work was finished, and I was alone.

I heard a door open and slam shut at the back of the church. Quick footsteps hurried along the carpeted floor. An exasperated young man looked around briefly and then sat next to me. He folded his hands and placed them on his lap. His eyes were brimming with tears. He began to sniffle.

"I'm late," he explained, though no explanation was necessary.

After several eulogies, he leaned over and commented, "Why do they keep calling Mary by the name of 'Margaret'?"

"Because that was her name, Margaret. Never Mary. No one called her 'Mary,'" I whispered. I wondered why this person couldn't have sat on the other side of the church. He interrupted my grieving with his tears and fidgeting. Who was this stranger anyway?

"No, that isn't correct," he insisted, as several people glanced over at our whispering, "Her name is Mary, Mary Peters."

"That isn't who this is."

"Isn't this the Lutheran church?"

"No, the Lutheran church is across the street."

"Oh."

"I believe you're at the wrong funeral, sir."

The solemnness of the occasion mixed with the realization of the man's mistake bubbled up inside me and came out as laughter. I cupped my hands over my face, hoping it would be interpreted as sobs.

The creaking pew gave me away. Sharp looks from other mourners only made the situation seem more hilarious. I peeked at the bewildered, misguided man seated beside me. He was laughing, too, as he glanced around, deciding it was too late for an uneventful exit. I imagined Mother laughing.

At the final amen, we darted out a door and into the parking lot.

"I do believe we'll be the talk of the town," he smiled. He said his name was Rick and since he had missed his aunt's funeral, asked me out for a cup of coffee.

That afternoon began a lifelong journey for me with this man who attended the wrong funeral, but was in the right place. A year after our meeting, we were married at a country church where he was the assistant pastor. This time we both arrived at the same church, right on time.

In my time of sorrow, God gave me laughter. In place of loneliness, God gave me love. This past June we celebrated our twenty-second wedding anniversary.

Whenever anyone asks us how we met, Rick tells them, "Her mother and my Aunt Mary introduced us, and it's truly a match made in heaven."

ROBIN LEE SHOPE

Marriage is the gold ring in
a chain whose beginning is a
glance and whose ending is eternity.
KAHLIL GIBRAN

Reprinted by permission of Robin Lee Shope.

AN ARRANGED MARRIAGE

It may be those who do most, dream most.
STEPHEN LEACOCK

hen people ask me how Roger and I got together, I tell them that ours is an arranged marriage. I say it's an arranged marriage because I know beyond any doubt that God arranged it.

Roger didn't catch my eye, at least not at first. We attended the same church and the same singles class. He remembers meeting me through a mutual friend, but my earliest recollection meeting him was at a singles class party at my sister's apartment. It wasn't a moment that stood out in my mind, even to this day.

Roger was sitting away from the action at the party, looking as if he felt out of place. Since we were at my sister's home, I felt as though I should help her out with hosting and making people feel at home. I approached Roger and tried to make him feel welcome. We chatted for a while, and he seemed like a nice guy. But I felt no interest in him.

Roger, on the other hand, knew from our first meeting that he was interested in a romantic relationship with me.

I met Roger during my first year of teaching, a year in which nothing seemed to go right for me. I was having a rough time with my new job, and it didn't look like things were going to turn around for me anytime soon. It turns out that the struggles I was enduring gave Roger just the "in" he needed to get to know me better.

Roger had volunteered to call and encourage the members of the singles class each Monday, and he always saved his last call for me. He must have sensed that I needed a shoulder to cry on for as the conversation slowed each week he would ask the question: "So how is work?" That would usually prolong the conversation another thirty minutes. It was good to have someone to talk to about my troubles.

I enjoyed talking to Roger and I appreciated his concern over how I was doing. But we didn't communicate much except over the phone. Obviously, if we were going to get together, God was going to have to arrange some help for us. He did just that.

Not long after we met, Roger decided to volunteer to help Wallace, the maintenance man at our church, on Saturday mornings. It just so happened that I lived across the street from the church and would often walk over to talk to Wallace. And, as long as I was there, I would visit with Roger.

One day, after one of my visits, Roger asked Wallace if he knew me. Wallace replied that he reckoned he knew me—pretty well, in fact. You see, Wallace is my father, and, with an intuition only a father could have, he could tell that Roger liked me... *really* liked me. Daddy approved of Roger's feelings for me too, and not only did he approve, he encouraged me to come visit him and Roger whenever I had the chance. Roger looked forward to the visits, and I began to enjoy being around him. I liked how easy it was to talk to him, and sometimes we would flirt with one another.

Roger was always careful not to seem pushy or overbearing, but I began to notice that things I said—even to other people—were getting his attention. I once remarked to a group of people that a pair of suspenders on any man makes him look more handsome. The very next week Roger showed up at church sporting a pair of suspenders! In fact, he made sure to take off his jacket when I was near so that I would notice them.

Roger was in the full-time Air National Guard and was often out of town for various trips. When Roger was away on one long trip—to Central America—our singles leader asked us to write him. I wrote once (I later learned that he read my letter many times a day) and was going to write again to ask him to bring me a rock from Central America for my rock collection. I never wrote the letter, but instead prayed that Roger would bring me a rock.

Roger, I would later learn, was making his own request of God.

Roger called me long distance from Central America. He claimed that he was homesick and that my number was the only one he could remember other than his brother's. I knew that wasn't true. This was when I became aware of Roger's feelings for me.

At Thanksgiving, after Roger had returned home from Central America, Daddy decided to invite Roger to dinner to thank him for his help at the church. My parents assured me that they were not setting me up, but I still called Roger that evening to see how he felt about spending the holiday in our home. He was not home, so I left a message.

I did not speak to Roger until his usual Monday call. This call was not like the others. There was something different in his voice. After the usual chitchat, I asked him what was wrong. He then told me of his feelings for me, feelings he had had from the time we met. Although he hadn't come close to proposing, I heard the word *marriage* going off in my head. I told Roger that I liked him, but that I wasn't sure how much or in what way, and that if he was going to buy wedding rings, the conversation was over.

Yet, by that Friday, I somehow knew that Roger would be my husband. Sometimes it's that way when God arranges something.

After that week, Roger and I started dating with the understanding that we knew that we would be married. On one of our first dates, Roger came over to my house to pick me up, and when he arrived, he said that he had something for me. It was a rock. No, not the kind fastened to a ring. It was the rock from Central America that I had prayed for Roger to bring.

Roger reached into his jacket and pulled out a heart-shaped rock. It was very unusual, particularly since there were so few rocks in that area. As strange as it may sound, Roger told me that the Holy Spirit had prompted him to pick up the rock and give it to someone special. He had been holding on to the rock for almost two months and now was giving it to me (I still keep that heart-shaped stone on the stand next to my bed).

Even though I knew Roger was the one for me, I was nervous about how fast this relationship was moving. Roger had already told me that he loved me, but I really did not know how to respond. After talking to a good friend, she explained that love is a decision, not a feeling. She said that Roger was waiting for me to make the commitment. I realized that the time had come for me to do just that.

I made plans and set up the perfect place to tell him I loved him. I asked him to drive us to the Marietta Square. I had planned for us to walk to a special spot I had picked out, but as we were getting out of the car, it began to rain—hard. I was crushed. My romantic moment was ruined. When we got back into the car, Roger saw the expression on my face and asked if I was okay. He asked several times and I finally told him that I had planned for everything to be perfect when I told him I loved him. He was quiet a moment, then smiled and said, "I want you to see something. I have kept this since we met."

He took a wrinkled, aged piece of paper from his wallet. He'd obviously carried it with him for quite a while. He handed it to me and I read these words:

God, please let me marry Melinda Ward.

At that moment, I didn't care about the rain. I didn't care that the moment hadn't unfolded according to my plans. This moment was far more wonderful than anything I could have imagined. This moment was perfect. We both knew that God had arranged this moment, and we knew that he had arranged for us to be together. Forever.

That's how it is with an arranged marriage—arranged by God, that is!

MELINDA ATKINSON

THE PUZZLE FITS

❧

Take away love and our earth is a tomb.
ROBERT BROWNING

ife is like a puzzle with thousands of tiny, fragmented pieces. Sometimes the pieces fit easily together; sometimes it takes time for the picture to make sense. So discovered Norma and Lon Day, whose puzzle pieces found an amazing fit.

Norma lost her husband of forty years, her high school sweetheart, Tom, when he suddenly died of a massive hemorrhage. One week later, Lon lost Dot, his wife of forty years, in a plane crash. Both Norma and Lon were steadfast believers who took comfort in God's grace and abundance. He had blessed both with wonderful marriages and three children each.

Both couples had belonged to the same church. When Norma lost Tom, Lon and Dot attended the funeral. A few days later, Lon and Dot presented Norma with a photograph album commemorating Tom's military service. Tom had been one of the Marines to make the initial assault on the beaches of Iwo Jima. Lon thoughtfully made three sets of copies for Norma's children.

Still grieving when her friend Dot died, Norma didn't attend the funeral. She sent flowers and mailed a note of condolence. She remembered Lon's kindness to her and her children and promised herself that later, when time had passed and her heart ached a little less, she would reach out to him and offer him the comfort he had first extended to her.

Months later, Norma's children urged her to do two things: first, to go to Palm Springs on the vacation that she and Tom had planned weeks before his death. And second, to call Lon to see how he was doing. They liked Lon and felt he could be a comfort to their mother.

Lon was incredibly happy that she called. A friendly, encouraging phone call led to a brief visit. Then Norma asked Lon to dinner.

When he came over, they laughed, cried, and reminisced about their marriages. Both felt relieved to talk freely about their experiences and the heaviness of grief. Two days later, Norma left for Palm Springs.

While she was away, Lon wrote several letters. He kept her abreast of the local news. He also asked if he could meet her at the airport, along with their pastor and his wife. As Norma came to the gate, their pastor gave Lon a little friendly nudge forward. "Go on. Give Norma a hug to welcome her home," the pastor urged. Lon did, and the courtship began with their pastor's blessing.

At Tom's funeral, Norma had promised herself to take a European trip. She and Tom had discussed the possibility before his death. Norma thought this was the perfect opportunity to remember her beloved husband while simultaneously going on with her own life. While she was on her trip, Lon called Norma first in London and then in Paris. By Paris, she realized she was falling in love with him. With this realization, Norma immediately cut her trip short and returned to see this man whom she believed was God's choice for her—her missing puzzle piece.

Norma and Lon courted for more than a year before they married. They both felt sure that their love, commitment, and trust in the Lord had brought them together and took the time to affirm it.

In the beginning, when Norma and Lon lost the ones they loved, the pieces in their lives just didn't seem to fit. But with time, healing, and God's abundant provision, they realized that God held all the pieces of their puzzles, and he alone could make them fit. And he did.

NORMA AND LON DAY

MR. WONDERFUL

Love is the gift of oneself.

JEAN ANOUILH

A new friend and I once asked the Lord to send her a husband. It's not as bizarre as it sounds. We didn't ask God to direct a certain individual her way; we asked him to send someone into her life who would bless her and bring much happy companionship into her life. She had been divorced quite a while and was lonely so we prayed very earnestly. We talked a long time afterward about how God loves to bless his children and restore to us the things we have lost. I felt strongly that her prayer would be answered and that her husband was on the way. Little did I know....

Not long after this prayer session, a friend invited me to a Presbyterian renewal program in Jonesboro, Georgia. I was living in Nashville, Tennessee, and I was Methodist, but something told me that I should definitely attend the renewal. Almost as soon as I arrived, I figured out why: I found him! I met "Mr. Wonderful"! I was so excited. His name was Joe and he was kind and gentle, a devout Christian and an elder in the church we were visiting. He told me that he had lost his wife after a prolonged bout with cancer. He spoke with great pride and love of his two grown sons and his love for God. Mr. Wonderful he definitely was.

Now all that remained was to get him together with my new friend and all prayers would be answered. Sounds easy, doesn't it? Guess again.

Joe invited me to breakfast one of the last days before the renewal ended. I took that opportunity to casually mention my friend, to illuminate her good points, and showcase her various talents. I even went so far as to hand him a piece of paper with her name and phone number, but he never seemed to take the hint. He just smiled and tucked the phone number in his pocket.

After the renewal, Joe came to visit me in Nashville. More and more, I began to notice and appreciate his unique qualities. We enjoyed getting to know each other better and after a short time, we realized that we were falling in love. Not long after, we were married.

I still call Joe Mr. Wonderful because that is who he is, and he always will be the answer to my truest heart's desire. God answered my unspoken prayer with a vast gift.

Months after Joe and I married, my friend called, wanting to know whatever happened to that Mr. Wonderful guy who was supposed to call her for a date. I had to laugh as I admitted to her that I had married him.

"Well," she said, "keep praying for me." We both kept praying and before long, my friend found herself married to her own Mr. Wonderful!

AS TOLD TO ANN PLATZ

I arise from dreams of thee
In the first sweet sleep of night,
When the winds are breathing low,
And the stars are shining bright.
PERCY BYSSHE SHELLEY

AN OLD-FASHIONED GIRL

The fleeting promise, chased so long in vain:
Ah, weary bird! thou wilt not fly again:
Thy wings are clipped, thou canst no more depart,
Thy nest is builded in my heart!

BAYARD TAYLOR

*M*y wife, Sarah, and I both looked for a long time for that special someone to spend our lives with. We had both been praying for spouses when we met and fell in love.

One evening not long after we had gotten engaged, I was visiting Sarah at her home. We had just finished dinner and we were cuddling on the sofa watching television when a show came on that we decided to watch. When a lovely girl appeared on the screen, I remarked to Sarah that when I had seen this very rerun years before, I prayed that God would bring me a wife just like the woman on the television...old-fashioned, pure, and kind.

My fiancée's eyes suddenly filled with tears.

"What's wrong, Sarah?" I asked, concerned that I had made my sweetheart cry.

"Fred...." She paused. "That's *me* on the screen.... I was the star in that television show."

You see, Sarah was not only soon-to-be my wife, but she *was* the actress on the screen. We both wept as we realized how God had answered my prayer! He didn't just give me a girl *like* the girl that played that part.

He gave me that *very* girl, a girl who is as old-fashioned, pure, and kind as the one on the television screen.

SARAH AND FRED BOVA, AS TOLD TO SUSAN WALES

How do I love thee? Let me count the ways.
I love thee to the depth and breadth and height
My soul can reach, when feeling out of sight
For the ends of Being and ideal Grace.
I love thee to the level of everyday's
Most quiet need, by sun and candle-light.
I love thee freely, as men strive for Right;
I love thee purely, as they turn from Praise.
I love thee with passion put to use
In my old griefs and with my childhood's faith
I love thee with a love I seemed to lose
With my lost saints, I love thee with the breath,
Smiles, tears, of all my life!—and, if God choose,
I shall but love thee better after death.

ELIZABETH BARRETT BROWNING

THE GREATEST CATCH

Ask me no more: thy fate and mine are seal'd:
I strove against the stream and all in vain:
Let the great river take me to the main:
No more, dear love, for at a touch I yield;
Ask me no more.

ALFRED, LORD TENNYSON

hen I was growing up, my mother would often finish my sentences for me—and rarely the way I intended. If I started to complain about homework, she'd pipe in, "But it sure is great to have teachers who want me to grow up smart." If I worried about my prospects for finding true love, she'd recite Psalm 37:4, "Delight yourself in the Lord, Nell, and he will give you the desires of your heart."

As a teenager, I sometimes felt she had my life all planned out before I even had a chance to live it. But by the time I went off to college, I'd learned to take comfort in knowing how much she cared about my future.

After college, I took a teacher's job in my hometown so I could live near my mother. I'd only been home a few months, however, when my father died suddenly of a heart attack. Now Mother wanted me to move even closer. For weeks on end she begged me to move in with her.

With more than a little reluctance, I finally agreed. To my surprise and relief, it worked out well for both of us. I enjoyed my mother's company, and on my modest salary, I was also quite happy to save on rent.

Having me around again seemed to give Mother new purpose. She had someone to cook for and fuss over on a daily basis. But above all, she was now in a better position to marry me off. "Nell, you just delight yourself in

39

the Lord, and…," she'd begin. Of course, I would finish the verse for her. I tried to convince her that, actually, I was perfectly content being an old maid school teacher, but she wouldn't hear of it. In her mind, I definitely needed to be married, and besides, her plan called for grandchildren.

Toward this end, my mother would invite another potential victim over for dinner at least once a week. The fact that pickings were extremely slim in our little town or that I wasn't terribly cooperative didn't give Mother a second's pause. Each of the young men was cordial, polite—and smart enough to know what Mother had in mind. Most ran for the door before we served dessert, even though my mother was famous for her homemade pies.

I was close to forty when we learned that mother had cancer. She was very brave. "I've had a wonderful life," she assured me. "My only regret is that I won't live long enough to see you married—and me a grandmother."

By that time, I agreed with her wish completely. But since I never let on, she had no idea how much I wished I could give her the desire of her heart. And I never let her know that I sometimes doubted her seemingly matter-of-fact faith in answered prayer. Hadn't I read in an article that women over forty were more likely to be abducted by terrorists than to meet a man and marry?

Never one to give up hope or put aside her mothering role, Mother spent our last conversation telling me how to tend to certain details in my life—and especially how to plan my wedding.

At Mother's funeral, more than 1,000 people arrived to celebrate her extraordinary life. No one was surprised to learn that Mother had planned her own funeral down to the smallest detail. For example, she had arranged for a helium balloon to be given to everyone in attendance. We were to write a prayer request—the desires of our heart—on a little card attached. When the minister prayed the final prayer at her gravesite, we were to release the balloons.

I wrote down the only thing I could think of. *Lord,* I wrote, *You know the desire of my heart. I want a husband. Nell.*

What a sight it was to see all those hopes floating up, up and away. For a few seconds, I believed that my prayer request would somehow reach heaven. Then I went home to pick up the pieces of my life.

About two months later, I received a phone call. "Nell? Is that you?" inquired a familiar voice.

It was Horace Van Heusen, the man who owned the pharmacy in our little town. Mother had had this confirmed bachelor over for dinner dozens of times it seemed. He and mother would talk all evening while I listened, probably with a pout etched across my face. Mother just couldn't see that Horace—cautious and mild-mannered—was definitely not my type.

Horace cleared his throat and asked how I was getting along.

"I'm fine, Horace," I told him. "But I'm rather busy grading papers. Thanks for calling."

I was preparing to hang up, when he exclaimed, "Wait! There's something I've got to tell you." After a long pause, he finally spoke up. "Last week I was fishing down by Mabreys Creek—"

"Catch anything?" I interrupted, trying to be more friendly.

"Oh, I caught something all right," he muttered.

"And what might that be?"

"Looks like I might of caught myself a wife," he said.

"You're getting married, Horace?" I tried to hide my surprise. "I'm so happy for you. Who is she?"

"Listen, Nell, this is too important to discuss on the phone. May I come over? Right now?"

I tried to say no, but the words wouldn't come out. In less than ten minutes, Horace was ringing my doorbell clutching a small velvet box. He must have read on my face the sudden dread I felt. But he plunged ahead anyway.

"When I was fishing, I caught the remnants of a balloon," he said. "Inside, there was a prayer request for a husband." He paused in his speech to place the box in my hands. "It seemed to me like the answer to my prayers, too."

I couldn't imagine being married to Horace. My heart softened a little as I looked into the eyes of this shy, blushing man, but he had to know that I couldn't entertain such an impossible idea.

"Horace, you can't think that...but really you don't think.... That's ridiculous!"

Horace calmly told me that he didn't think it was ridiculous at all. He had accepted the balloon as a sign from God, and he wanted me to pray about it.

In the months that followed, I did pray. And if I forgot, it seemed that my mother completed my sentences from the grave. *I need to pick up milk, stop at the dry cleaners...and pray about Horace.*

To my surprise, each day the idea of Horace and me seemed less ridiculous than before. Finally, I invited him over to dinner, warning him that I couldn't cook like my mother had. What I didn't say was that I needed to see if my feelings really had changed.

They had. In his patience, I thought I saw courage and steadfastness. In his shyness, I suspected a humble heart.

We cautiously began to date. By the time our wedding day arrived, Horace and I were madly in love. Who would have ever thought?

At our wedding reception—you guessed it—everyone released a helium balloon with the desires of their hearts attached. This time as I sent my balloon up to heaven, I asked God for a baby girl.

A year later we had our precious baby girl. I named her May, for my mother. Horace brought me a big bouquet of pink balloons.

Today whenever I see a balloon, it reminds me to teach my daughter, like my mother taught me, *Delight yourself in the Lord, and he will give you the desires of your heart!*

NELL VAN HEUSEN, AS TOLD TO SUSAN WALES

SING ME A LOVE SONG

*Those who bring sunshine to the lives of others
cannot keep it from themselves.*

JAMES M. BARRIE

found my husband at the Steak and Ale. It's not as easy as it sounds.

To reach the point when I was ready to commit the rest of my life to someone special, I had to travel a long, hard road that was confusing and sometimes terrifying. But through the grace and love of God, I made it and learned many valuable lessons. And when I did finally make it to that Steak and Ale I was ready to meet Tom and for him to meet me.

I was born and raised in Murray, Kentucky, the oldest of three children. My mother insisted that I attend college and earn my degree. By the time I was a junior in college, I had been seriously dating a young man for almost four years. We planned to get married, so I dropped out of school. But two days before the wedding, I got cold feet. I called off the wedding and returned all of the presents.

I decided then to fly to Atlanta and try to make my way in the big city. I had exactly one hundred fifty dollars in my pocket and a suitcase filled with all the clothes it could hold. A girlfriend offered me a room in her apartment—so much for glamour in the big city!

I went to Atlanta with the goal of pursuing a career as a professional singer. Once again, though, cold feet foiled my plans. Instead I became an executive secretary with General Motors. Not surprisingly for someone who loves to sing, it was a disappointing job. I added to my misery by suffering through a bad relationship and then found myself at rock bottom, where I even considered suicide. At that point, the only place for me to go was back to Kentucky. I knew my family would welcome me and I would find my balance again.

Back home, I finished my schooling in the college's new television and communications department. I earned my degree with honors. When I stood at graduation, tears of joy and gratitude clouded my eyes as I located my parents in the crowd.

I moved back to Atlanta, this time with the resolve to do things right. I was determined to follow my heart and pursue the job I really wanted. I returned to my love of singing and got my first job at a supper club. One evening, a nice-looking man dressed in a yellow sports coat and white pants approached me during a break.

"My name is Vic Varconi and I am really enjoying your singing," he said. "But I have to ask, and I know it sounds clichéd, but what's a nice girl like you doing in a place like this?" He smiled.

"Singing and making money to pay my bills," I replied. "What's a nice guy like you doing here?"

Vic told me that he was a Presbyterian ministerial student at the local seminary and that as part of his psychology project, he was visiting clubs trying to find out why people went there in the first place. I laughed when he told me his answer. Soon after, we became really good friends. He was just the kind of friend I needed.

He introduced me to a new church, Mount Paran Church of God. The very first time I went there, the entire church sang "Hallelujah" in rounds. I must have cried buckets of tears. The sound was so beautiful and seemed to fill my soul. I knew I had found my church. I felt that God was making sure that this time around, my life was going to work. He was leading me in the best possible direction.

I started praying with Charlotte, a wonderful woman from Mount Paran. I told her that I wanted to be married and that this time I was ready. Charlotte prayed that God would send me the right man; she added that he needed to be tall because I was. I laughed at the last part of her prayer.

Enter the Steak and Ale, where I got a singing job. One night, as an introduction to my next song, I asked the audience if they had heard of Elton John. A man answered my question with, "Yes, but have you heard of Tom McGarey? He's at the end of this table and he is dying to meet you." Tom was six-feet, four inches and wonderfully handsome. I decided to make the most of the opportunity!

I sang a love song to him and a friendship bloomed, then blossomed effortlessly into true love. We were married in October of 1979 in the beautiful Blue Ridge Mountains.

Even twenty years later, the sight of a Steak and Ale makes us smile and squeeze each other's hand.

DIANNE MCGAREY

Across the threshold led,
And every tear kissed off as soon as shed,
His house she enters, there to be a light,
Shining within, when all without is night;
A guardian angel o'er his life presiding,
Doubling his pleasure and his cares dividing.

SAMUEL ROGERS

IT STARTED WITH TOMATOES

*To Love is to place our happiness
in the happiness of another.*

GOTTRIED VON LEIBNITZ

In 1941, a pretty blond thirteen-year-old named Mary Ellen Shives saw more tomatoes in any one day than a girl could possibly count, more tomatoes than a girl had minutes in a day, or dreams to fill them with.

You see, she was working at a tomato cannery near her family's farm in Fulton County, Pennsylvania. The job brought Mary Ellen extra money after her farm chores were done at home. Besides, it was wartime, men were scarce, and energetic young women more than welcome in the work force.

One day, Mary Ellen impulsively wrote her name and address on a label and packed it carefully among cans of tomatoes about to be shipped. People sent notes across the seas in bottles, didn't they? But she was nowhere near the sea, so tomato cans would have to do.

That night she lay in bed wondering and dreaming where her label might end up. Would a handsome, decorated soldier find it? Or just a crabby cook in some elementary school cafeteria? There was no way to know. Probably the label would disappear without a trace.

Weeks passed with no response, and Mary Ellen decided it had been a silly, immature thing to do. In the coming months, her attentions shifted to important teenage concerns—clothes, social events, and new crushes. In time, she forgot about the label.

Meanwhile, across the Atlantic, a teenager named Nick Tyssens was suffering through the war in German-occupied Netherlands. After working as a slave laborer in Germany, he was sent to a concentration camp where he became desperately ill and frail. By the time the war ended in 1945, Nick weighed only ninety pounds.

After he recovered, Nick became one of the first men to enlist in the newly founded Dutch Marine Corps and he was sent to Camp Lejeune, North Carolina, for training. That summer, he offered to help out a buddy who had mess hall duty. When they opened a crate of canned tomatoes, both soldiers spotted a label with a girl's handwriting on it. It had been in the crate for four years.

In their eagerness to grab the label, the two men tore it in half. But Nick's half had the girl's name and address. Anyway, unlike his buddy, Nick was fluent in speaking and writing English.

Nick decided to write to the girl. Or, for all he knew, perhaps "Mary Ellen Shives" was an old woman.

One day in September Mary Ellen Shives stopped to get the mail as she came in from working in the fields. She was surprised to find a letter written in red ink addressed to her. The envelope contained a photo of two young men, one of whom was circled in red.

The enclosed letter was short. The writer, Nick Tyssens, explained that he was a Dutch marine stationed in America for training. He told her he'd found her label in a case of tomato cans. *What kind of girl would do such a thing?* he wondered. If she was interested, he'd like her to write back.

Mary Ellen felt a shiver go up her spine. She had always wanted to visit Holland. That evening, she stared at the photo for at least an hour. In the morning, she eagerly returned his letter with her own, along with the most flattering picture of herself she could find.

Before Nick's return letter reached Mary Ellen, he had already been whisked off to the Pacific for more training. Each week for two and a half years, Nick and Mary Ellen corresponded. Through their letters, they became friends and confidants. Then friendship turned to love. Nick concealed a ring in a bar of soap and sent it to Mary Ellen, asking her to marry him.

Delighted, she accepted, even though she knew that Nick was about to be shipped back to the Netherlands. When and how would she ever meet her new fiancé?

Nick decided to go to his commanding officer and try to persuade him to let him return to America. The officer listened impassively to the obviously love-sick soldier—until Nick told him the part about the tomato can label. Then he burst out laughing—and decided to grant Nick permission.

Nick traveled by freighter for more than fifty days before finally disembarking in New York City. He set off for Pennsylvania by bus. By the time he arrived at Elwood Shives's farm, he was in a taxi and completely broke. His future father-in-law had to pay his cab fare.

In front of Mary Ellen's family (and quite a few family friends who just had to witness the event), the nervous couple finally met for the first time. Mary Ellen had planned to stay back, look calm, and keep her poise. But as soon as Nick stepped out of the cab, she flew into his arms. They didn't let go for a very long time.

Nick had only a two-month visitor's visa and had to be out of the country by September 24. Everyone wondered if the adventurous couple would still want to marry after they'd met, and if so, wouldn't a wedding date by the twenty-fourth be too soon?

The answers were yes and no, respectively. Mary Ellen Shives and Nick Tyssens were married on September 22, 1948, in the parsonage of St. Paul's Methodist Church in Hagerstown, Maryland. They spent their wedding night riding a bus to New York City in order to catch the ship that would carry them to the Netherlands.

To Mary Ellen's surprise and amazement, Nicky's hometown of Maastricht, Holland, welcomed them with a banner and music. Both of them agreed, however, that America would become home. Six months later, the couple sailed back to America with a stowaway—Mary Ellen was expecting their first child.

The Tyssens, who now live in Hagerstown, recently celebrated their golden anniversary. They enjoy a large family of children and grandchildren. But Grandma Mary Ellen is always dismayed when she hears of a new little Tyssens who doesn't like tomatoes. "Doesn't like tomatoes!" she cries. "They should eat tomatoes for dessert. How do you think all this began?"

DENISE TYSSENS, DAUGHTER-IN-LAW

A Dedication To My Wife

To whom I owe the leaping delight
That quickens my senses in our wakingtime
And the rhythm that governs the repose of our sleepingtime,
The breathing in unison

Of lovers whose bodies smell of each other
Who think the same thoughts without need of speech
And babble the same speech without need for meaning.

No peevish winter wind shall chill
No sullen tropic sun shall wither
The roses in the rose-garden which is ours and ours only

But this dedication is for others to read:
These are private words addressed to you in public.

T. S. ELIOT

THE FIRST NOEL,
BUT NOT THE LAST

Christmas is the kindling of new fires.
GLADYS TABER

*O*nce again my fellow workaholic and I were the last lawyers to leave the office. "Merry Christmas, Sister Scrooge! You'd better get outta here before Santa Claus comes!" Jack warned.

"Happy holidays to you, too, Ebenezer. See you next year," I replied.

After Jack was gone, I turned back to some work on my desk. I was in no hurry to get over to my parents' home to celebrate the holiday weekend with my family. My two married sisters and their families and my brother and his family had arrived earlier in the day. I knew they would all greet me with their yearly barrage of questions: "Met anybody interesting, sis?" "Why don't you got out with Ralph again?" "Why don't you join a dating service?"

I had prayed feverently throughout the year that this year would be different, and that God would provide a special guy for me to invite to my parents' for Christmas dinner. Up until the last week, I'd still felt hopeful, somehow sure that God was going to grant me a positive answer to this prayer.

But once again, Christmas was almost here and I was alone.

At thirty-five I was beginning to believe that I might never marry. I had plenty of friends who love being single. But I longed to meet someone to share my life with—and have children with. By now, my biological clock was clanging for all the world to hear, especially my younger siblings who were all married with children.

When the clock struck six-thirty, my work was finally finished. I gathered all the gifts I had received from my coworkers and headed for the elevator. As I hopped on, I was not surprised to find myself the only one going down. Everyone else was probably at home with their families preparing for Christmas Eve by now.

Down, down I went from the forty-seventh floor—until the elevator stopped suddenly on the thirty-ninth floor and another holiday workaholic joined me. "Merry Christmas," the stranger said.

I barely got a glimpse of him over my stack of packages but I returned his greetings with as much enthusiasm as I could muster.

Down, down the elevator continued until it jerked to a sudden stop. I looked up at the monitor. We were on the twenty sixth floor and presumably another late worker was about to join us. But when the doors didn't open, I exchanged a nervous look with the man next to me.

My companion began to punch the buttons on the panel. Nothing happened and suddenly the entire elevator car went black. I was seized with a sudden panic. *What if I am trapped in an elevator in the dark with an ax murderer on Christmas Eve?* I thought.

We both began trying to dial our cell phones in the darkness even though we knew we couldn't get service inside the elevator.

My companion spoke first. "You wouldn't happen to have a match?" he asked.

We both laughed, realizing I was holding an armload of packages— and he had just uttered a clichéd come-on line.

I knelt to put my packages on the floor. Lucky for us, I collected matchbooks from restaurants. I retrieved several small boxes and smiled in the darkness when I realized I could do even better that. "I even have a couple of candles," I offered.

"You're kidding! That's great," he said.

I began going through my boxes and bags of gifts and retrieved two large scented candles. I lit one and held it by his side as he groped for the elevator phone to call the service company. He gave them our location and looked over at me as he hung up.

"Everyone's away for Christmas, so they're running a skeleton crew," he said. "I'm afraid it will be a couple of hours before they can get here." Then he tried to reassure me. "I'll sound the alarm in the meantime and someone is sure to find us even before the elevator folks get here."

"On Christmas Eve?" I blurted. "You really think anyone's left in the building?"

"Sure," he said confidently. "We can't be the only crazy people working late on Christmas Eve."

While the alarm blared, I began to make myself comfortable in my corner of the elevator. I lit the other scented candle. *Thank you for the gift, Jill*, I murmured, and placed it in the middle of the floor. He held onto the other candle checking the controls on the panel until he finally decided he'd done all he could. Finally he turned and sat down.

"I'm Chad Hunter," he said with an outstretched hand.

"I'm Greta Green," I replied.

"I don't know about you, but I'm a praying man," Chad announced. "Would you like to pray with me that we will be rescued soon?"

I couldn't believe my ears. Here was a guy, a successful business-man—and he prayed! I wondered if he was single. I sat there dazzled as he prayed the most beautiful prayer I'd ever heard.

We exchanged pleasantries and I mustered up my courage to ask, "Your wife and children are probably worried and waiting for you at home?"

"Nope, I'm single," he replied. My heart began to beat a little faster. As we kept talking, I learned that he was unable to go back East to spend the holidays with his family because of a new client he had acquired for the firm. "I was planning a quiet Christmas Eve at home," he confided, "so no one is going to come looking for me until tomorrow when I don't show up for dinner at one of my partner's homes."

"Don't worry," I assured him, "my family's expecting me for a Christmas Eve supper tonight. Of course, they'll expect me to be late as usual. But in a couple of hours they'll probably send out the National Guard."

Chad then observed that our situation was nothing compared to what Mary and Joseph must have felt when there was no room at the inn on the first Christmas Eve. He regaled me with funny stories of his childhood Christmases back in New England. And he laughed at my own tales of Christmases past.

Over an hour had passed and I hadn't even thought about how hungry I was until Chad suddenly pulled out a bottle of wine. "I bought this for tomorrow to take to my partner's house for dinner, but there's no reason that we shouldn't celebrate Christmas right here and now." He pulled out a Swiss Army knife and pulled the cork out.

Okay, I can match that, I thought. So I shuffled through my bags and retrieved a coffee mug and an assortment of Christmas goodies the girls at the office had prepared—cheese straws, cookies, fruit, and even homemade bread and jelly. We enjoyed our Christmas Eve feast by candlelight. At one point we sang his favorite Christmas carol, "The First Noel."

For the first time in years, my heart was filled with the Christmas spirit and hope. And when the elevator service people arrived, shouting to tell us they were going to get us out soon, my heart sank. I felt like Cinderella must have felt when the clock struck twelve. I didn't want this Christmas Eve to end.

Hours after the elevator first stopped, the doors opened and my brother and my father were standing there waiting. As we hugged, I sniffled back a few tears. They assumed I was emotional because of my ordeal. But the real reason for the tears was that I didn't want to say goodbye to Chad.

When we exchanged farewells, Chad handed me his card and I gave him mine. "Merry Christmas," he said and disappeared out into the parking lot.

The next morning, our family attended our church's Christmas service as usual. But I hardly heard a word the minister said. I couldn't stop thinking about the stranger who'd become my friend in an elevator. When the organist began to play the "The First Noel," my eyes filled with tears.

As I walked up the aisle after communion, I glanced up to see Chad sitting on the right side of the church. I was stunned. *My eyes must be playing tricks on me!* I thought. But there he was, smiling broadly as he waved.

It was almost impossible to sit through the rest of the service. At the close, he rushed over to greet me.

"Merry Christmas, Greta," he said.

"I didn't know you went to church here!" I exclaimed.

"I don't," he said. "I came to see you."

"How on earth did you know you would find me here?" I asked with amazement.

"Remember, you told me that your family comes here every Christmas morning. I knew I'd find you here," he said.

My heart was beating wildly, and my sister began smirking and poking me in the side. My father leaned over and gave me a wink while my mother mouthed, *Invite him for dinner.* I just stood there speechless but beaming.

"I don't know about you," Chad began, "but after spending Christmas Eve with you, I couldn't wait. I just had to see you again."

Chad cancelled his dinner plans to join me and my family for Christmas dinner. God had heard those prayers I had prayed throughout the year. I was not alone that Christmas. Nor have I been alone any Christmas since then. Chad and I were married on Christmas Eve the following year. The next year, our first child was born on Christmas Day. We named her Noel.

To this day, whenever Chad and I find ourselves in an elevator together, we still hum "The First Noel." And we give thanks to God for the many wonderful Noels that have followed.

GRETA HUNTER, AS TOLD TO SUSAN WALES

The Moment We Met

God knew his chosen time:
He bade me slowly ripen to my prime,
And from my boughs within the promised fruit,
Till storm and sun gave vigor to the root.

BAYARD TAYLOR

"I KNEW THE FIRST TIME I SAW HER..."

"I'D KNOWN HIM AS A FRIEND FOR THE LONGEST TIME, THEN ONE DAY..."

"TO TELL YOU THE TRUTH, AT FIRST WE DIDN'T REALLY LIKE ONE ANOTHER THAT MUCH. THEN, OUT OF NOWHERE..."

TALK TO ONE HUNDRED HAPPILY MARRIED COUPLES AND YOU'LL GET ONE HUNDRED DIFFERENT STORIES ABOUT HOW TWO PEOPLE RECOGNIZED THERE WAS SOMETHING SPECIAL BETWEEN THEM. GOD MAKES MATCHES THE WAY HE MAKES SNOWFLAKES: NO TWO ARE EXACTLY ALIKE.

WE ALL KNOW COUPLES WHO MET, KNEW THEY WERE RIGHT FOR EACH OTHER ALMOST INSTANTLY, AND MARRIED AS A MATTER OF COURSE. THEN THERE ARE THE TWO PEOPLE WHO FOR THE LONGEST TIME HAD NO ROMANTIC FEELINGS ABOUT ONE ANOTHER, BUT ENDED UP CRAZY IN LOVE.

OTHERS HAVE HAD TO OVERCOME INSURMOUNTABLE OBSTACLES LIKE DISTANCE, OR DIFFERENCES IN CULTURE AND FAMILY BACKGROUND IN ORDER TO MAKE IT TO THE ALTAR. WHAT A VARIETY OF STORIES THERE ARE ABOUT THE TRIUMPH OF RELATIONSHIP WHEN GOD BRINGS A MAN AND A WOMAN TOGETHER.

THE LORD KNOWS EXACTLY WHO BEST SUITS YOU AS FRIEND AND LIFELONG LOVE. HIS WAYS ARE MYSTERIOUS AND FULL OF GRACE. BEFOREHAND, YOU HAVE NO WAY OF KNOWING WHAT BEAUTIFUL MOMENT HE IS DREAMING FOR YOU. BUT WHEN TIME, CIRCUMSTANCE, AND YOUR INWARD PREPARATION ARE JUST RIGHT, HE CONSPIRES TO DO THE IMPOSSIBLE—IGNITING THE FIRE OF INTEREST AND ATTRACTION.

HE LEAVES IT UP TO YOU TO GENTLY FAN THE FLAME.

A CHRISTMAS REMEMBERED

Love took you by the hand
At eve, and bade you stand
At edge of the woodland,
Where I should pass;
Love sent me thither, sweet,
And brought me to your feet;
He willed that we should meet,
And so it was.

J. B. B. NICHOLS

My youngest brother Joe had dreamed of serving his country since he had been a young boy. When Joe graduated from high school, he immediately joined the armed services—much to our family's concern, since our country was at war. Our fears were confirmed when soon afterward, he was shipped to Vietnam. Joe convinced us that he felt it was his calling and his duty to serve his country.

It was 1968, and large numbers of Americans were protesting the Vietnam War. As I read the letter from Joe, my heart began to break. The news of the unrest and the antiwar protests had slowly swept across the ocean to our soldiers. The men in his platoon who were bravely serving their country and fighting the war were not only discouraged, but deeply hurt by their country's reaction to the war they were fighting and many of their friends were giving their lives for.

The young men were also painfully lonely and heard little from the folks back home. A few of these men didn't receive any letters or packages from home.

I was outraged by the lack of support our country was showing our men. A large number of these soldiers had no choice in the circumstances that took them to Vietnam.

After receiving my brother's letter, I worked hard to persuade the city council of San Mateo, California, to adopt my brother's company, which was made up of men who were virtually orphaned by their country's protests.

The town joyously reacted, and patriotism and appreciation soared. Little old ladies were baking cookies, and teenagers were corresponding with the men. Each one of the men in my brother's company was adopted by a citizen of our town. By a proclamation of the city council, the town officially adopted Company A of the 1st Battalion, 327th Infantry, 1st Brigade, 101st Airborne Division known as the famed Screaming Eagles.

In mid-March of that year, Joe wrote an enthusiastic letter of thanks to both my mother and me for organizing the outpouring of love in the San Mateo community. But that was about the last we heard from Joe, because less than two weeks later, we received the devastating news that my brother's company had been ambushed and that many of the young men were killed, including Joe.

The entire town of San Mateo went into shock. Joe was the town's first adopted son and the news of his death brought the reality of the war to our doorstep. Our family was shattered, but I dealt with my grief by plunging into the Company A adoption with more vigor than ever before. I would not allow my brother's life to be lost in vain. I would make a difference in the lives of others!

When Christmas approached, the city of San Mateo agreed to send me to Vietnam to represent the town bearing gifts for the platoon. I was excited about meeting Joe's buddies.

The city had struck medallions for the platoon and asked me to personally deliver them to their adopted sons. The money was raised and provided for my trip. I was eager to go and talk to the members of the platoon.

Joe had been halfway around the world when he was killed. It was not only important for me to witness the spot where he'd died, but to talk to the men who had been with him when he was killed. I knew this would provide enormous comfort to my family and me.

When I landed in Vietnam, Joe's platoon leader was called to escort me to the men's camp. The platoon leader had only two more weeks left in Vietnam, and escorting a woman into dangerous territory was not exactly what he wanted to do. He thought my coming there was the most ridiculous thing he'd ever heard of, and he let me know it. He was irritated when the call came, but he grudgingly made his way to meet me at the airport.

This was his second tour of duty in 'Nam and he had been gravely injured during this last tour. I learned later that he was injured in the same ambush that had killed my brother. He was literally counting the hours until he could go home, so he was grumbling all the way of his journey to greet me.

No one could have prepared either of us for the moment we met. Steve's attitude took a 180-degree turn, much to the amusement of the soldiers around him. We bonded the very moment our eyes met, and his enthusiasm increased remarkably. It's impossible to describe what happened, but it was obvious to us and all the men that something special was occurring between the two of us, something almost magical. My hopes soared. The entire experience was just too special to put into words.

I soon learned that Steve had not only been my brother's platoon leader, but he had been there helping a soldier who was wounded in the process of trying to save my brother's life. Steve was wounded while he aided that soldier and still bears the scars today. It seemed like a miracle to me at the time that Steve was able to give me every detail of my brother's last days and more importantly, his last hours.

When we arrived at our destination and I first saw the young soldiers, tears moistened my eyes as I was struck at how very young they were. As I looked into their eyes, I saw the look of love, and some shyness, loneliness, and fear. I saw my brother. Every one of them looked like my brother.

It was Christmas Day when I arrived and the company held a memorial service for Joe, followed by the soldiers singing "Silent Night." No Christmas before or after has ever touched my life like that one.

When Steve drove me back to catch my plane back to America, my life had changed. I had changed. I was fighting my emotions and the strong feelings that had developed for the young lieutenant who had accompanied me.

When Steve saw me off, I knew he had feelings too, because to my utter surprise, he kissed me good-bye. "I'll call you when I come home," he promised. I knew in my heart that he would. Just the same, it was painful to leave him.

My heart was heavy as I left Steve standing there. He finally disappeared from my sight as I flew away. As I sat back in my seat on the plane I knew that the trip had been a tremendous healing process. My visit with the appreciative soldiers changed my life.

Company A became an extended family for me and my city. I am still in touch with those surviving men today. When I returned home, I received a hero's welcome. I reported all the details of my trip to the city but held secretly in my heart the love I felt for the young lieutenant I had met.

Just as he promised, weeks later I received a phone call from the young lieutenant who had escorted me. He was home from Vietnam and wanted to see me. My heart fluttered at the mere sound of his voice.

Steve eventually settled in my area, and proposed soon afterward, but we weren't married for eight years. It never bothered me that we had such a long engagement because I was aware that Steve required a lot of healing from his experiences in the war. He had witnessed a lot of his men dying—young men—and desperately needed to come to terms with the war before he could be made whole and ready for marriage. I am thankful that we were both mature enough to accept this.

We were also faced with the dilemma that Steve wanted to get as far away from the war as he could. He didn't want to talk about it, hear about it, or think about it, and yet the woman he loved was still attached to and heavily involved in her adopted Company A.

After we were married and the years went by, Steve healed and eventually got involved in my adopted platoon as much as I had. When Desert Storm began, I began organizing again and my ideas soon grew into a national organization.

While I realize that my efforts have made a difference in the world—especially with the young men and women who serve our country—the greatest gift was that I was blessed with the most wonderful husband. Steve has become my life's partner and the love of my life.

Since that time, there has not been nor will there ever be a Christmas like the one I spent in Vietnam. My brother Joe's short life not only had a great purpose, but it brought such meaning to my life in so many ways. I made the Christmas trip to Vietnam to seek the gift of healing, but in addition, I returned with the gift of love for a lifetime.

What could be more fitting at Christmastime considering the ultimate gift of love that mankind received on that very first Christmas.

CAROL, AS TOLD TO ANN PLATZ AND SUSAN WALES

THE HEALING DREAM

⌒

I have found the paradox that if I love until it hurts,
then there is no hurt, but only more love.
MOTHER TERESA

was having breakfast at a local drugstore in Palm Beach, Florida, when I first saw her. She came in with an older couple and needed directions. They were lost, but suddenly I felt quite found. They got the directions they were after and left. But I couldn't get her out of my mind. I wanted to know everything about her. I wondered what she did, what her voice sounded like, what her favorite hobbies were. I had it bad.

Driving home about a week later, I saw her crossing the street in front of the Palm Beach Elementary School. I thought my heart was going to explode. I was positive that God had brought me to this place, just as he had brought her to the drugstore that day. This was *it*. It required some detective work on my part, but I convinced the sister of a good friend of mine, who happened to know the mystery woman, to introduce us.

I arranged for my friend's sister to bring her to my office. She could introduce this attractive lady to me sort of by accident. The meeting was magnetic. We started dating immediately and were married two years later in 1966. Our daughter was born in 1969. Life was perfect.

In 1970, perfection was interrupted. My wife was diagnosed with breast cancer. Being a teacher, she taught our daughter everything she could get into her head until she died, at age thirty-two, in 1974. My wife was an outstanding woman, beloved by her community, her colleagues, and her students. She was an inspiration to all who knew her.

When we were in the hospital for the last time, she told me she loved me and that she trusted me to do the best I could for our daughter. She knew I would love our daughter enough for the both of us.

My wife was far too young to die. It took me a long time to accept her death—thirteen years, in fact. It was then that I dreamed about her. In this dream, she and I were walking through a shopping mall together. You see, my wife loved clothes. She had been a beauty queen in high school and college. She made most of her clothes. Easily, she could have been a dress designer. She would see an evening gown in the window of a shop, go straight home, and make it herself.

In the dream, I was so happy to be with her, so content to be holding her hand. I had almost forgotten what that felt like. She was dressed in a blue double-knit pantsuit circa 1970. I laughed and told her, "Darling, you need some new clothes!" She smiled at me.

I jerked awake from the dream. I reached for her beside me. I had to remind myself that she wasn't there except in my imagination. I thought a long time about that dream. *Why now?* I wondered. The dream haunted me, and slowly I began to understand its healing value.

My mind was telling me that both my wife and our relationship belonged to the past. I had never let her go and so I was still stuck with one foot in the present, the other planted firmly in the past. I had to move forward. I had to continue with my life. So in my mind I finally told my wife that I had loved her from the first moment I saw her in the drugstore that morning, that I loved the way she used to make me laugh and how she looked at me with love in her eyes, that, most important, she always seemed to teach the people around her the greatest lessons. And I told her good-bye.

Sometime later I was having a business lunch when I noticed a woman sitting a few tables away. She was seated with a group of six people and she appeared to be in charge of the meeting. I couldn't stop watching her. I wanted to meet her. But how could I? I was about to leave. I couldn't interrupt her meeting. I decided to jot a short note inviting her to a lunch or dinner. I included my office and home telephone numbers on the note. As I left the restaurant, I slid it under her plate. When I arrived at my office, I told my secretary that if a woman called to inquire about me, patch her straight to me.

Nothing happened.

I waited and waited. I waited a little more. Nothing. Then a call came from a lady who asked my secretary, "Would you tell me who Bill Smith is?" My secretary told her my position in our company. "Thank you very much," she replied, then hung up.

Two weeks later, she called me at the office. We agreed to meet, but she lived in Charlotte, North Carolina, and I was in Atlanta. We were trying to get our schedules together and finally we saw that we were both going to be in Florida at the same time. I was to be in Boca Raton and she would be in Miami. So we made a date for dinner in Miami.

We were both kind of nervous when we first saw each other. It was more or less a blind date. After dinner, I heard music coming from the lounge so I asked her to dance. After dancing with her one time, I knew she was right for me. It felt so natural.

She eventually told me about her response to my note. She put it straight into her purse without even reading it. The president of her company was sitting to her left and she didn't want him to think that people were flirting with her when she was out of town, so she acted like it didn't happen. At the airport, the president asked her if she was even slightly curious about the note. "Let's look at it," he said. She pulled it out and they all read the note. The president commented that he liked a man with strong handwriting.

We dated for about two years and I took her back to the same restaurant where I met her and asked her to marry me. We were wed at my house with our children and relatives present. My wife and I now go back every year to that restaurant to celebrate our anniversary. Our children, all three of them, get along wonderfully. We made a new family full of people and full of love.

And it was all because of a healing dream. Had God not helped me to let go of my beloved first wife, I might never have met the woman who fills my life with blessings now. With my history, I don't believe in "chance" encounters—at drugstores, restaurants, or in dreams. God's plan is wonderful.

AS TOLD TO ANN PLATZ

SEND MIKEY
RIGHT OVER!

I'm glad it cannot happen twice,
the fever of first love.

DAPHNE DU MAURIER, *REBECCA*

The blond-haired blue-eyed kindergartner surveyed her classmates on the other side of the playground. Who should she choose? Who should she call? She studied the faces of each one of the gangly boys and then she surveyed the group of giggling girls.

There stood Mikey, tall and proud. Diane was drawn to Mikey's big blue eyes and smiling face. Her decision was made: she would choose Mikey. Shyly, Diane called out, "Red rover, red rover, send Mikey right over."

The young boy grinned with a smile that stretched all the way across his face, and ran across the lawn to her.

Later that year, when Mike fell off the swing at Diane's birthday party, it was she who came to his rescue and nursed his scrapes (and bruised pride). Her tenderness made Mikey feel all better.

After kindergarten, Mike and Diane went to different elementary schools. They did not meet again until the sixth grade. But even after all those years, they hadn't forgotten one another. They continued to exchange glances in class and the cafeteria.

In the seventh grade, Mike's parents allowed him to have his first boy-girl party. Mike invited Diane as his special date. Throughout high school, they were rarely apart again.

Diane proudly wore Mike's class ring their senior year. The couple enjoyed all the fruits of their young first love. Sadly, after graduation, Diane and Mike, like many other high school sweethearts, parted ways.

Diane was leaving for Macalester College and Mike had been accepted at Yale. They were both ready to experience all college had to offer, but that didn't lessen the pain of their farewell. As they walked away, they both knew in their hearts that their relationship probably would not survive. They agreed to cherish the memories but look to the future.

College was an exciting adventure for the two of them. "I was very active on campus and began dating immediately," Mike explains. "It was a very exciting time in my life. I was meeting people who were so sophisticated and attractive. My ego swelled with all the choices of outstanding women to go out with.

"There were many times when I would begin to get serious about a certain girl—until I would compare her to Diane. The answer was always the same, no matter how special the new woman in my life might seem: *No one* could hold a candle to Diane!

"Diane's character, intelligence, kindness, and gentle ways were always a cut above the rest. She also had such a deep and genuine faith in God. At the time, I was considering going into the ministry, so that was one of Diane's most important assets. Diane was all a man could ever hope for in a wife. She exuded so much self-confidence and such strong values that I never felt I was competing with her, as I did with so many of the other women I was seeing.

"Plus, I knew I wanted to marry and have a family. I was dating with that goal in mind. Whenever I dated someone seriously and got to know her, I would ask myself: 'Would I want this woman to be the mother of my children?' I highly recommend this litmus test for any potential marriage partner. The only woman I could ever answer 'yes' to that question was Diane.

"I could hardly wait to get home that summer to tell Diane that I knew without a doubt that she was the girl I wanted to marry. I had played the field for a year and Diane was the only one left standing!

"When I arrived home, my first stop was Diane's house. Unfortunately, there she stood at the door with a guy she'd met at college who had dropped by to meet her parents. My heart began pounding in my chest. I was devastated. Worse yet, he had a shiny new Corvette standing at the curb. How could I ever compete with that?

"I got out of my old clunker and went up to the door. What I really wanted to do was punch the guy, but instead I extended my hand."

Here Diane takes over the narration. "As I watched Mike's behavior in comparison to my college friend's I thought, 'This guy is history!' I asked him to leave the next morning. I knew then without a doubt that Mike was the man with whom I wanted to spend my life."

Just before his senior year of college, Mike proposed to Diane. They were married following their respective college graduations. The entire town of Estherville, Iowa, turned out to see the hometown sweethearts become man and wife.

Mike and Diane have been married thirty years. They love to show their faded kindergarten class picture in the hallway of their home. It's like many of the black and white photos from the fifties: Davy Crockett coonskin caps and cowboy hats with chin straps rest on the heads of the boys, and the girls are adorned with big bows and hair ribbons. Pretty Diane is standing next to the wide-eyed young boy who even at five is making eyes at her. And who would have dreamed that Diane's Red Rover choice would become a lifetime partner?

DIANE AND MIKE RHODES, AS TOLD TO SUSAN WALES

Editor's note: Mike and Diane Rhodes live in Pacific Palisades and have two daughters, Sarah, a teacher, and Katie, a missionary in Russia. Mike is an award-winning director and producer for many television shows and movies including the CBS series, *Christy*, *China Beach*, and the Fox series *Beverly Hills 90210*, as well as several television movies of the week and the feature film, *Dorothy Day*.

HAMBURGER HEAVEN

He that is of a merry heart
hath a continual feast.

PROVERBS 15:15

From time to time they bumped into each other in the library, the cafeteria, and other spots around campus, but they rarely exchanged anything more than a brief greeting.

One night after the dinner meal on campus, Jim and Shirley found themselves standing near one another in a circle of friends. Capturing the moment, Jim sidled up to Shirley and said, "See this nickel? I'm gonna flip it in the air. If you can call heads or tails correctly, I'll buy you a hamburger. But if you lose, you'll owe me one."

How's that for a new approach? Jim would be a winner either way because he got a date out of the arrangement. Shirley liked the idea and said, "It's a deal." She called heads as the nickel went into the air, but it landed tails.

"Good," said Jim. "when do you want to pay off?"

"Hey, wait a minute!" Shirley protested. "Give me a fighting chance. Let's go double or nothing."

Jim flipped the coin and Shirley lost again.

"Great," said Jim. "I like hamburgers. Now I get two of them."

"Let's go one more time," she demanded.

Jim checked the nickel. "You now owe me four hamburgers," he said.

Before they had completed the game, Shirley owed him one hundred twenty-eight hamburgers, and she's been frying them ever since.

SHIRLEY AND DR. JAMES DOBSON, EXCERPTED FROM
DR. DOBSON: *TURNING HEARTS TOWARD HOME*, ROLF ZETTERSTEN,
1989, WORD PUBLISHING, NASHVILLE, TENNESSEE.

Thou art my life, my love,
My heart, the very eyes of me,
And hast command of every part
To live and die for thee.
ROBERT HERRICK

MAN'S BEST FRIEND

✍

A door is what a dog is
perpetually on the wrong side of.

OGDEN NASH

Jimmy Stewart was one of the biggest stars as well as the most eligible bachelor in Hollywood in the late '40s. Women everywhere were pursuing the charming bachelor but at forty he appeared in no hurry to marry.

One night when he attended a dinner party at the home of his friend Gary Cooper and his wife the matchmaker, Rocky, he was seated next to the lovely Gloria McLean. Obviously interested, he offered to drive Gloria home and as he walked her to her door, he invited her for a golf date.

Their courtship is vividly described below from *Jimmy Stewart, A Wonderful Life* (Pinnacle Books, Kensington Publishing Company).

When the two played golf, Gloria beat Jimmy and he didn't seem to mind at all. When he drove her home he declined her invitation to come in but not because he didn't want to! He was afraid of her enormous dog who growled at him at the door.

"Only as I drove away did I realize how smitten I was by Gloria. I wanted to see her again but I knew I would have to win that dog over because Gloria was obviously devoted to it," Jimmy recalled.

To woo Gloria, he had to woo her dog, too. Jimmy went about schmoozing both with typical thoroughness. He would show up for a date with a steak from Chasen's under his arm as a peace offering for the German shepherd. The dog was no gourmet and continued to growl at him. He tried talking baby talk to him, patting him, praising him. "It was terribly humiliating, but I finally got to be friends and was free to court Gloria.

"It took me a year to get her to say yes." He didn't say how many chateaubriands from Chasen's it took to get the German shepherd to agree to the union.

Maybe the dog never became Jimmy Stewart's best friend, but the marriage was a success! The Stewarts' long and happy marriage was legendary and one of the great role models in Hollywood.

LETTERING IN LOVE

*Your letters are always fresher
to me than flowers
Without fading so soon.*

MARY RUSSELL MITFORD

*I*t was the spring of '42 and they were two kids living on two continents when pen and paper—and a school assignment—brought
them together.

She was fourteen, a student in Miss Frady's class here, when the
eighth-graders were asked to select a pen pal from a list of kids in
England. It was a small way of uniting teens during the war.

He was fourteen, too, a grocery errand boy outside London when he
began writing her.

They had little in common but the two found enough to write about
for years.

When the war ended and he was in the Royal Navy, he wrote to say
he wanted to visit her in Iowa. She told her fiancé, who quickly laid down
the law: No more letters.

It seemed the pen pals would never cross paths again.

*Dear Sir or Madam,
I am writing to see if you can help me in my plight. During the war
years, I was writing to a girl (as a pen friend). Her name was then*

Miss Colleen Lee. If you could by any chance trace her for me, I would be very grateful.
Yours truly,
Geoffrey W. Lake

The letter was dated October 19, 1989, and now, almost ten years later, Geoffrey still can't say precisely why he decided to look up his old pen pal.

He was sixty-one, happily married for decades to his wife, Eileen, with a grown son, Michael. But something tugged at the retired factory worker.

He didn't remember Colleen's address but couldn't forget her hometown's distinctive name: Soldier.

With just 250 souls in Soldier, there are no strangers. It turned out Colleen was now Colleen Straight, having long ago married her childhood sweetheart, Harvey, and their three children were adults.

Geoffrey and his wife were planning to visit the United States when his note arrived in Soldier.

Dear Geoff,
What a surprise! I believe it's been forty-five years since we corresponded.

Where to begin? Colleen dashed off a breezy three-page letter describing her family and where they had lived over the years. She also invited Geoffrey and Eileen to Soldier.

And so, they began corresponding again. They always signed their letters as couples.

Then in December 1992, Colleen had sad news.

This is not an easy letter to write. I lost Harvey…I know I must not dwell on his passing, but I do think of it a lot.

Geoffrey responded with a condolence card, and one each year on the anniversary of Harvey's death.

Geoffrey and Eileen's plans to visit Colleen the next year fell through, but the letters continued.

Then in November 1997, Geoffrey's wife of 45 years died.

This time, Colleen did the consoling.

Dear Geoff and Michael,
It's difficult at this sad time to find the right words to comfort you. You will find yourself thinking of all the things you have done together and that helps a lot...just be thankful you had a good life together.

On a January night a year ago, a downcast Geoffrey dialed his phone. He was tempted to hang up before a little girl answered.

"Grandmother, somebody I can't understand wants to talk to you," ten-year-old Ashley said.

"Hello, Colleen, do you know who this is?" the caller asked.

For the first time in fifty-six years, the childhood correspondents spoke to one another.

They talked for a while and at the end, Colleen recalls, "He said, 'Good-bye, love.' I really took that to heart. I thought, boy...he means business!"

Geoffrey wanted to visit her, though Colleen felt it was too soon for the new widower. So she delicately put him off.

But their calls and letters picked up.

"We more or less—" Geoffrey begins

"Struck up a romance," Colleen finishes his sentence.

My darling Colleen,
It sounds a bit ridiculous the way we feel about one another. Here we are, both approaching the age of seventy and carrying on as though we are teenagers, but honey, I've got a young heart and cannot express my feelings any other way. I love it and I love you, honey. Roll on May 28!

That was the date they agreed to meet in New York.

"It was love at first sight," Geoffrey adds.

They spent three days touring New York before heading to Iowa, where he met her family. Then it was off to Mount Rushmore—where they bought friendship rings decorated with hearts.

Everything clicked. There was no tension, no shyness, no awkwardness.

In no time, Geoffrey decided to move to Iowa. He returned home to settle some personal matters, then on his first night back last September, he bent on one knee and proposed to Colleen.

"I said yes!" she recalls, turning to Geoffrey as they sit at their kitchen table. "I didn't even stop to think about it, did I?"

On November 28, the wartime pen pals became husband and wife. They sent out word to friends and family: "A reception honoring the newlyweds Colleen and Geoff will be on Saturday…"

It was their first joint correspondence.

SHARON COHEN
USED BY PERMISSION OF AP,
THE ASSOCIATED PRESS

LOST AND FOUND

&

Marriage is a sweet state,
I can affirm it by my own experience,
In very truth, I who have a good and wise husband
Whom God helped me to find.

CHRISTINE DE PISAN

You're going to bring home a nice man from Korea to marry!" This prophecy relayed by a well-meaning neighbor frustrated twenty-four-year-old Susan as she prepared for her first overseas missions trip. *I'm NOT going halfway around the world to look for a husband,* Susan thought indignantly. And indeed, she wasn't. She was traveling the long distance to serve God and the people of South Korea as a medical missionary. Susan had received God's call to serve him overseas at the young age of ten. And now, fourteen years later she was embarking on this exciting adventure to a foreign land. Looking for a husband was the last thing on her mind!

Susan's tenure in Korea was filled with great challenges and great rewards. All too quickly, her two-year project had come to an end. As she packed a very large steamer trunk full of her belongings and all her mementos from her Korean experience, she chuckled as she recalled her former neighbor's good-bye. *How many people will be disappointed that I didn't find a husband here?* Susan wondered. After all, it was the hope of most women of her mother's generation to see the next generation of young women married. And two years in Korea didn't produce that result.

Susan arrived back in the United States without incident—almost.

She arrived safely, but her steamer trunk was MIA (missing in action). Somewhere on the way from Asia, the shipping company had lost the trunk including any clue to its whereabouts. Susan anguished over the fate of her trunk but kept praying it would turn up. Why would God have allowed all her belongings and all her personal treasures to get lost? Meanwhile, she began her next adventure—pursuing a master's degree in missions at a small Christian college in South Carolina.

Almost a year had passed when, out of the blue, Susan received a phone call from the shipping company. They had located her long-lost trunk. Susan's heart leaped with joy and thanks.

"When can you get it here?" she asked excitedly.

"It's on its way as we speak," the man informed her. "Ought to be pulling up there in about thirty minutes, ma'am."

"Thank you, thank you!" Susan gushed.

"But ma'am," the man said, "you'll need to get someone over there to unload it."

"Can't the driver—?" Susan suggested.

"Nope," said the man. "The union doesn't allow the driver to do that work, and besides that trunk is the size of a refrigerator. It will take several big guys to get it off the truck and into your house."

Susan panicked. She had only recently moved to the small college town. How in the world could she recruit three or four "big guys" in a matter of minutes? As soon as she hung up, she feverishly dialed an acquaintance, Paul, who lived in one of the college dorms. The small college did not have private phones in the dorm rooms. Instead, it had only one phone in each dorm hallway. Understandably, the residents were loathe to answer the phone as this invariably involved the time-consuming activity of tracking down or taking a message for the person for whom the call was intended.

On this particular day, when the phone rang Dave Hedberg was alone in the hall on his way to class. He heard the phone ring and ring. He hesitated, but, having a few minutes to spare (this day anyway), he decided to pick up the phone.

"Hello."

Susan was relieved when the phone was answered. "Is Paul there?" she asked breathlessly.

"No, Paul has moved off campus," came the response.

"Moved? Really? Do you know where he lives now?" Susan inquired anxiously.

Sensing how distraught the caller was, Dave replied, "No, but is there anything I can do to help you?"

Susan knew she must sound desperate, but she was. "I hate to ask this of a perfect stranger, but…how big are you?"

"How big am I?"

Knowing how strange the question she posed was, Susan quickly explained her predicament to the stranger she had just met on the phone a few seconds before. Always one to help whenever he saw a need, Dave assured her that he and the friends he would recruit were big enough to help. They arranged to meet on the steps of the campus student center.

As he told it later, when Dave arrived at the student center and got a glimpse of the attractive blond who had been at the other end of the phone, he was especially delighted that he'd answered the dorm hall telephone earlier that day.

Sure enough, Dave's muscles proved big enough to help Susan move her newfound trunk of treasures. But ultimately, it was his love for Christ and his love for Susan that were big enough to win her heart.

Two years after their first meeting, Dave proposed on the same steps where he first laid eyes on Susan. And so, while Susan didn't bring home a "nice man from Korea to marry," she did find true love through the misadventures of her steamer truck and its journey to South Carolina from Korea.

SUSAN HEDBERG, AS TOLD BY HER SISTER PAM ZELEK

Editor's note: Susan Zelek and David Hedberg were married and today serve as missionaries to South America.

LEFT INSTEAD
OF RIGHT

*A man's heart plans his way
but the Lord directs his steps.*

PROVERBS 16:9

W hy did I turn left instead of right in the alley that Friday
night? Was there an angel blocking my path as I came out
of the underground restaurant, causing me to walk up inexplicably
toward Harvard Square, rather than downhill toward my apartment?

I had begun graduate school only a few weeks before. While I
enjoyed the John F. Kennedy School of Government and was learning to
survive on fewer hours of sleep than I had dreamed possible, I was aching
for the family and friends I had left behind in my hometown of
Washington, D.C. I missed my church and the close bonds forged in our
single-adults group. I missed singing and my ego was still bruised by my
almost comically horrible audition and subsequent rejection from the
Harvard Collegium choir just two days before. Harvard was an experience
of a lifetime—but it was also new territory, sometimes cold, and often
lonely.

That crisp fall evening, I had looked forward to the first meeting of the
Harvard Graduate School Christian Fellowship (HGSCF), a monthly gathering of all the Christian fellowship groups within the university's many
graduate programs. For three years, my relationship with God had been
the most important thing in my life, and I was yearning to find others who

shared that priority. I was also looking for friends among my classmates, and that day I had jumped at the opportunity to go waterskiing with three of them.

Tired and disheveled, I returned late to my apartment, realizing there was no way I would make the HGSCF meeting before it ended. For some unfathomable reason, I showered, changed, and walked the two miles to the campus meeting site anyway, arriving just as the last few people were turning out the lights.

I recognized Virginia, a second-year student at the Kennedy School. She mentioned that some of the others had asked her to get a big table at a nearby underground restaurant, where they would meet for a late dinner. Would I like to join her?

I was thankful that after all I would get to meet people from other graduate programs, but when the whole group arrived en masse at the restaurant, there were too many. From across the room, I could see them crowded on the steps down into the restaurant, talking to the hostess, who was regretfully shaking her head. My eyes fell on one particularly good-looking guy in a striped shirt. Because Virginia and I were both tired, we elected to stay at the restaurant while the others went elsewhere, but I grinned and told her that I sure would have loved to have met a few of the nice young men in that group!

It is funny how things work. For the next ten minutes, Virginia and I tried unsuccessfully to be served. Waiters bustled all around us but would not stop and give us menus, take our orders, or bring us water. After our fifth fruitless attempt to flag down someone, we joked that we must be invisible and decided to call it a night.

We walked up the steps and said our good nights at the entrance to the restaurant. Virginia's bike was parked in Harvard Square, which we could see at the end of the alley to our left. My apartment was on the campus of the business school, downhill and to the right. I turned left.

Unbeknownst to me, as I was walking up the alley, another person was walking down an intersecting street toward me. On Friday nights, Harvard Square is as crowded as Grand Central Station at rush hour, and suddenly I found myself nearly bumping into someone. I recognized the striped shirt. We both looked at each other and said in unison, "Say, weren't you just at the restaurant?"

He introduced himself as Jeff. He was in his last year at the law school, had been in the HGSCF group that left for a less-crowded restaurant, and was out looking for anyone who'd lost the group. He pointed me toward the new restaurant. An hour into dinner, the topic turned to singing. Jeff was in the Law School Christian Fellowship's a cappella singing group, which was looking for a soprano! A friendship was born, and a romance followed.

Almost exactly two years later, Jeff and I were married at my church in Washington, D.C. We both look back on that fall night with amazement. Events had to have been perfectly synchronized for us even to have met. Because of his schedule, Jeff did not attend another HGSCF meeting until right before he graduated. If I had given up on going to the meeting despite the late hour; if Virginia had left the building one minute earlier; if a waiter had served us; if I had turned right instead of left; if Jeff had been ten seconds earlier or later on his path through crowded Harvard Square—Jeff and I would never have met. God did it all, and he did it well.

A man's heart may plan his way, but thank goodness, the Lord truly does direct his steps.

SHAUNTI CHRISTINE FELDHAHN

And the fruit that can fall without shaking
Indeed is too mellow for me.
LADY MARY WORTLEY MONTAGUE

SHE ROPED
HIM IN

Twice or thrice had I loved thee,
Before I knew thy face or name.
JOHN DONNE

I spent the summer after my high school graduation with my sister and her husband at the campground in Cedar Falls, Iowa. My sister had invited me to come and help care for her new baby, and I was thrilled to enjoy a summer vacation by the river.

Every afternoon when the baby napped I enjoyed the luxury of swinging out on the front porch in the hammock, reading a good book. I was relishing my last few months of freedom before I began school at the local college.

Every day, a dashing young man would hurry by the house on his way to work and I would peek up from my book to get a glimpse of his handsome face. I later learned that he was responsible for firing up the stove in the dining hall and that was why he came by our house each afternoon. How I longed to catch his eye so that we could meet!

As the summer wore on, I observed him watching me as he passed by, but it took several weeks before he finally smiled and said hello, but there was no other contact. I longed to meet the stranger with the friendly face but I was much too shy to initiate a conversation. I wished that he would.

One sunny afternoon just at the very moment the young man passed by, I had an opportunity to meet him, as the rope on the hammock suddenly broke and I tumbled out onto the floor of the porch. What a stroke of luck! My knight-in-shining armor immediately dashed up on the porch to rescue me.

At last, we met. His name was Leon Krafft and he told me that he attended the local college where I would be going in the fall. From that day forward we chatted every time he came by. I found myself looking forward to his brief visits that became the highlight of my afternoons.

Much to my disappointment, though, the summer romance that I'd been dreaming of never developed. Leon never invited me to go out.

After the summer ended, college began and I would run into Leon occasionally. He was always smiling and friendly, but he still didn't ask me out. I kept praying that he would.

One Friday afternoon when we ran into one another on campus, he asked me if I would like to go to a party with him that evening. "Yes, I would love to go with you!" I answered breathlessly. I had daydreamed about going out with him every afternoon as I swung in the hammock when he walked past me. My dream had finally come true!

I practically floated home on a cloud that afternoon to get ready for my date that evening, But when I announced to my mother that I was going to a party with the boy I had met over the summer at the campground, she promptly extinguished my enthusiasm. Mother was not pleased and she delivered a scorching lecture to me.

"Don't you know that a proper young lady never accepts an invitation for the same evening? You are obviously his second choice."

I frankly didn't know if I was his first, second, or third choice, but it was too late to do anything about it now…and was I sure glad it was!

Leon and I had a wonderful time that evening, and when I told him that my mother had scolded me, he confessed to me that I had, indeed, been his second choice. He had been seeing the campus queen, but she was suddenly called away for the evening. When he ran into me, his problem of finding another date at the last minute was quickly solved. Too bad for the campus queen, because after that evening, Leon never left my side.

A year later we were married and remained happily so for more than fifty years. My dear husband always teased me about tampering with the rope so the hammock would fall at the exact time he walked by. For the rest of our lives, Leon told everyone the story of how I roped him in. Truthfully, I couldn't have planned it that way if I'd tried!

I would tell anyone that it's not necessarily a bad thing to be second choice, just as long as you're the *right* choice. And, as in my case, with a little help from above, you can be roped right into first place before you know it!

RUTH KRAFFT, AS TOLD TO SUSAN WALES

There is a garden in her face
Where roses and white lilies blow;
A heavenly paradise is that place,
Wherein all pleasant fruits do flow;
There cherries grow which none may buy
Till "Cherry-ripe" themselves do cry.
THOMAS CAMPION

Will You Marry Me?

Prithee, pretty maiden
will you marry me?
SIR WILLIAM SCHWENCK GILBERT

HE HAS BEEN FEELING OUT THE EMOTIONAL ENVIRONMENT WITH THE ONE HE LOVES. THEY HAVE TALKED ABOUT WHAT THEY LIKE, WHAT THEY WANT, WHAT THEY DON'T. THEY HAVE TALKED ABOUT WHO THEY ARE AND HOW THEY BELIEVE. THEY SHARE A COMMON COMMITMENT TO WALK IN GOD'S WAYS. HE IS CERTAIN THAT HE WANTS TO SPEND THE REST OF HIS LIFE WITH HER. HE IS SURE THAT THE INTENTION IS MUTUAL.

HE IS READY. IT IS THE CULMINATION OF MONTHS—OR YEARS—OF GETTING ACQUAINTED, PRAYING FOR DIRECTION, NURTURING A RELATIONSHIP, LEARNING THE GIVE AND TAKE OF LOVE, AND SEEKING THE WISDOM OF FRIENDS AND FAMILY.

HE HAS REHEARSED THIS MOMENT IN HIS MIND A THOUSAND TIMES, AND IS NOT ABOUT TO ASK THE ALL-IMPORTANT QUESTION ON A WHIM.

WHY, THEN, DO HIS LIPS QUIVER AND KNEES KNOCK? WHY IS THIS MAN'S HEART POUNDING?

A CHRISTMAS PORTRAIT

☙

Christmas isn't a season.
It's a feeling.
EDNA FERBER

Steve and I met and fell in love while we were in law school. We often talked about marriage, and I fully expected Steve to present me with an engagement ring at graduation. But the only thing presented that day in May were diplomas.

I brushed off my disappointment, convinced that Steve would propose to me on my birthday in July. That would be much more romantic anyway, I decided. I looked forward to the day with great anticipation. The night before, I could hardly sleep. I was too busy planning how I would accept the proposal—happily, of course, but not too desperately.

Sure enough, when Steve handed me my gift, it was in a small jeweler's box. I opened it with baited breath—to discover a beautiful gold locket. "It's beautiful, Steve!" I gushed. But honestly, it was a struggle to hide my disappointment. *What was he waiting for?*

It didn't help that my little sister had gotten engaged the year before. Not only that, but her fiancé planned the most romantic proposal. He took her on a scavenger hunt and at the end of the evening she discovered the sparkling diamond tied to the stem of a pink rose—her favorite kind.

Steve, a more serious type, probably wasn't capable of such creativity. But I did expect a proper proposal. Not that I needed to worry about that.

Raised in a Southern family, he had impeccable manners and always knew the proper thing to do. He would certainly ask my father for my hand in marriage. But *when?*

Now with Christmas fast approaching, I mustered up my courage and asked my father if Steve had mentioned anything.

"Like what?" my father asked.

"Like my hand in marriage," I replied.

"I've hardly laid eyes on Steve since he began working at the law firm," Father said. "You two aren't still serious are you?"

My heart sank. It looked like Christmas, too, would pass without a proposal. I began trying to drop subtle hints—like dragging him past the window of jewelry stores, or asking him what style of decorating he'd prefer in a home. But I only received blank responses. "I don't know," he'd say, and change the subject.

My best friend, Betty, suggested that I try a little something to wake him up. "Tell him you think the two of you should date other people," she suggested. The thought devastated me, but maybe Betty was right. If he thought he was losing me then just maybe he'd propose. Then again, I didn't want to manipulate something as important as a marriage proposal.

I finally decided that if the ring didn't appear at Christmas, I'd have a heart-to-heart talk with him about my feelings. In the meantime, I had a hard time getting into the Christmas spirit. Each year, since my sister Sarah and I have been little, our entire family has gotten dressed up, and with our dog, Puddin', in tow, marched off to the mall to pose with Santa. Mom puts the picture on our Christmas cards and sends them to family and friends all over the world.

But this time when Father announced that we were having our annual Christmas photo taken on Saturday morning, I balked. "Dad," I protested, "aren't we all getting a little too old for this? Why can't we just have our picture taken in front of the Christmas tree like normal people?"

Dad pretended not to hear me, and Mom was oblivious. "This year," she gushed, "your sister's fiancé, Ted, is coming along. So you'll have the honor of sitting on Santa's lap all by yourself."

"Oh yippee," I moaned.

"And next year," Mom added, "maybe Steve will be in our picture."

"I don't think so, Mom," I said. *Maybe,* I thought, *Steve has realized that I have a wacky family and that's the reason he hasn't proposed yet.*

When I saw Steve that Friday night, he invited me to accompany him to pick out his mother's Christmas present the next morning, but I had to decline.

"I have to have my picture taken with my family," I told him. I was sorely disappointed because helping a guy buy a present for his mom is quite a wifely chore.

"They aren't still going to see Santa, are they?" he asked.

"Yes, I'm afraid so," I confessed, "but maybe I can meet you afterward."

"I doubt it," he said, "Have you ever seen those lines waiting to see Santa on Saturday mornings? You'll be lucky if you make our date at eight."

The next morning when Sarah's fiancé arrived we all crowded in the family car along with Puddin', who was decked out in his finest Christmas sweater.

"Are you sure you want to marry into this crazy family, Ted?" I asked my sister's fiancé.

"Sure," he replied, "I think this is really cool!"

At least my father had arranged for us to arrive early and have our pictures made before the line of screaming children descended upon Santa Claus. As we waited for Santa to be escorted by an elf to his throne surrounded by a gaudy miniature toyland, I glanced at this year's Santa.

"Wow, they sure picked an awful Santa this year!" I whispered to my sister. "He's a puny looking thing and that beard is about as fake as any I've seen."

Sarah looked him over and disagreed. "I think he's kinda cute," she replied.

My parents were making cheerful chatter with one of the elves as I stood alone pouting. "Let's get this over with," I complained a little too loudly. The other elf must have heard me because we were immediately invited up to Santa's throne.

"Ho, ho, ho!" bellowed Santa as he looked in my direction.

Our dog, Puddin', took one look at this ridiculous Santa Claus and began to growl.

"My sentiments exactly, Puddin'," I whispered.

"Ho, ho, ho!" Santa hollered again, louder this time because of Puddin's growling and yapping. "Come sit in Santa's lap, little girl," he said in a fake Irish accent, looking in my direction.

"Isn't Santa taking this a little too far?" I protested. My mother shot me a look that could kill. So I climbed up in Santa's lap praying I wouldn't squish the skinny impostor.

The elves arranged my mother and father behind Santa. Sarah and her fiancé sat at his feet holding onto Puddin', who had finally calmed down. And there I sat, a twenty-four-year-old on Santa's bony lap. The children in line started to giggle. It seemed as though the photographer would never get the camera adjusted. We all waited.

"Ho, ho, ho!" said Santa. "There seems to be a problem. In the meantime, why don't you just tell Santa what you want for Christmas."

"You've got to be joking," I objected.

"Go on, tell me," he said.

"Well, if you must know," I said, "I want an engagement ring. If you can arrange that, Santa Claus, I actually might believe in you."

"I think I can manage that," he mumbled, "and who's the lucky bloke so I can put a wee bug in his ear?"

"My boyfriend, Steve," I answered. "But good luck, Santa—I've been waiting forever."

The photographer was finally ready again and I managed to smile through several photos. It was finally over, or so I thought. Santa reached down into his big bag and pulled out some presents for my parents, my sister and Ted, even a bone for Puddin'. Next he handed me a Christmas stocking bulging with candy.

"Well go on, darlin'," he insisted, "look inside."

Amid the candy canes and chocolate kisses, I spotted a tiny box. "It can't be!" I screamed. The photographer was snapping away as I opened the dainty satin box. It was the most beautiful engagement ring I had ever seen in my entire life. "But where is Steve?" I asked.

"Ho, ho, ho!" Santa said again, dropping his accent. "Will you marry me?"

It was Steve! I couldn't believe that my sweet, prim and proper Steve was disguised as Santa Claus!

"Aren't you going to get on your knees, Santa Steve?" I teased.

"I would but you're sitting on them," he said. So to the cheers of all those waiting in line, I turned around and gave Santa a big kiss, polyester beard and all.

Today our children squeal with delight when they see the pictures of Mommy on Santa's lap, kissing Santa. I must confess, every Christmas season without fail our whole clan still dresses up in our finery and meets at the mall for our annual photo. And right before the camera goes pop, I always turn to Steve and give my sweet, skinny Santa a well-timed kiss.

AS TOLD TO SUSAN WALES

O my Luve's like a red, red rose
That's newly sprung in June;
O my Luve's like the melodie
That's sweetingly played in turn.
As fair art though, my bonnie lass,
So deep in luve am I;
And I will luve thee still, my dear,
Till a' the seas gang dry.
ROBERT BURNS

WHAT ABOUT FRED?

❧

He used to say to me in his soft language:
"God brought you to me,
Sweet Lover, and I think he raised me
To be of use to you."

CHRISTINE DE PISAN

When I was single and not in a relationship, which was more often than not, I often bemoaned to my friends, "There's nobody for me to go out with!" My friends were always sympathetic, knowing how much I wanted someone to share my life with.

I hung out with a crowd of actors and musicians in Los Angeles who were committed Christians. There was one guy in our group named Fred Bova. I'd only met him once, but we had friends who suggested that we go out. I'm an actress, Fred's a musician, and our friends prayed for both of us that God would bring someone special into our lives. They would often suggest my name to Fred just as they suggested his to me, as a possible date, but Fred would always say, "I don't really know Sarah." And I would say, "He's definitely not my type."

During the time Fred and I hung out in the same crowd, we rarely saw one another. We both were in other relationships. But just as a special boyfriend dumped me on Christmas Eve, my friend Daisy insisted that I come to her party alone. She told me that Fred was going to be there, playing his guitar.

There's nothing worse than to have just broken up with your boyfriend at Christmastime. Also I was so distraught that I was almost crying my eyes out, and I didn't want to make a spectacle of myself. So I sat in a corner and held my personal pity party, crying buckets of tears. I never heard from Fred.

After that disastrous romance, I decided to give up dating and concentrate on my career. I wasn't looking for anyone, but during those next two years, my friends kept asking, "What about Fred?" I would protest, telling them I'd given up dating.

That following summer I got a leading role in a play in Pittsburgh. Before I left, I promised my friends I would get to know Fred when I returned. They didn't forget, either, and I agreed to go to a party where I would have a chance to chat with Fred.

"Everyone's saying that the two of us should get to know one another," Fred said cautiously.

"I know," I told him, "they've told me that, too."

"Would you like to go to lunch?" Fred asked.

We met for lunch several times, but there was something wrong. I finally confessed, "I just can't do this anymore...I'm too nervous."

Fred told me he felt the same way and that really broke the ice. For some reason, both of us knowing that the other one was nervous put us both at ease. At that moment, he asked me for a real date.

We went to dinner, and as the evening unfolded I was mesmerized by this kind and gentle man. He appeared to be enchanted with me, too.

When my birthday rolled around a few days later, Fred gave me a vintage birthday card. He had no way of knowing that I'm an old-fashioned girl, so I was overjoyed to discover that he, too, shared my passion for antiques and, more importantly, my faith in God. We were discovering what our friends had known all along...it had just taken a us a few years!

We had dated little more than a few months when Fred asked me a shocking question: "Is it too soon for me to propose?"

I became all tongue-tied because it *was* too soon. Fred could sense my apprehension and said, "Maybe Christmas?"

He didn't wait for Christmas but proposed in November. At Christmas, Fred gave me a lovely antique engagement ring. Celebrating this happy Christmas with Fred made me think about how three years earlier I was crying over a guy who wasn't right for me when God had my future husband right there under my nose.

Less than a year later Fred and I were married surrounded by our friends—our matchmakers. But there is more to this story, much more.

When I was helping Fred move out of his apartment into our new home, he took me by the hand and pointed out something on the sidewalk. There scrawled in concrete obviously written years ago, the name, *Sarah*.

"God has been trying to tell us and show us this for a long, long time," he grinned as he took me in his arms. Fred had lived in the apartment quite a while and had walked over the name *Sarah* several times a day.

"I thought about you every time I walked past your name. It was only a few months later that I realized there was another name there, too." We looked down at the sidewalk and there in plain view above my name, Sarah, was the name *Fred* faintly visible.

It seems that God was not only trying to show and tell us something when he brought Fred and me together; he made sure what he was telling us was written in concrete.

SARAH RUSH AND FRED BOVA, AS TOLD TO SUSAN WALES

TIME IN A BOTTLE

The voice of the sea speaks to the soul.
The touch of the sea is sensuous,
enfolding the body in its soft, close embrace.
KATE CHOPIN

Every August of my childhood, my family gathered at my grandparents' beach house on the North Carolina coast. It was two
weeks that I looked forward to each year, especially being with my cousin
Marilyn from Connecticut. She and I were the same age.

From morning till night Marilyn and I played in the sea. As children
we loved riding the waves and building sand castles. When we became
teenagers, we loved the romance of the ocean as we took long walks down
the beach, daydreaming about our future. The summer we celebrated our
sixteenth birthdays we decided it would be wildly romantic if we tossed a
bottle filled with a note from each of us into the sea. We spent days com-
posing our letters for our bottles. Marilyn wrote the following:

> *When you open this bottle and discover my letter*
> *I hope you'll agree that fate has brought us together.*
> *Write me and we will see*
> *If our love is meant to be!*

"Clever, don't you think?" she asked.

I, on the other hand, decided to be very daring. I wrote: "Will you
marry me?" I also included my name, address, and phone number. The

evening before we left for home, we went to the beach where we tossed our bottles into the sea at sunset. We staged quite a little ceremony that evening on the beach.

For years afterward, we talked about who would find our bottles. I told Marilyn that I hoped he would have blond hair and blue eyes. She was hoping her Prince Charming would be tall and dark.

To our disappointment, there was no news from our bottles. "They're probably somewhere on the ocean floor," I speculated.

The years went by. I moved to New York where I shared an apartment with Marilyn until she married. My advertising career was flourishing but my social life seemed to be at a standstill. My parents, knowing I had a little extra money and some time off, convinced me to spend my vacation with them at my grandparents' beach house.

When I arrived a couple of days before my parents, it was lonely and I longed for the days of my youth when the house was full of cousins and laughter. My grandparents had passed away and the rest of the family rarely made time to visit the beach house. Everyone had busy lives and all my cousins had their own families now—except for me.

I was feeling incredibly lonely as I walked the beach each morning. My parents arrived a few days later and my mother announced that a mysterious letter addressed to me had arrived at their home.

"Debbie, I didn't know you knew anyone from Charlotte," she said.

"I don't." I thought it might be someone I'd met at college.

"Does the name Tom O'Neil sound familiar?" my mother asked.

"Nope. Don't know any O'Neils."

"Well, don't just stand there," my father urged. "Open it!"

I ripped into the letter. As I read it, a wave of emotion swept over me. I was both embarrassed and intrigued at the same time.

"Well?" Mom asked. "Aren't you going to tell us who it's from?"

"I...It's...oh, no!"

"What? What?"

"Somebody found my bottle!"

"Your what?"

"My bottle! The bottle I threw into the ocean ten years ago."

"What?"

I made myself read the words. "It's this guy, Tom O'Neil. He found my bottle, and—"

"And what?"

I looked at them woodenly. I'm sure my face was white. "He's accepted my marriage proposal."

Two mouths fell open.

"And he wants me to call him. Here's his number."

Mom and Dad made me go back to the beginning and explain everything. I told them I'd imagined the bottle had made its way to Spain or some exotic island. "Can you believe it only made it down to the next beach?"

The next morning, at my parents' urging, I dialed Tom O'Neil. There was no answer (thankfully), so I left my name and the number at the beach house on his voice mail. *It's all some prank,* I told myself.

He called me the next evening.

"Hi Debbie," a strong male voice said. "This is Tom O'Neil. I'm not at home. I called and checked my messages. You're not going to believe this, but I'm here at the beach, too! Want to have dinner at the Crab Shack tomorrow night?"

I was so shocked I could hardly speak. But before we hung up, we agreed to meet for dinner the following evening. I mean, how could I not?

When the hostess led me to his table, I was stunned. There sat this handsome young man—with blond hair and blue eyes.

Meeting Tom was just too good to be true. It turned out he worked as an attorney in Charlotte. He had been coming to the neighboring beach with his family for his entire life, just like I had. He had found my bottle ten years before, but never contacted me until now.

"I was just getting to the point in my life where I wanted to meet someone," he said. "I figured you would be a good place to start. I always knew I would contact you one day—when I was ready to get married. For ten years I've dreamed about the girl who put the note in that bottle."

I was suddenly self-conscious. "I hope you aren't disappointed."

"Absolutely not. You're far more than I ever dreamed. Besides, you've already proposed! That makes things a lot simpler."

We laughed like old friends.

Over the next two weeks, we had a lot of fun getting to know one another. Our friendship grew, but didn't progress beyond that. My parents referred to the experience as my "summer romance." But that was pushing it—we hadn't even held hands.

When I returned to New York, I didn't really expect to hear from Tom. I figured I'd see him next summer if we were both still available, but I knew long-distance relationships were impossible. I did find myself thinking about him, however. Often.

Two weeks later, I came home from work and found a letter from him. "He misses me," I reported to my cousin Marilyn. I'd called her about the mystery man right away.

Tom came to New York to visit me a couple of times. And we ran up a sizable long-distance phone bill. *And* we wrote letters once a week.

We met at the beach again the next summer. The night before we were leaving, we walked down the beach at sunset. Tom had brought a blanket. When we got a spot near my family's beach house, Tom insisted that we pause so that I could dig in the sand for a surprise.

I dug where he indicated and found the same old bottle I'd thrown in the ocean eleven years before. There was a note inside. It read, "Will you marry me?" And that wasn't all. At the bottom of the bottle was a beautiful engagement ring!

Exactly two years from the time Tom first contacted me, we were married at the little church in the beach community with my cousin Marilyn as my matron of honor. Every summer we bring our children to the beach house.

Next summer our daughter turns sixteen, and she's already working on the letter that she plans to place in her bottle.

MARGARET O'NEIL

SILVER JUBILEE

Brief is life, but love is love.
ALFRED, LORD TENNYSON

Harper and I were approaching our silver wedding anniversary. We'd had twenty-five years of wedded bliss and we both felt the desire to share our joy with our closest friends and family. We decided the perfect way to celebrate our love was to get married for a second time.

We invited our original bridesmaids and groomsmen to attend. Our guests—friends and family we had collected through the years—came from all over the country. I felt like a young, blushing bride again in a beautiful gown with silver thread woven through it. In my hair, we used silver gray net for a small veil. I carried a bouquet of white calla lilies down the aisle.

For the most important part, the vows, Harper and I carefully repeated the ones we'd made to each other twenty-five years before. We promised to love and cherish each other all over again. The best part of our second wedding was that we weren't the least bit nervous. We enjoyed our meaningful ceremony to the fullest and were thrilled that we could share it with all our friends and family.

Our daughter came home from college to help us celebrate. She thought we were joking about taking a second honeymoon. We kept trying to tell her we were serious and she kept rolling her eyes and laughing.

She stopped laughing when we waved good-bye to her from the car, leaving her to entertain all of the guests at the reception.

Marge Piercy wrote, "Life is the first gift, love is the second, and understanding the third." Our second wedding honors all three: the life God gave us, the depth of feeling that joins us, and our realization of both as gifts. Twenty-five years marks a very important anniversary. We've come through so much, learned so much, and loved so much. Harper and I both think that marriage should be celebrated, so why limit yourself to just one wedding? Who knows—we may even get married a third time!

DR. ANNE GASTON

I arise from dreams of thee
In the first sweet sleep of night,
When the winds are breathing low,
And the stars are shining bright.
PERCY BYSSHE SHELLEY

ONE DAY YOUR PRINCE WILL COME!

❧

An engaged woman is always
more agreeable than a disengaged.
She is satisfied with herself.
Her cares are over, and she feels
that she may exert all her power
of pleasing without suspicion.

JANE AUSTEN

At the age of five, many girls love playing with dolls and imagining the joys of having a family. But how many of them start praying for their fantasies to come true?

At five years old I was already eager to meet Prince Charming, get married, have kids, and live happily ever. And even at that young age, every time I kneeled to pray I asked God to send me a husband.

Through all my growing-up years, the prayer remained the same. By the time that I graduated from college at twenty-three, I had kissed a lot of frogs but none had turned into Prince Charming. I decided my fairy tale was probably still en route, but for the time being, I'd better get serious about a career.

I pursued another goal, this one to become an agent in Hollywood. As the years passed I found success in my career but faced failure in the dream department. I discovered that Hollywood was not the place to find husband material. Few men of faith crossed my path. Friends who knew how much I wanted to get married were astonished when I ended promising relationships, turned down dates and even a couple of marriage proposals because the men involved weren't believers. My friends thought I was being too picky, but as much as I wanted to marry, I refused to compromise on the faith issue.

By the time I turned thirty, I accepted the fact that I might never marry, and I relinquished my hopes for marriage to God. After much prayer, I did finally find peace and contentment as a single career woman. The deep desire in my heart for a husband was not removed, just dormant, so I figured I couldn't do any harm by continuing to pray for a husband...just in case!

When I was thirty-three I was in a hotel lobby just before attending the Golden Globe Awards. An attractive young man approached my dear friend, Cathy Brown, and asked to see her program. They begin chatting and he happened to mention that he was a Christian. Hearing those words, Cathy grabbed him by the hand and led him in my direction.

Cathy was so proud of herself. She thought she had found "one." I was interested and amused until I learned that Will was only twenty-six and was a guest at the hotel from Oklahoma City. I politely gave him a business card and walked off to rub shoulders with Kevin Costner, Brad Pitt, and the other movie stars that had assembled for the Golden Globes.

Cathy, though, both a relentless matchmaker and a genuinely nice person, was not about to let this Christian guy—a rarity in Hollywood—get away! She arranged for him to get into the Golden Globes and the aftershow parties.

After those events, almost a year passed before I thought of Will Rogers again. Cathy called one day and said, "Remember the cute guy from Oklahoma City? He's in town for the week—wants to know if we can get together with him!" I flipped through my calendar; it was jammed, so I suggested that she invite him to hike with a group of our friends on Saturday.

Everyone enjoyed the hiking trip except Cathy, who was busy darting between Will and me. She whispered, "Victorya, you should go out with Will. He likes you!" and "Will, you should ask Victorya out." Neither of us knew she was coaxing the other.

Later that evening Will joined Cathy and me and my parents for a concert. When Cathy went to the ladies' room with my mother, she announced, "This is the one—just watch. Victorya is going to marry Will Rogers."

My mom just humored her and said, "Yeah, sure, Cathy."

But something had clicked. Will and I began e-mailing one another every day and within three weeks, he came back to Los Angeles to see me. After that, he visited every few weeks. I began to hope and pray that maybe Cathy was right. When Will invited me to fly out to meet his family for Thanksgiving, I knew things were getting serious.

That weekend, my hopes began to soar when Will told me that he wanted to marry me one day, but when he didn't officially propose, I was devastated. Afterward I prayed: "Lord, why did this guy have to come along who apparently cares for me but isn't ready for marriage? I've waited for so long to meet the right person. If he knows he wants to marry me, why doesn't he just propose?"

The next time I saw Will, I honestly told him how much I wanted to get married. Much to my disappointment, he replied, "Victorya, I love you and I know without a doubt that one day I want to marry you, but I'm just not ready yet. Trust me, when the time is right—I'll propose!"

Yeah, yeah, yeah, I thought. *I'd better get used to being single again!*

From then on, I grew exceedingly anxious every time Will came to Los Angeles. I always wondered if this would be the time he'd propose. By the time he arrived, I was so uptight that it began affecting our relationship. Every moment I was with him I expected him to pop the question, but he never did. Each time he left without a proposal, I was in tears. To make matters worse, when I showed up at the office on Monday morning, everyone was anxiously waiting to see if I was wearing a ring!

Will always apologized and explained that he felt bad, but he just wasn't ready to get married. One week he called to say that he wanted to come for the weekend, but he didn't want his visit to cause any anxiety. "I'll just tell you up front that I'm not going to propose," he said, "so if you would prefer I not come, I won't."

"Of course I want you to come," I assured him. Knowing not to expect his proposal actually took a lot of pressure off, and we had one of our best visits ever. Just before we left for an Angels baseball game, Will began acting a little strange. He asked me to sit down on the couch and after a dramatic pause, he finally spoke. "If I were to propose to you without a ring, would you still consider us engaged?"

I asked suspiciously and anxiously, "Is that a proposal?"

"Maybe, but answer the question," he ordered.

"Of course we'd be engaged. I don't need a ring," I assured him.

Then he said again, "Even without a ring, we'd be engaged?"

By this time I was so excited I could barely whisper, "Yes."

Will continued, "So, will you marry me even without a ring?"

I had a big ear-to-ear grin and my eyes begin to tear up as I answered, "Yes!"

Suddenly, Will whipped out a ring and said, "Well, how about with the ring?"

At that moment I totally lost it—I shed a gallon of tears. It was finally true: I was officially engaged!

After I had cried for a few minutes, Will laughed and told me that I could look at the ring. It was so gorgeous that it took my breath away!

I became Mrs. Will Rogers on January 31, 1998, at the Crystal Cathedral in Garden Grove, California. It was the happiest day of both of our lives.

As we drove away to our honeymoon destination, Will took my hand and tenderly revealed, "When I was a little boy about five years old, I dreamed about the girl I would marry. And when you walked down the aisle today—do you know that you were that girl in my dream?"

Then I told Will how I'd prayed for my husband since I was five years old and now he was there…by my side! Will and I both cried as we saw with clarity that God hears and honors the prayers and dreams of even the youngest of hearts.

VICTORYA MICHAELS-ROGERS, AS TOLD TO SUSAN WALES

PEN PALS

Submit yourselves one unto the other as unto the Lord.

PAUL'S ADVICE TO CHRISTIAN COUPLES
EPHESIANS 5:21

When do you ask a girl to marry you?"

The man remembered asking his mother long ago, and her answer came again to his mind: "When you can't live without her."

This was now that time, but the question still caught in his throat.

He had met her years before at a Christian student conference in New Mexico. At the time, he was an undergraduate student in Mississippi. She was from Texas, and was attending school in Massachusetts.

For the next three years after they met, they saw each other just once a year, staying in touch by writing back and forth. While each believed God had a special partner for them, and while both had prayed to be led to a Christian spouse, they simply regarded each other as pen pals. Through monthly letters they exchanged thoughts and began to discover special qualities in each other. It was a sort of correspondence course in companionship.

He finished college and began graduate school in Kentucky. That same year, she began her junior year abroad in Geneva, Switzerland. While there, she was led to a student retreat in the Swiss Alps. The retreat was led by a yet-unknown theologian, Francis Schaeffer. The exciting spiritual and intellectual atmosphere lured her back many weekends to the place called *L'Abri* (The Shelter), where she felt close to her special friend across the Atlantic.

Upon the completion of her year in Switzerland, she and her pen pal reunited and discovered, much to their own surprise, that their relationship had advanced to a deeper level.

Although still separated by hundreds of miles, they saw each other on holidays until her graduation from college. As a graduation gift, her parents presented her with a trip to a Christian student conference in the Holy Land. She chose the tour group led by her pen pal!

At the end of the tour, she took him to visit *L'Abri*, where he met Francis and Edith Schaeffer and saw the place that had been so special to her. That weekend, Schaeffer led a worship service in his chalet for the people of the village of Huemoz. That evening there was a communion service with students from five continents sitting cross-legged in a circle. Afterward, the young couple took a walk alone in the crisp alpine air. On that bright night, with the moon shining off the snowcapped Mont Blanc and the hint of Swiss cowbells in the higher pasture, they walked along, hands clasped, in a seemingly serene silence. Actually, he was nervously rehearsing the question that he had been considering for many months, and she was wondering if that "feeling" she had that he might propose was more than wishful thinking.

Completely unaware of their surroundings, they found themselves back in the chalet kitchen sipping hot chocolate. She had perched herself on top of the running washing machine.

Suddenly, he got up, positioned himself in front of her as if to block her escape, and blurted out, "Will you marry me?"

There! He had finally said it! He could breathe again, but the words had seemed too puny for the commitment it expected and inadequate to demonstrate the devotion he felt toward her. Before she could respond, he blurted again, adding the words his father said had worked for him thirty-five years earlier: "I mean it. This is not a trial. This is forever."

She only smiled. It was a tender smile, but it revealed nothing affirming. Then she shook her head slowly and told him, "I always wondered what this would be like." Holding his hands and looking into his eyes, she said nothing for almost five minutes—perhaps considering each option, or relishing the moment, or even wondering how to say no painlessly. He listened to the washing machine begin its spin cycle and held his breath again.

"Yes, yes, I will," was the long-awaited answer. It came so simply that he couldn't believe that it was settled. She jumped down from the washing machine and smiled again. They embraced as the spin cycle stopped and rushed off to share their joyful news with their hosts.

The next morning after breakfast they sat in the grass of the high pasture, praying together. He showed her a letter that he had written to her parents back in Texas, asking for their daughter's hand in marriage. He was struck again by the description of real commitment that his own parents' words had shown him. Thirty-six years later, that commitment, first made during a moment in Edith Schaeffer's kitchen, is remade daily in deeper and broader dimensions.

DORSEY AND PAM DEATON

Kindness in women,
Not their beauteous looks,
Shall win my love.
SHAKESPEARE

BEGINNING TO
BEGIN AGAIN

✑

*A diamond is a chunk of coal
that did good under pressure.*
MOUNTAIN SAYING

I had been married a few short years when my husband walked out on me, leaving me alone with little money and a young daughter to support. We had been living in California, where my husband was a cinematographer/director in the movie industry. Then, suddenly, this world stopped. After the divorce, things turned from bad to worse for me. I thought long and hard about what to do, and leaving California seemed to make the most sense. So, I packed up my daughter and moved to New York in the hopes of making a new start. To escape the world and life of the West Coast, I fled across country to the world I had once known.

In New York, my daughter and I temporarily lived with friends of the family. But you can only be a guest for so long. I knocked on many doors trying to find a place to live. Apartments are hard to find in New York.

Because of my mother's social connections, I was invited to the many parties that New York society held, but I felt loneliness even in the midst of this sophisticated world. Something was missing in my life, but I didn't know what. Since the divorce, I felt like I'd been floating, just barely going through the motions of life. This was definitely the lowest point of my life…I couldn't get a credit card. I was ready for a change.

It was about then that my friend, Lee, took me to a prayer group that she attended. I was busy trying to start my own business as a personal shopper and a fashion consultant. I was working very hard, and what few moments I had at the end of the day I happily gave to my daughter. However, I forced myself to make room for the growth of my faith. I wanted a place to live and more importantly, a purpose for my life. After the first meeting at the prayer group, I prayed to accept the Lord. I could immediately feel things in my life start to change for the better. After such an exhausting period, I finally felt rejuvenated. I felt alive.

My life began to turn around. I found an apartment and my business prospered. But the biggest change happened when I surrendered my life to the Lord. The leaves and the flowers even looked different. It seemed that I could see, taste, smell, hear, and touch life for the first time.

Lee wanted me to meet a gentleman from Georgia. I kept saying no, that the timing was all wrong, but Lee wouldn't listen. She persuaded me to go out with him. "He's only here for two days. You'll like him and be doing me a huge favor at the same time."

Lee had done so much for me. I owed her at least this small favor. But, the timing was still awful. Oh well, I thought to myself, what could it possibly hurt. I knew I wasn't interested in a relationship at this point. In fact, I had completely given up on the idea of marriage at all and my life was going so well that I didn't really know if I wanted a serious relationship.

Guy was a true Southern gentleman and I liked him right away. He made me feel comfortable and spending time with him was a pleasure. He made me laugh, which I needed so desperately. He just seemed to fit into the new picture of my life. I could tell immediately that Guy was an incredible Christian. He was definitely one of the good ones!

We went to dinner both nights that he was in New York. After that, he'd fly up to see me and go along with me to my prayer group. I was amazed at how easily and effortlessly our lives seemed to fit together.

We had dated for a year when Guy invited me to join his mother, aunt, sister, and children at his North Carolina mountain house. I remember that it was pouring down rain. I was busy baking an apple pie, complete with an apron tied about my waist, when Guy suggested we go for a ride.

"I've got flour all over me," I laughed.

"It doesn't matter. Come on," he whispered. I quickly tried to dust most of the flour off me and then followed him out the door.

We had been driving for a few minutes when he looked at me and smiled. "Ginny, I can't live without you. I don't want to live without you," he said. "I want you to marry me. I want you to be my wife."

I was absolutely speechless. "Can't we keep dating?" I asked, feeling panicked.

Guy smiled. I suppose he had already anticipated my anxiety. "I don't want to rush you. Take as much time as you need. A week? A month? How long do you need? I'll wait."

I couldn't breathe and my ears were burning. I was so excited. I felt like a schoolgirl. I realized that I was smiling at him then. I knew that I was really in love with him. I had known it for a while but I hadn't expected a proposal that afternoon. But as I looked into his eyes, I knew that he was the one God had for me. "Okay," I agreed. "I'll do it!" That was Labor Day weekend and we were married that December in New York.

It's been eleven years now and we are still madly in love. When I look back on the tough times in my life, I realize that the struggles, those dark and confusing times, make us who we are meant to be. They make us grow stronger. I am so thankful for those lessons.

When I least expected it, God sent a husband to me. Looking back, I can see the hand of God working in my life at that time. God placed the people I needed the most at the right time and place in my life. Even in the darkest moments of my life, God was always with me, urging me forward to fulfill his plan for my life. He made sure that I met the people who would help me along my path until I was indeed ready to meet the most wonderful Guy in the world.

GINNY MILLNER

THE APPLE OF HIS EYE

What greater thing is there
for two human souls
To feel that they are joined...
so strengthen each other...
to be at one with each other in
silent unspeakable memories.

GEORGE ELIOT

Clothed in rags, the emaciated form of a young boy, in an effort to stay warm, shuffles back and forth in front of the barbed wire fence of a Nazi concentration camp in Germany. Like so many Jews before him, he wonders, "Will I survive?" The year is 1943 and I am that young boy.

As I look across the barbed wire, I suddenly catch sight of a young farm girl hurrying by. Her eyes are drawn to my sad figure. Embarrassed, I struggle to turn away, but our eyes are destined to meet. Without any words, a connection is made through our shy glances.

Bravely, I call out to her, "Do you have anything to eat?" The girl searches for any sign of the guards, and seeing none, she reaches in her pocket, pulls out an apple, and tosses it over the fence. My heart leaps with joy as the shiny red apple flies through the air, bringing with it both nourishment and hope. Food has become only a faint memory for me. How long has it been since I had tasted an apple? As I hold the fruit in my hands it seems to thaw my frozen fingers as well as my soul.

"Come back tomorrow," I ask.

The same time the next afternoon, I make my way to the fence. I wait.

In the distance the tiny speck grows larger. As she comes closer, our eyes embrace. She tosses another apple in my direction. I can see by the look I in her eyes that she, too, is being fed by our stolen moments.

The next day she came again bringing with her another apple, and then the next day a crust of bread. Our secret rendezvous continued for seven months, and the young girl became the apple of my eye. Through my pain and sorrow her visits supplied the hope that I needed to carry on.

Then one day I overhear that we were being moved to another concentration camp. My heart breaks knowing that I will never see those eyes again. When we meet that afternoon I tell her I'm going away and not to come again.

The next day I am shipped to another camp. The endless days pass by and then the months stretch into years. Each night when I am awakened by the recurring nightmares filled with the horrors of all I have endured, I weep for I am alone. My mother and father have died. But then I am comforted by the memories of the young girl's eyes as I dream of the precious moments we shared.

At last the war is over. The Russian Army descends upon our camp and frees us.

The years go by and I am living in New York City. In 1957 a good friend arranges a blind date for me with another immigrant. Reluctantly I go, and as I chat with my date in the back seat of the car on the way to the restaurant, she asks me the question often shared by immigrants, "Where were you during the war?"

"A concentration camp in Germany," I reply. "And you?"

"My family and I were spared. We had Aryan (Christian) papers and were fortunate to work on a farm in Germany," she answered. Then a faraway look came upon eyes.

"What is it?" I ask.

"Oh nothing," she replied, "Just a memory."

"Go on," I encourage her.

"Our farm was located near a concentration camp," she explained, "and every day I visited a young boy there and secretly tossed an apple over the barbed wire to him. We rarely spoke a word…but I can tell you, there was love between us. One day he was gone and I never saw him again. I assume he was killed but I cherish the memories of those months we shared.

"Were his feet covered with rags?" I ask. "And did he tell you one day not to come again?"

"Why...why, yes," she replied. "How do you know that?"

I felt as though my heart would explode as I took her hand in mine. I composed myself and spoke, "You fed me when I was hungry, you gave me hope when I had none. It was you who saved my life. Destiny has brought us together again. This time we are free...no longer separated by the barbed wire, and I never want to be separated from you again. Will you marry me?"

Without any hesitation she replied, "Yes," I will marry you." Roma suddenly knew, too...that I was that young boy, as I knew that she was the apple of my eye.

AS TOLD TO SUSAN WALES BY HERMAN ROSENBLAT

Used by permission of Herman Rosenblat. Mr. Rosenblat tells his life story in *The Will To Live* to be published in 2000 by Adam's Media Corporation, Holbrook, Massachusetts.

With This Ring

Go little ring to that same sweet
That hath my heart in her domaine.
GEOFFREY CHAUCER

It's THE MOST RECOGNIZED SYMBOL OF COMMITMENT IN OUR CULTURE. IT IS THE ULTIMATE TOKEN OF LOVE BETWEEN A MAN AND A WOMAN. IT IS THE VISIBLE MESSAGE TO ALL THAT THIS WOMAN OR THIS MAN IS NO LONGER LOOKING, BUT NOW AND FOREVER BELONGS TO A CERTAIN SOMEONE. THE WHITE OR YELLOW BAND OF METAL, SOMETIMES SET WITH BRILLIANT STONES, IS A TREASURE WHOSE VALUE FAR EXCEEDS ITS PRICE TAG.

Your WEDDING RING, ADORNING THE THIRD FINGER OF YOUR LEFT HAND, SAYS TO FRIENDS, FAMILY, AND THE REST OF THE WORLD, *I HAVE FOUND THE LOVE OF MY LIFE. I HAVE MADE UP MY MIND THERE IS NO ONE ELSE FOR ME.*

THE DAY A HUSBAND AND WIFE PLACE A RING ON EACH OTHER'S FINGER, IN THE PRESENCE OF GOD AND WITNESSES, ITS PERSONAL MEANING OUTWEIGHS ITS BRILLIANCE AND BEAUTY. AS YOU WALK WITH THE ONE YOU LOVE INTO THE FUTURE, YOU WILL NOT ALWAYS BE AT THE SAME PLACE IN THE SAME PATH AT THE SAME TIME. ALL KINDS OF WEATHER

WILL FIND YOU. THERE WILL BE STUMBLING BLOCKS. OBSTACLES MAY BRING DOUBT AND FEAR. LET YOUR RING ALWAYS REMIND YOU OF THE DAY YOU SEALED YOUR DECISION TO CLEAVE TO ONE ANOTHER, BE FAITHFUL, BECOME ONE FLESH.

YOUR RING IS YOUR SYMBOL OF FOREVER-AFTER SHINING COMMITMENT.

A COSTLY KISS

&

Pussy said to the Owl, "You elegant fowl!
How charmingly sweet you sing!
O let us be married! too long we have tarried;
But what shall we do for a ring?

EDWARD LEER

One thing was obvious as they approached married life. They needed a newer car. For years Jim had been driving a dilapidated heap he called "Ol' Red." This 1949 Mercury convertible was a disaster on wheels. The top wouldn't go up or down, the electric windows didn't work, the lights sometimes went out unexpectedly, and the engine dozed off every now and then. Jim never knew if he would get where he was going. A typical scene around town was Shirley steering the wreck while Jim pushed it. Once they got it started, people would drive alongside and point frantically at the wheels, which appeared to be falling off. It was a humiliating experience.

Furthermore (and most frustrating to Shirley), the front seat of the car was disintegrating. Springs stuck up at various angles, snagging her clothes and puncturing her backside. Shirley hated that car with a passion, but Jim didn't want to go into debt to buy a newer one. Tension was obviously brewing between Dobson and Deere over the pile of junk he used to transport her.

This conflict culminated one day as Jim came to the dorm to get Shirley. They had scheduled important job interviews that day, and she had spent two hours getting dressed. She was wearing her best outfit—a black suit she had just retrieved from the cleaners. So off they went. As they flew down the road at fifty miles per hour, the rotted old convertible top suddenly blew off. Bits of string and canvas beat them about the head and shoulders, and dust settled everywhere. The remnants of the top hooked onto the back of the car and flapped outward like Superman's cape.

Shirley had absolutely had enough. She screamed at Jim from the floorboard, where she crouched to escape the flogging. Jim was angry, too, not just at his car but at Shirley. For Pete's sake! It wasn't *his* fault. So he just kept on driving, with the ribs of his convertible top glistening in the sun, the ragged canvas flapping out the back, and his fiancée yelling at him from under the dashboard. Passersby must surely have thought these folks were crazy.

Given this background, it was a minor triumph for Shirley to get Jim to agree to buy a newer car. They picked out a gleaming white, 1957 Ford with white sidewall tires and a hard top. They drove Ol' Red up to the used car lot, where the engine sighed once and gave up the ghost. Somewhere in a salvage yard sits a lonely red Mercury with no top. On a spring protruding from the front seat are tiny woolen fibers ripped from a coed's skirt.

But that inconvenience was finally over for them. Jim and Shirley climbed into their shiny new (three-year-old) car and patted the dashboard. They could not have been more proud if they had just bought a new Rolls Royce. Down the road they drove in their chariot, feeling like a king and queen. They had gone only five blocks when Jim leaned over and kissed Shirley to celebrate the happy moment, but just as he did, the two cars in front of them made an unexpected stop in the middle of the block. Jim was on top of them by the time he looked up. He slammed on the brakes, but it was too late.

The events of the next few seconds have been preserved in their minds like an old videotape. "I can still hear my tires screeching and then the awful sounds of metal crunching against metal, and breaking glass tinkling as it fell to the pavement," Jim recalls. "I can see the hood and fenders of my beautiful car rising in slow motion toward me. At the same time,

Shirley and I are falling forward as our heads hit the sun visors."

It was actually a three-car collision since Jim knocked one car into the next in line. Fortunately, no one was hurt. The stunned couple got out of the car and surveyed the wreckage. They were sick over what they had done. Moreover, they were afraid someone might have seen the careless kiss that caused the accident. They weren't afraid to admit their fault in the matter; they just didn't want the whole world to know that an untimely kiss was really to blame.

While Jim was exchanging information with the two irritated drivers, Shirley overheard two little boys talking on the sidewalk.

"What happened?" one of the lads asked.

"Oh, that guy over there kissed the girl and hit two cars in front of him," the other responded matter-of-factly. Shirley held her breath!

Then the boys rode off on their bicycles, thereby concealing until this moment the embarrassing truth.

Although the damages were covered by Jim's insurance policy, he had to reckon with a $100 deductible—precisely the amount they were planning to spend for Shirley's wedding ring. On the wedding night she had to settle for a silver band, but Jim surprised her on their first anniversary with the ring she should have received twelve months earlier.

FROM DR. DOBSON: TURNING HEARTS TOWARDS HOME, ROLF ZETTERSTEN, 1989, WORD PUBLISHING, NASHVILLE, TENNESSEE. ALL RIGHTS RESERVED.

POP THE QUESTION...
NOT THE CORK!

It isn't beauty, so to speak
Nor good talk necessarily
It's just It.
Some women'll stay in a man's memory
If they once walked down the street.

RUDYARD KIPLING

What a difference a day can make! When I woke up that morning, I never dreamed that I was about to meet *Mr. Right*. I had almost given up on love when *he* walked into my life. It happened when I least expected it. The distinguished film producer was expected in Atlanta for a fundraiser. It was a miracle that our paths even crossed.

Ken had been an eligible bachelor for many years and was an unlikely candidate for the husband I had prayed that God would one day bring into my life. I was a far cry from the women he usually dated. Ironically when we met, I was wearing no makeup, my hair pulled back with a ribbon. There I stood before this handsome man, looking far from my best. "Why hadn't I at least put lipstick on?" I chastised myself.

I knew it was a special moment and feared I'd lost it because of my appearance. And yet when our eyes locked, we knew. It was as though God reached down from heaven and placed my hand in Ken's. There was never any doubt after that moment. I'm convinced that I could have had a paper bag over my head, and he still would have fallen in love with me.

That's because God was our matchmaker. It didn't matter to Ken what I looked like, what I was wearing, or even what I said. God revealed our hearts at that special moment. Our lives would never be the same. My head was spinning and my routine life suddenly took off on an exciting adventure.

Our fateful meeting was the beginning of a great romance followed by many crosscountry flights for both of us. I knew it was just a matter of time before Ken would propose. Ken was a professional at making beautiful films, and I knew he would plan an unforgettable proposal with the same thought and creativity that he planned his movies.

At Christmas I found the airline ticket he'd secretly sent to my mother to place in my Christmas stocking. When I called Ken to thank him, he explained that he wanted me to be in Los Angeles for Valentine's Day. *This must be it!* I told myself.

When February 14 arrived, Ken, every woman's dream of a romantic, had planned a very special evening for me at Saddle Peak Lodge, a romantic out-of-the way restaurant nestled in Malibu Canyon. Ever the producer, Ken drove me up the coast along the ocean's edge just as the sun was setting while Ken played our favorite love song, Rachmaninoff's Second Piano Concerto. Mesmerized by the beautiful setting, I must admit that I had to pinch myself to make sure I wasn't dreaming. Ken made me feel as though I was his star in a very romantic movie he was producing. I just couldn't wait to see what happened next in his script.

When we arrived at our destination and I stepped inside the 1929 hunting lodge, my fairy tale began to unfold. The maître d' seated us in front of the massive stone fireplace. The crisp white tablecloth held two dozen of my favorite Sonya roses. Ken had remembered. We just sat there gazing into one another's eyes and basking in the warm glow of the fire and the candles. Because of the distance that separated us, this was a rare opportunity for the two of us to be alone. I never wanted this evening to end but we were suddenly interrupted by the maître d'.

He reappeared at our table with waiters carrying a bottle of champagne

from the restaurant's renowned vintage collection. "This is a rare champagne," he announced, "and I want to share a glass with the two of you
for Valentine's Day."

Not wanting to break the romantic spell, I politely refused, but when
Ken and the man insisted I try the rare champagne, I accepted. The maître
d', the wine steward, and the waiters lingered as if they were waiting for
me to comment on the taste. I decided if I was ever going to get rid of the
entourage and be alone with my sweetheart that I would have to take a
big sip. *They're going to stand there and watch me drink this whole glass*, I
thought, so I purposely took a big gulp this time.

The look on Ken's face, and the faces of the little group that had
congregated around us, suddenly changed to horror as the sparkling
engagement ring that Ken had arranged for the restaurant to place in the
champagne disappeared. I never even saw the ring. My mind was on
making eyes at Ken!

Thanks to a quick little cough, the ring resurfaced. Everyone was
greatly relieved that I hadn't choked to death or worse yet, swallowed my
beautiful ring. In all the confusion, Ken momentarily forgot to propose.
When he recovered, he uttered the most beautiful proposal ever offered to
a woman in my opinion.

Mother always told me to look before you leap. I had looked into my
heart and knew that God had brought Ken into my life. Mother forgot to
add…look before you sip!

Today when we celebrate our anniversary, the two of us reserve our
same table at Saddle Peak Lodge and reflect on all the miracles God has
brought into our lives—especially the miracle of his matchmaking. And
when the waiter comes round, Ken says, *No champagne for Susan, please!*

SUSAN WALES

THIS TOO SHALL PASS

Young bride, a smile for thee,
To shine away thy sorrow;
For Heaven is kind today, and we
Will hope as well tomorrow.

MARTIN FARQUHAR TUPPER

My girlfriend, Rebecca, and I had struggled through the worst year of our lives. My mother died in January, Rebecca was laid off from the job she loved in February, and a fire destroyed my apartment building in March. When April arrived, my company downsized and I assumed the duties of three employees; in May Rebecca discovered a lump in her breast (fortunately, it was benign).

Trial after trial, we leaned hard on our faith and it sustained us. As we sought solace in the Lord we developed a motto: "This too shall pass."

Though I had planned to propose to Rebecca for some time, after such a tragic year I wanted to create a moment so fabulous and overwhelming that it would erase all our bad memories. I began to plan the perfect romantic proposal.

I considered all the ways my friends had proposed to their wives. My college roommate had hidden his wife's engagement ring in a box of chocolates. One friend hired a pilot to write his proposal, along with puffy hearts, in the sky. Another friend rented a billboard for a day and painted his love in huge block letters. My friend Joey's proposal beamed from a baseball field's scoreboard lights. All those proposals were memorable, but none seemed appropriate for Rebecca and me.

When I dropped by Rebecca's apartment one evening after work in June, I found her in tears. It seemed our tough times weren't ended yet. She explained that her dog, Buzzy, had been hit by a car earlier that afternoon and had died. She was inconsolable. Buzzy had been my pal as well, so I didn't feel much better. As I kissed Rebecca good-bye that night, I promised that we would visit the pound and get her another dog over the weekend.

As I was driving home feeling despondent over Buzzy's death, I had a sudden inspiration. I now knew exactly how I would pop the important question! The next morning I hurried over to the pound and found an adorable black lab puppy. I promptly adopted him for Rebecca and took him home for safekeeping until the weekend.

When Saturday finally arrived, I loaded a picnic basket with a catered lunch, flowers, and a blanket. Then I attached the engagement ring, an heirloom that had belonged to my mother, to a gold ribbon and tied it around the puppy's neck. I put the puppy in a second picnic basket and packed everything in the car.

I picked up Rebecca that morning for a day at the beach. Still grieving over Buzzy, she asked, "Jessie, when are we going to the pound?"

"Monday," I told her with a straight face.

"I won't feel better until I get another dog," she said sadly. "There's such a big hole in my heart."

"I know," I replied. "I feel the same way, but remember: This too shall pass."

When we got to the beach, I took the two picnic baskets from the back of my car. Fortunately the puppy was asleep. I prayed silently that he wouldn't wake up until we arrived at the water's edge.

Placing the flowers in a vase in the center of the blanket that I had spread out on the sand, I brought out my boom box to play some of Rebecca's favorite romantic songs. The setting was perfect as the waves lapped along on the sand with their own special melody.

"Oh, Jessie," Rebecca said, "this is so sweet of you, to try to make me feel better about Buzzy."

I smiled. *You just wait,* I thought gleefully, *you're going to be the happiest girl in the world.* I knew that when I gave Rebecca the new puppy she'd feel better, but when she saw the ring and I proposed, she'd be ecstatic.

It couldn't have been a more beautiful day. There was a cool ocean breeze and the sun was shining as we sipped lemonade. Suddenly I heard the puppy whining and I knew it was time.

"What's that?" Rebecca asked innocently.

I opened the picnic basket and brought out the puppy.

Rebecca jumped up and down as she cried, "Oh, Jessie! I love you! Just look—he's the cutest dog I've ever seen. And you—you're the greatest guy in the whole world."

My heart pumping, I placed the dog in Rebecca's outstretched arms and waited. As she cuddled the dog, I put my arm around her. "Rebecca, there's something very special for you tied around the dog's neck."

She looked up at me quizzically. "There's nothing around the dog's neck," she replied.

"It's on the gold ribbon," I said.

She felt along the ribbon. "There's nothing here."

My heart sank. I grabbed the dog and looked all through his fur. Nothing! Inside I panicked. *So much for my perfect proposal,* I thought. *Now the ring is missing!*

After a frantic search of the sand, I confessed to Rebecca that her engagement ring had been tied on the ribbon. She started to cry. I felt like crying too, but I said, "Don't worry. We'll find it."

"Oh, I'm not crying because you can't find the ring," she said. "I'm crying because you were going to propose to me."

"That ring's worth crying over!" I informed her. "Without it, I can't propose to you. And besides, it belonged to my mother."

Sensing my distress, Rebecca knelt alongside me in the sand and helped me search again for the diamond. It was hopeless. The ring was nowhere to be found.

"The dog must have bitten the ring off the ribbon," I told her as I turned the picnic basket upside down.

"He's only a puppy," she reminded me. "What did you expect?"

Through tight lips I told her, "I thought you'd think it was romantic."

Great, I thought. *What was supposed to be the happiest day of our lives is turning into a heated discussion.*

In unison we realized what had happened and said together, "He ate it."

Gathering our belongings, we left the beach and raced to the vet's office. The doctor laughed as I described our dilemma—until he noticed that neither of us was laughing. Without another word he took the puppy to x-ray.

When the vet returned, he held up the film for us to see. There inside the puppy's tummy was my mother's ring. "Oh, no," we moaned.

"Don't worry about a thing," the vet assured us. "Leave the puppy with me and I'm sure we'll have your ring back by the morning—maybe sooner."

"Will you have to operate?" Rebecca asked sheepishly.

"No," the vet answered, chuckling.

Rebecca then asked, "Then how will you—"

"This too shall pass," the vet assured us.

We burst into laughter. Our familiar words of comfort were to be applied to yet another amazing circumstance.

"I'll call you," promised the vet.

Later that afternoon the vet did call and I picked up the ring. I proposed to Rebecca over a candlelight dinner. She said she'd love to be my wife.

With our troubles finally behind us, a year later we were married. When the minister asked our attendants to "pass the rings," Rebecca and I exchanged a knowing smile. I spoke the vow on cue: "With this ring, I thee—" Then I burst out laughing, remembering the journey of the ring. Rebecca couldn't keep a straight face either when she said the same vow. The minister, puzzled by our reaction, frowned.

Throughout our marriage God has been faithful. Each time we run into to trouble, we gaze upon Rebecca's ring and remind each other that our troubles will pass...one way or the other!

And by the way, we named our black lab Ringo.

AS TOLD TO SUSAN WALES

WITH THIS RING

"With this ring…"
your strong, familiar voice
fell like a benediction
on my heart, that dusk;
tall candles flickered gently,
our age old vows were said,
and I could hear
someone begin to sing
an old, old song,
timeworn and lovely,
timeworn and dear.
And in that dusk
were old, old friends—
and you,
an old friend, too,
(and dearer than them all).
Only my ring seemed new—
its plain gold surface
warm and bright

and strange to me
that candlelight...
unworn—unmarred.
Could it be that wedding rings
like other things,
are lovelier when scarred?

RUTH BELL GRAHAM

Used by permission. Ruth Bell Graham, *Ruth Bell Graham's Collected Poems*, Baker Book House Company, 1995.

FOLLOW YOUR HEART

The best and most beautiful things in life
Cannot be seen or even touched...
They must be felt with the heart.

HELEN KELLER

After graduation from college I moved with two of my friends, Megan and Leslie, to Kansas City, where we were seeking jobs and—more truthfully—where we each hoped to find our Prince Charming.

I found a great job as a marketing assistant in a large company. One of my coworkers arranged a blind date for me with Carl Young, a salesman with a telecommunications firm. Carl had just arrived in town and needed a date for a company function.

Carl and I had a wonderful time and I was greatly encouraged when I learned that Carl also shared my faith in God. When he saw me to my door, I realized that Carl was very shy, so I mustered up my courage and said, "I'd really like to see you again." That's when Carl gave me the news—news to me anyway!

Carl blushed and said, "Katie, I have a girl back home, but I'd really like to be friends."

Fat chance, I thought to myself. We said good-bye and I mumbled, "Have a nice life."

The next weekend Carl and I showed up at the same party, and we had a chance to chat. Carl told me he had tickets for the ball game and asked me if I'd like to join him. My head said no, but my heart said yes. My heart won the argument, and, against my better judgment, I agreed to accompany him.

Once again I had a wonderful time with Carl, and I invited him to a party. Megan and Leslie both chastised me. "If you want to get married, you're wasting your time." I reasoned that having a friend like Carl wasn't such a bad thing. Maybe he would introduce me to some nice guys.

I enjoyed Carl's company and it was easy for us to talk for hours about our faith in God. Before long, we were seeing one another every week. The weeks of seeing one another turned into months. Being a very forthright kind of guy, on several occasions Carl tried to bring up the subject of the girl back home, but I would always say, "Let's not discuss it...let's just have fun and enjoy our friendship."

Carl and I continued seeing one another on a regular basis until November rolled around, and he told me that he was going home to Tennessee for Christmas. His announcement brought me back to reality. I was then reminded of the girl back home. I stopped accepting his invitations. The time had come to use my head and not my heart.

Carl kept calling but I made up every excuse imaginable not to see him, even though I missed him terribly. He was persistent and said that he just wanted to talk, but I prayed that God would give me the strength to refuse him every time. Megan and Leslie were applauding my newfound courage to say no to him, but unbeknownst to them, my heart ached.

Just before Christmas, Carl called to invite me to dinner. When I refused, he asked me if he could drop by to give me a Christmas present before he left for home. Megan and Leslie gave me a hard time for letting him come by, but I couldn't refuse. This time I listened to my heart!

I had spent months knitting Carl a cashmere sweater for Christmas, but the wrapped package now sat under my tree with my brother's name on it (luckily they were the same size). I scurried around and put Carl's name on a tin of cookies, my standard Christmas gift for my friends, and told him he could come over one Saturday afternoon.

"Katie, you look spectacular," he said when I answered the door.

I knew I looked good because I had spent hours getting ready since my female pride wanted to show him what he was missing when he went home to his girlfriend.

"I'm going home tomorrow and I wanted to see you before I leave," he announced.

Because I knew he'd be seeing *her,* those words pieced my heart. I felt shattered at the thought.

We sat on the sofa and I handed him the tin of cookies. "My favorite," he replied politely. "Chocolate chip."

"They're everyone's favorite," I said sarcastically.

He then reached inside his coat and pulled out a beautifully wrapped package. He handed it to me, and when I opened it, I gasped at what was inside. It was a velvet box containing the most beautiful strand of pearls I'd ever seen. I was speechless. And puzzled.

"They're my grandmother's," Carl told me.

"Carl," I said, "I can't possibly accept these!"

"But my grandmother wants you to have them," he said.

"But your grandmother doesn't even know me!"

Carl dropped his head for a minute and then continued, "Katie, my grandmother wants the girl I marry to wear these on our wedding day."

My heart began to beat wildly. *The girl I marry? Is this a proposal?*

"But what about your girlfriend back home?" I asked.

"I've been trying to tell you for months," he explained. "After our second date, I knew that God was showing me that you were the girl that I wanted to spend my life with. I was just too shy to tell you, but then when I realized that I was losing you…I couldn't wait any longer. I love you."

With those words it was as though God reached down from heaven and knitted all the pieces of my shattered heart back together again!

I was stunned. I couldn't hold back my tears as Carl reached down and fastened the pearls on my neck and then got on his knees and proposed. "I had hoped for a more romantic proposal, but when I couldn't talk you into going out with me…well, this will have to do!"

When Carl returned from the holidays, he invited me to a romantic dinner at our favorite restaurant and presented me with his grandmother's ring. The next Christmas we were married.

After years of marriage, with my encouragement and God's help, Carl eventually outgrew his shyness.

I have learned a lesson of my own, too: There are times when it's better to keep listening to your heart!

As told to Susan Wales

If ever two were one, then surely we.
If ever man were lov'd by wife, then thee;
If ever wife was happy in a man,
Compare with me ye women if you can.
I prize thy love more than whole Mines of gold,
Or all the riches that the East doth hold.
My love is such that Rivers cannot quench,
Nor ought but love from thee, give recompense.
They love is such that I can no way repay,
The heavens reward thee manifold I pray.
Then while we lived, in love let's so persevere,
That when we live no more, we may live ever.

Anne Bradstreet,
from "To My Dear and Loving Husband"

A HEART OF STONE

*In courtesy I have chiefly learned
that hearts are not given as a gift
but hearts are earned.*

It was Valentine's Day and also our first anniversary. I had planned a romantic candlelight dinner for my husband, Tom, that evening to celebrate our love and our first year of wedded bliss. I had rushed home from work to make his favorite dish, lasagna, and brought out our wedding china and my grandmother's silver. The candles were on the table and the stereo was playing our song as I soaked in a fragrant bubble bath waiting for Tom to come home from work. Just as I heard the door open, I squirted Tom's favorite perfume behind my ears and rushed down to greet him.

It was the perfect evening, at least until I glanced down at my left hand when I was clearing the table. I let out a cry of distress, "Tom, my diamond is missing from my engagement ring." We both left the table to frantically search everywhere for the tiny stone: the kitchen, the dining room, and the bathtub. I worried that it had gone down the drain.

"We'd better call the plumber," Tom resigned himself.

"But honey, it's nighttime. Do you know how much a plumber charges after hours?" I was torn with indecision.

"Believe me, we'll pay a much higher price if we don't find your diamond," he told me, unleashing the guilt.

I thought back to the day when Tom had purchased my ring. He had wanted it to be a token of our love that I would treasure for a lifetime so he had stretched to spend far more than he could comfortably afford. Truthfully, I would have been satisfied with the pop top off a soft drink can—I was just so happy when he asked me to be his wife. But when I first looked at the beautiful diamond, it took my breath away, and I knew that the sacrifice that he had made was worth every penny. It was an exquisitely cut heart-shaped diamond. We had had our first date on Valentine's Day so the ring had great sentimental value for both of us. In fact, after we set a date, we were married on the next Valentine's Day.

At the time my husband had purchased the ring, he was a college student, and I knew he had made a great sacrifice to buy this ring for me. He had sold his ancient Volkswagen bug for a few hundred dollars in order to purchase the ring. After the proposal, he was forced to take the bus everywhere until he graduated and landed his first job and could buy another car.

We had insurance but we had a very large deductible. So large that it would be impossible for us to replace the diamond. We continued to search high and low, but no diamond. Tom shrugged his shoulders and dialed the plumber.

While we waited for the plumber to arrive, I cried until my eyes were swollen shut while we continued to look for the diamond. It was nowhere to be found. When the plumber finally arrived, he spent a couple of hours taking the drain apart. No diamond but a bill that could have probably paid for another ring. Tom was forced to pull out his VISA card.

By now it was almost midnight but I decided that we had to salvage what was left of our disastrous first anniversary dinner. I brought out the beautiful heart-shaped strawberry cake that I had made for our dessert to the table. I thought that surely this cake would make us feel better until Tom confessed, "I'm sorry, Jenny, I'm afraid I've lost my appetite." He was obviously still concerned about the ring and the plumber's bill. I'd spent hours baking that cake and I was secretly crushed when he barely looked at it and then refused it. He hadn't even commented that I had written our names in hearts in pink icing on the top of the cake.

Trying to sound cheerful, I sidled up to Tom in front of the fire and tried to reminisce about our first date and our wedding day. "Next time," he ordered in an accusatory tone, "don't wear your ring while you cook or take a bath."

He had uttered the words that initiated a historical event...our first fight! It wouldn't be our last either but was by far our worst.

I shouted that he had ruined our first anniversary.

He retorted, "I wasn't the one that lost the ring!"

"We don't need to find the diamond," I replied angrily, "because you...you have a heart of stone!"

I covered my beautiful cake and returned it to the refrigerator. Our perfect evening was in shambles and we could hardly kiss one another good night as we turned off the lights. True to our wedding promise, we agreed not to go to bed angry, each muttering a forced, I'm sorry. I cried myself to sleep dreaming of the perfect anniversary.

The next morning, still pouting, we headed for the breakfast table. Reluctantly, we agreed to share the morning devotional. We were incredulous as Tom read the Scripture for the day, "For where your treasure is, there will your heart be also." (Matthew 6:21, KJV). Instantly, we were both convicted.

"We lost sight of our real treasure," Tom said. "It's not the heart-shaped diamond, but our hearts that really matter."

"That's the real treasure," I agreed.

Tom took me into his arms and asked, "Can you forgive me for breaking your heart?" Those words not only melted my husband's heart of stone, but mine, too. The diamond didn't seem to matter much as we walked into the kitchen to prepare breakfast.

"Say, Jenny, I have a great idea," Tom told me. "Let's do something wild and crazy to celebrate our anniversary this morning! Why don't we have a piece of that cake you made instead of fruit and cereal for breakfast," he suggested.

He *had* noticed my beautiful cake. I sliced two large pieces giggling at the wickedness of having such a gooey sugary dessert for breakfast. We even blew out the candle and uttered a prayer of forgiveness and thanksgiving.

No sooner had Tom tasted his first bite of cake, than he jumped up excitedly.

"Now that's the enthusiasm I wanted to see for my cake," I teased.

"Is this cake supposed to have nuts?" he asked.

"No," I answered curiously.

Reaching inside his mouth, Tom pulled out the heart-shaped stone! Tom had found my diamond! "If only I hadn't been so stubborn," he admonished himself, "we could've found the diamond last night and still celebrated our anniversary."

Today whenever we run into problems, God has taught us that our *real* treasure can only be found in our hearts, and not in the diamond heart on my finger. The ring is the only heart of stone that we have allowed in our marriage since that first anniversary.

AS TOLD TO SUSAN WALES

The face is the mirror of the mind,
And eyes without speaking confess
The secrets of the heart.
SAINT JEROME

THE RING BEARER

And all at once a pleasant truth I learned,
For while the tender service made me weep,
I loved thee for the tear thou couldst not hide,
And pressed thy hand, and knew the press returned.

ALFRED, LORD TENNYSON

Marie and I had met our freshman year in college, and as time went on we knew that one day we would be married. I had proposed our senior year at Christmas and now that our graduation was near, we were making plans to become man and wife.

It may come as a surprise to some people, but not everyone loves weddings. I, for one, despised them. But when it came time to set a date, as a prospective groom I had to inform my bride-to-be that I wasn't prepared to endure the frills, pomp, and circumstance of a big wedding. As we began to broach the subject of our wedding day, I told Marie that I personally was in favor of eloping. The look of horror in her eyes told me that I was in for a big debate—one I was going to lose.

"But, Jeff, I've always dreamed of a wedding with all the trimmings," Marie said, doing her best to convince me.

I, on the other hand, was afflicted with a deep fear of walking down the aisle in front of all those people.

She continued, "Those people are our family and friends…they love us and want to share our special day."

Marie persuaded me to discuss my wedding phobia with our pastor.

Reverend Smith was a compassionate man who understood both sides of our dilemma.

"Perhaps you'd like to set up a private session, Jeff, to discuss your fears," he urged me when he realized that our wedding plans had reached an impasse.

The next week I spent two hours with Reverend Smith, who helped me uncover the source of my apprehension as I revealed to him my deep-rooted fears. Although I had a better understanding of my wedding phobia, I still wanted to elope.

"Why don't you discuss this with Marie, and the two of you pray about it and come back in a week. Perhaps we can reach a compromise," he suggested.

I dropped by Marie's house and told her that I had been traumatized as a child...at a wedding.

"Tell me about it," she urged.

I sat back on the sofa facing the woman I wanted to marry, while she perched hopefully on the edge of the nearby chair.

I silently prayed that Marie would understand and abandon her plans for a big wedding. So I began to pour out my heart, determined to persuade her to see it my way. I began, "When I was a kid, about eight years old, my father forced me to be the ring bearer in the wedding of one of his friends. I was determined to do my very best and make him proud of me.

"Over and over, my mother stressed the importance of my job. I had to dress in a funny looking suit and carry a pillow with the rings for the bride and the groom. A real nice lady, the wedding director, gave me all the instructions on the night of the rehearsal. It was a cinch! All I had to do was carry that pillow down the aisle. The only thing about the job that alarmed me was that I was going to have to walk back up the aisle with a girl...the flower girl. I was eight years old and I *hated* girls!

"When the night of the actual wedding arrived, I overheard the groomsmen discussing, 'Who's got the ring?' I tried to tell them that I did, but nobody would listen. I offered my pillow that held two rings to one of the men, but he told me those weren't the *real* rings; he would put the real ones in his pocket.

"When the minister asked for the rings, I remembered that my mother had told me that the rings were my responsibility so I walked over to one of the groomsmen and reached inside his pockets. No ring but everyone in the congregation began to laugh. Unfortunately for me, all the guys were dressed just alike and I couldn't remember which one put the rings in his pocket so I continued down the line reaching into every one of the groomsmen's pockets. The flower girl finally came over to me and took me back to where I had been standing and the wedding continued, but I was humiliated beyond belief."

Marie suddenly interrupted me with her laughter and tears.

"Jeff," she said. "We didn't meet in college, after all!"

She suddenly jumped up and didn't return for a long time as I sat perplexed on the sofa. When Marie finally reappeared she was carrying an old photograph. Because of her hysterics, she silently thrust the picture toward me. I could hardly believe my eyes. It was a picture of me at the wedding I had just described to her. On my arm was the little flower girl.

"That's me, Jeff," she exclaimed as she pointed to the flower girl.

Until that very moment Marie and I hadn't known we'd first met as children at the wedding of her mother's cousin and my father's friend. We decided that we were destined to marry, even as children, as we walked down the aisle together.

The picture settled it. Marie could have the wedding she wanted. It was a sign from God. And he healed the trauma of my first big wedding because our wedding day—with all the pomp and circumstance—was the happiest day of my life.

Once again I escorted the flower girl up the aisle...this time as my bride.

AS TOLD TO SUSAN WALES

I Thee Wed

Then before all they stand, the holy vow
And ring of gold, no fond illusions now,
Bind her as his. Across the threshold led,
And every tear kissed off as soon as shed,
His house she enters, there to be a light,
Shining within, when all without is night;
A guardian angel o'er his life presiding,
Doubling his pleasures and his cares dividing.

SAMUEL ROGERS

JUST THREE WORDS.

WHEN THE THREE WORDS ARE SPOKEN, THE COURSES OF TWO INDIVIDUALS CHANGE FOREVER. THE DREAMS AND DESTINIES OF A MAN AND A WOMAN MERGE.

JUST THREE WORDS.

TWO BECOME ONE.

WHEN A GROOM RECITES THE WORDS *I THEE WED* TO HIS BRIDE HE PAYS THE HIGHEST COMPLIMENT. HE IS—WITH GOD, HIS FAMILY, AND BEST FRIENDS—LOOKING ON, SAYING TO HER, "THERE IS NO OTHER, NOR WILL THERE EVER BE. YOU ARE

THE PERSON I HAVE CHOSEN AS MY PARTNER, MY BEST FRIEND, MY LOVER, MY COMPANION...FOR LIFE."

WHEN A BRIDE SAYS *I THEE WED* TO HER GROOM, SHE IS REVEALING THE DEEPEST PLACES OF HER SOUL, GIVING HIM THE KEY TO HER OWN PERSONAL GARDEN OF EDEN. SHE IS CHOOSING HIM TO BE THE FATHER OF HER CHILDREN, HER COMFORTER, PROTECTOR, AND ALLY IN LIFE. SHE SAYS, "NEVER WILL I WANT ANOTHER. NEVER WILL I WALK AWAY. NEVER WILL I ALLOW MY LOVE FOR YOU TO DIE."

JUST THREE WORDS.

I HEARD THE VOICE
OF AN ANGEL

*Her angel's face
As the great eye of heaven shined bright,
And made a sunshine in the shady place.*

EDMUND SPENCER

y younger brother Tom called me one day to make an exciting announcement I didn't want to hear: He was getting married.

After my long pause, he asked, "What's wrong, Ted? Aren't you happy for me?"

A huge lump moved up from my heart to my throat and I could barely speak. Now the youngest of my five siblings was going to take the walk down the aisle before me. It was a walk that I so badly wanted to take myself.

After the long, uncomfortable silence, I managed to compose myself and offer my sincere congratulations.

"Of course," my brother continued, "we want *you* to sing at my wedding."

I had sung at almost every wedding in the area so there was no way I could refuse my little brother.

I was genuinely happy for my brother, but I dreaded his wedding day because I knew I would once again walk down the aisle alone.

Always the singer…never a groom, I thought to myself as I hung up the phone.

"But, Lord," I cried out, "what about me? Haven't I been praying for years for you to bring a wife for me? How could you let this happen…my younger brother getting married before me?"

My brother's big day finally arrived and as I drove to his wedding, I was in pretty bad shape. This was one wedding I didn't want to attend. I thought about the fact that I had no love in my life, not even a prospect. I prayed on the way to the church that God would give me the strength to get through yet another wedding.

I was going to be singing a duet with a friend of Tom's, so I arrived at the church early to rehearse. The moment I stepped inside I heard an angelic voice melodiously filling the sanctuary. It was as though the voice was calling to me. Without noticing the others who had gathered early, I walked down the aisle in the sanctuary to see the source of that beautiful voice. I looked up and gazed upon a face that was every bit as beautiful as the voice I had heard. And she was rehearsing the music for *our* duet.

I stood there, mesmerized by her voice and her face that at that moment I thought were surely sent from heaven.

"Hi, Ted," my brother welcomed me. But I didn't even hear him...I was in a world all of my own that was filled with the sight and sound of her.

All during the ceremony, I could think of nothing else but the angelic singer. When the time came for our duet, I found myself falling in love at the melodious sound of her voice while we sang "We Are One in the Bonds of Love" for my brother and his bride.

After the wedding, I didn't waste any time. I arranged to spend time with my new friend. It wasn't long before I knew she was the woman I wanted to spend my life with, and fourteen months later, I married the angel.

God had a special plan for me all along. On the day I dreaded most, the Lord turned my sorrow into joy as he brought Kim into my life.

And to this day Kim and I continue to celebrate God's bringing us together as we sing for young couples on their wedding days.

TED ENGSTROM, AS TOLD TO SUSAN WALES

A HEAVENLY HAM

℘

Small cheer and great welcome
Makes a merry feast.
WILLIAM SHAKESPEARE

Throughout history during wartime, betrothed couples have often had to sacrifice or forego the weddings of their dreams. The following is a tale of a post Civil War bride written by Cynthia Blyth Halsey in Worth, remembering to celebrate the one hundredth anniversary of the United Daughters of the Confederacy by the New York Chapter in 1963.

There should be a special dish for a wedding dinner…but heaven only knew where it was to come from when Major Charles Seldon married Miss James. Rations were thin in Northern Virginia after April of 1865. The bride and her mother combed the smoke house, ransacked the cellar…and finally rested from their search in front of the great hall fire. "Only heaven knows where we'll get anything. It looks like a choice of johnny cake with bacon…or without." But heaven did know, because as they stood there a fifteen-pound ham fell down the chimney and landed with a crash at their feet.

No, it wasn't a miracle. It seems that they'd hung the ham to cure in the old chimney because the smoke house was unsafe. This one had been forgotten…and the suspending rope had frayed through just at the right time. A merry wedding followed.

Sounds like a miracle to me!

THE MISSING CANDELABRA

There are two ways of spreading light;
To be: The Candle or
The mirror that reflects it.

EDITH WHARTON

It was one of the largest weddings ever held at Wilshire. Fifteen minutes before the service was scheduled to begin, the church parking lots were overflowing with cars and scores of people were crowding into the foyer, waiting to be properly seated. It was the kind of occasion that warms the heart of a pastor.

But that was fifteen minutes before the service.

At exactly seven o'clock the mothers were seated, and the organist sounded the triumphant notes of the processional. That was my cue to enter the sanctuary through the side door at the front and begin presiding over the happy occasion. As I reached for the door a voice called from down the hall, "Not yet, Pastor. Don't open the door. I've got a message for you."

I turned and through the subdued lighting I saw the assistant florist hurrying as fast as she could toward me. Her speed didn't set any records for she was about eight months pregnant and waddled down the hall with obvious difficulty. She was nearly out of breath when she reached me. "Pastor," she panted, "we can't find the candelabra that you are supposed to use at the close of the ceremony. We've looked everywhere, and it just can't be found. What on earth can we do?"

I sensed immediately that we had a big problem on our hands. The couple to be married had specifically requested that the unity candle be a part of the wedding service. We had gone over it carefully at the rehearsal—step by step. The candelabra, designed to hold three candles, was to be placed near the altar. The mothers of the bride and groom would be ushered down the aisle, each carrying a lighted candle. Upon reaching the front of the sanctuary, they were to move to the candelabra and place their candles in the appropriate receptacles. Throughout the ceremony the mother's candles were to burn slowly while the larger middle one remained unlighted. After the vows had been spoken, the bride and groom would light the center candle. This was designed to symbolize family unity as well as the light of God's love in the new relationship.

I felt good about all this at the rehearsal. I had a special verse of Scripture that I planned to read as the couple lighted the middle candle. We had it down to perfection.

We thought.

The notes from the organ pealed louder and louder as I stalled in the hallway. I knew that the organist by now was glancing over her left shoulder wondering where in the world the minister was.

"Okay," I said to the perplexed florist, "we'll just have to 'wing it.' I'll cut that part out of the ceremony and improvise until the close."

With those words I opened the door and entered the sanctuary, muttering behind my frozen smile, "What on earth are we going to do?"

The groom and his attendants followed me in. The bride and her attendants came down the left aisle of the sanctuary. When the first bridesmaid arrived at the front, she whispered something in my direction.

The puzzled look on my face was a signal to her that I did not understand.

She whispered the message again, opening her mouth wider and emphasizing every syllable. By straining to hear above the organ and through lip-reading I made out what she was saying: "Go ahead with the unity candle part of the ceremony."

"But how?" I whispered through my teeth with a plastic smile.

"Just go ahead," she signaled back.

We made it through the first part of the ceremony without any difficulty.

Everyone was beaming in delight because of the happy occasion—except the first bridesmaid who had brought me the message. When I looked in her direction for some additional word about the candelabra, she had a stoic look on her face and her mouth was tightly clamped shut. Obviously, she was out of messages for me.

We continued with the ceremony. I read a passage from 1 Corinthians 13 and emphasized the importance of love and patience in building a marriage relationship. I asked the bride and groom to join hands, and I began to talk about the vows they would make. There wasn't a hitch. I was beginning to feel better, but I still had to figure out some way to conclude the service. Just now, however, we needed to get through the vows and rings.

"John, in taking the woman whom you hold by your hand to be your wife, do you promise to love her? . . ."

"That's the funniest thing I've ever seen," the bride interrupted with a loud whisper. I turned from the bewildered groom to look at her and noticed that she was staring toward her right, to the organ side of the front of the sanctuary. Not only was she looking in that direction, so were all the attendants, and so was the audience! One thousand eyes focused on a moving target to my left. I knew it was moving, for heads and eyes followed it, turning ever so slightly in slow motion style.

The moving target was none other than the assistant florist. She had slipped through the door by the organ and was moving on hands and knees behind the choir rail toward the center of the platform where I stood. The dear lady, "great with child," thought she was out of sight, beneath the rail. But in fact, her posterior bobbed in plain view, six inches above the choir rail. As she crawled along she carried in each hand a burning candle. To make matters worse, she didn't realize that she was silhouetted—a large moving, "pregnant" shadow—on the wall behind the choir loft.

The wedding party experienced the agony of smothered, stifled laughter. Their only release was the flow of hysterical tears while they fought to keep their composure. Two or three bride's attendants shook so hard that petals of the flowers in their bouquets fell to the floor.

It was a welcome moment for me when the vows were completed and I could say with what little piety remained, "Now let us bow our heads and close our eyes for a special prayer." This was a signal for the soloist to sing "The Lord's Prayer." It also gave me a chance to peep during the singing and to figure out what in the world was happening.

"Psst! Psst!"

I did a half turn, looked down, and saw a lighted candle being pushed through the greenery behind me.

"Take this candle," the persistent florist said.

The soloist continued to sing, "Give us this day our daily bread…"

"Psst. Now take this one," the voice behind me said as a second candle was poked through the greenery.

"…as we forgive those who trespass against us…"

I was beginning to catch on. So I was to be the human candelabra. Here I stood, with a candle in each hand and my Bible and notes tucked under my arm.

"Where's the third candle?" I whispered above the sounds of "…but deliver us from evil…"

"Between my knees," the florist answered. "Just a minute and I'll pass it through to you."

That's when the bride lost it. So did several of the attendants. The last notes of "The Lord's Prayer" were drowned out by the snickers all around me.

I couldn't afford such luxury. Somebody had to carry this thing on to its conclusion and try to rescue something from it, candelabra or no candelabra. I determined to do just that as I now tried to juggle three candles, a Bible, and wedding notes. My problem was complicated by the fact that two of the candles were burning, and the third one soon would be.

It was a challenging dilemma, one that called for creative action—in a hurry. And there was nothing in the *Pastor's Manual* that addressed this predicament. Nor had it ever been mentioned in a seminary class on pastoral responsibilities. I was on my own.

I handed one candle to the nearby hysterical bride who was laughing so hard that tears were trickling down her cheeks. I handed the other one to the groom who was beginning to question all the reassurances I had passed out freely at the rehearsal. My statements about "no problems," and "we'll breeze through the service without a hitch," and "just relax and trust me," were beginning to sound hollow.

I held the last candle in my hands. They were to light it together from the ones they were each holding. Miraculously, we made it through that part in spite of jerking hands and tears of smothered laughter. Now we had three burning candles.

In a very soft, reassuring voice, I whispered, "That's fine. Now each of you blow out your candle."

Golly, I said to myself, *we're going to get through this thing yet.*

That thought skipped through my mind just before the bride, still out of control, pulled her candle toward her mouth to blow it out, forgetting that she was wearing a nylon veil over her face.

"Poooff!"

The veil went up in smoke and disintegrated.

Fortunately, except for singed eyebrows, the bride was not injured.

Through the hole in the charred remains of her veil she gave me a bewildered look. I had no more reassurances for her, the groom, or anybody. Enough was enough.

Disregarding my notes concerning the conclusion of the ceremony, I took all the candles and blew them out myself. Then, peering through the smoke of three extinguished candles, I signaled the organist to begin the recessional...now! Just get us out of here! Quickly!

Everything else is a blur.

But I still turn pale when prospective brides tell me about "this wonderful idea of using a unity candle" in the ceremony.

BRUCE McIVER
FROM *STORIES I COULDN'T TELL WHILE I WAS A PASTOR*
© 1991, WORD PUBLISHING, NASHVILLE, TENNESSEE.
ALL RIGHTS RESERVED.

KINDNESS THROUGH MUSIC

❧

Music has charms to soothe the savage beast,

To soften rocks,

Or bend a knotted oak.

WILLIAM CONGREVE

Our wedding was special because we were surrounded by friends and family who shared in the celebration. It was a beautiful outdoor wedding, under a bower in the rose garden at a Victorian mansion in California's wine country. The guests all assembled. Classical flute and guitar music of our choosing filled the air with a melodious tribute to our love. A processional welcomed each member of the wedding party. We stood in front of the rabbi and nervously but joyously said our vows.

We turned, now man and wife, joined with great hope and happiness. We walked down the aisle past our beaming families and friends. Suddenly, I noticed what the chamber musicians were playing: "Zippedy-Doo-Dah." I was stunned. I whispered, "'Zippedy-Doo-Dah?' Is that what you asked them to play?"

My darling bride smiled happily and said, "Want to skip down the aisle, honey?"

Skip down the aisle we did.

The light-hearted tune was Meladee's gift to me—the promise of a lifetime of humor and laughter as well as serious love.

MELADEE MCCARTY AND HANOCH MCCARTY
FROM *ACTS OF KINDNESS*

THE LOOK
OF LOVE

A loving heart is the truest wisdom.

CHARLES DICKENS

or many years, the word *family* always meant pain. I grew up in an alcoholic home, and my mother died when I was sixteen. A month later, my father committed suicide. I was sent to live with my eighty-eight-year-old grandfather, who soon passed me to an all-girl school in Mississippi. At that early age, I was forced to leave behind all that was familiar and was left on my own, struggling to find my way.

At twenty-one, I thought I had finally found my way. I got married and was blessed with two beautiful children. For a while everything seemed to fall into place. But then the marriage soured and I spent ten difficult years trying to salvage the unsalvageable. We finally divorced.

Terrified and alone, I desperately tried to raise my children with a strong sense of family and comfort. But I felt helpless and exhausted. I kept asking myself where I could turn, whom I could turn to. One Sunday, a friend encouraged me to attend a church service with her.

I remember most vividly the music...the wonderful music. The people were amazingly friendly and embracing. I felt like I was being welcomed into a family for the first time in my life.

The minister spoke words that reached straight into my heart. As I listened to him preach about God's infinite love and grace, I realized that

I had never known Christ on a personal level. The minister said what I desperately needed to hear. I accepted the Lord as my Savior.

It was at that precise moment that my life began to change for the better. Immediately God's magnificent love began to heal the deep scars in my life. I could feel the effects instantly, yet the process was a long one that required dedication and complete openness.

During my eight years as a single mother, my two children and I had worked extremely hard to rebuild and reorder our lives. For the longest time, my children were all I had in my life—they were my reason for living. When I accepted God into my heart, I began to see that life was worth living for myself *and* for my children, that life was a precious gift to all of us.

During those years, my sixteen-year-old son declared that he was the man of the house. He was determined to protect both me and his sister from all harm. He informed me that we were a secure family unit, and if I ever remarried, he would leave home. But by the time I had accepted the Lord and my son was ready to leave for college, he had changed his mind. He wanted me to find someone with whom to share my heart. He wanted me to be okay; he wanted me to be happy.

I prayed very hard, asking God to send me someone. I prayed for a man who would love and accept me and my children. I wanted to have the kind of marriage and family that God designed.

A friend I hadn't heard from in ages called one night and suggested we meet for dinner and talk. On a Saturday night, we met at a restaurant and began catching up on each other's life. My friend mentioned a wonderful man she wanted me to meet. I had to laugh; this same friend had set me up on a disastrous blind date some years earlier.

I told her that she had already lost all of her matchmaking credibility. She ignored my protests and continued to talk about this man. The more she talked, the more interesting this man became. She decided to call and invite him to join us that very night. He agreed to come for coffee after dinner.

I never believed in love at first sight, but when Gene walked in—tall, slim, gray just at the temples—I was instantly convinced! Gene spoke with the polished voice of a professional speaker, but it was the gentleness in his eyes that made the biggest impression on me. I could see immediately that there was a lot to this man. Unlike his predecessor, this blind date looked promising.

The three of us laughed, talked, and laughed some more—I couldn't remember when I had laughed so hard. I enjoyed myself immensely. Gene suggested that we all go hear a jazz performer after dinner. My friend excused herself gracefully. Personally, I didn't want the evening to end.

Gene called the next day and asked me out for Valentine's Day, only two nights away. I eagerly accepted. I purchased two Valentine's cards: Card A was inscribed to a friend, Card B was more special and romantic. When Gene arrived for our date with beautiful red roses and a romantic card, I quickly produced Card B. We were off to a candlelit, extremely romantic Valentine's dinner celebration.

Gene made me feel beautiful and brilliant. He showed a great deal of interest in me and wanted to know everything about my life. At one point, he turned to me and whispered, "You're wonderful." I had never felt the way Gene made me feel: safe and secure, protected and comforted.

Our next date was two nights later and it was another fabulous evening. I knew already that I was falling in love with him. When we went back to my house, Gene blurted out, "Lynn, I believe that I'm going to end up marrying you."

"You know, I believe you're right," I heard myself saying.

As time passed, we both could see the hand of God at work in our lives. My son totally approved. Our families meshed smoothly. I realized that God had answered every detail of my prayers. Three months later we were married in the chapel at our church, attended by our children.

Since that day—for nineteen years now—*family* has meant only love.

AS TOLD TO ANN PLATZ

ROCKING CHAIR WEDDING

❧

Focus on making things better, not bigger.
Be your best, be yourself.
ANONYMOUS

One of the blessings of being a pastor is to perform weddings. On June 17, 1999, a lovely wedding was held on the front porch of our home, a log cabin in rural Georgia. This ceremony was the shortest, simplest, and most relaxed I have ever performed.

The bride was the eighty-year-old grandmother of our daughter-in-law, and her eighty-one-year-old groom was her eighth-grade sweetheart. They had fallen out of touch, but a high school reunion had reacquainted them after sixty-seven years.

The happy couple made an appointment to see me and asked me to marry them. They wanted a simple, no-fuss wedding. No flowers. No guests. No fanfare.

The day of the ceremony, they arrived in the early afternoon dressed very casually in slacks and shirts. Katie had a white baseball hat with BRIDE on the front. Dick's hat had GROOM written on it. The "nervous" couple came right up on the porch, sat in our rocking chairs, and began to rock.

While getting acquainted, I learned that they both were active outdoors people. She loved swimming, walking, and fishing and he intended to (and did, in fact) buy a van that pulled a camper for their trips after a

Callaway Gardens honeymoon. All during our conversation, Dick and Katie continued to rock.

I began the ceremony by asking, "Have you both duly considered this relationship which you are about to enter?"

"We sho have!" Dick said loudly. He took Katie's hand in his and continued to rock.

I continued with the ceremony while the bride and groom continued their rocking. Earlier they had requested not to repeat the vows and we agreed that they would simply say "I do" after I read them. Each one answered in turn—and continued to rock.

They bowed their heads as I prayed this benediction.

"Our Father, we thank you for the joy of living and especially the joys of love and marriage. You have loved us and you have made us so we can love and be loved in return.

"Thank you that we need not walk the road alone, but that you provide someone to share our dreams and comfort us in our sorrows. Bless these two as they begin their lives together. In Jesus' name, amen."

After I pronounced them man and wife, they each smiled, leaned toward each other, and sealed their union with a kiss.

Then they continued to rock!

REVEREND BILL LAWRENCE

THE WEDDING MARCH

✍

Marriages are made in heaven
and consummated on earth.
MOTHER BOMBIE (1590) ACT IV, SCENE 1
JOHN LYLY

*W*eddings throughout the world are celebrated with the magnificent strains of the Wedding March from a Midsummer's Night Dream. The oft-played wedding tune was written by the great German composer Felix Mendelssohn in the age of romanticism. What inspired the young composer to write such an extraordinary piece? Perhaps it was the story of his grandparents' romance.

Mendelssohn's grandfather, Moses, was born with a deformed and twisted body. In fact, he was a hunchback. People would avert their stares to avoid looking upon the grotesque young man as he would walk through the streets of Hamburg, Germany. Despite his freakish appearance, the sensitive young man was the same on the inside as everyone else, with the same desires in life—purpose, happiness, contentment, and most of all love. But who would ever have him?

Early one spring, Moses accompanied his father to the tailor to have clothes made for his misshapen body. As Frumtje, the tailor's daughter, walked down the stairs into her father's shop, Moses' heart stopped as he gazed upon the most beautiful creature he had ever seen. At that very moment, Moses knew with all his heart that this lovely girl must be his future bride. But how? Like everyone else, she averted her eyes at the mere sight of him and quickly excused herself.

When her father dismissed him, Moses rushed up the stairs in search of Frumtje. When he found her he mustered up every ounce of courage inside of him and blurted out, "Do you believe that marriages are made in heaven?"

"Why, yes," the flustered young woman replied. "Do—do you?"

Moses knew he had to seize the moment or lose her forever so he began, "When a baby boy is born in heaven, the Lord shows him his future bride—and you see, he told me that you were to be my bride."

Horror clouded the face of the shocked young girl as she heard the words of the young man with the twisted body. "I?" she gasped. "I, your wife!"

Undaunted by the look of astonishment on her face, Moses continued. "When the Lord showed me that you would be my wife, I cried, 'No! A hunchback woman is a tragedy! Please let me carry the hump for her.'"

Upon hearing his words, the young woman's heart was filled with love and her mind with a deep revelation. Moses and Frumtje were later married and they lived happily ever after. They were blessed with children and, later, grandchildren, including Felix Mendelssohn, whose music delights couples everywhere as they walk up the aisle together in the first moments of their marriage, as man and wife.

RETOLD BY SUSAN WALES

THE NERVOUS GROOM

The art of being wise is the art of knowing what to overlook.

WILLIAM JAMES

One of the greatest joys of living in a small town is that it's easy to get to know your neighbors well. Small-town people seem to connect with one another in a way that is impossible in a big city. My parents lived in such a town in South Carolina, and they genuinely loved and cared about all the local citizens. This—and the fact that my father was influential in state politics—gained them an invitation to nearly every wedding in the county.

For many years Mother and Daddy ate their evening meals at a popular local restaurant where everyone knew each other. They often chatted with the waitresses and knew all about their families…especially one in particular, who was a little older than the rest.

This woman was very anxious to get married. In fact, she was desperate. One evening, when my parents came in to dine she informed them that she was engaged. She invited them to the wedding, which was to be held in mid-August, just a few months away. They assured her that they would be there.

The wedding day arrived and it was very hot, nearly 103 degrees! The ceremony was held in a small country church that was not air-conditioned. Nevertheless, it was clear to everyone as the wedding party began their procession down the aisle that this was a very happy occasion for the bride. She had saved for many years to have the funds to make her wedding everything she dreamed of. Her dress was exquisite and had so many layers of ruffles that there was barely room for her father to stand next to her in the aisle. She had gone all out with flowers, her bouquet, and a beautiful candelabra.

The groom was very nervous standing at the front of the church. He had been in an automobile accident the week before and had been determined, despite some lingering pain, not to distract in any way from the bride, the various prewedding activities, or the importance of this day.

As the minister began to say the marriage vows, the groom's nervousness started to get the best of him, and he started swaying.

"Oh, my, I think he is going to faint," Mother whispered to Daddy. Before she could finish the sentence, the groom passed out and fell against the stand that held dozens of lighted candles. Flames went everywhere, including the organ keys. The veteran church organist, however, did not miss a note and played on calmly as the ushers gingerly picked lighted candles from around her.

The bride was in tears. Her beautiful wedding was being ruined. To the rescue came the bride's father, who jumped to his feet and caught the groom. He tried to steady the hapless man, who was still swaying. He looked dazed and disoriented, and his eyes were rolling around. He wasn't responding intelligently to anything anyone said to him.

Guessing (and hoping!) that the combination of heat, nerves, and pain medication was to blame for his future son-in-law's odd condition, the father propped him up by standing against his back, and signaled for the minister to go ahead with the ceremony. The bride smiled bravely and tried to look as if everything was normal.

"Do you think that this will be legal?" Mother whispered again to Daddy. "Poor thing, I don't think he even knows where he is."

Daddy smiled a sweet smile and whispered back, "Oh, I don't think anyone here would tell. Let's just get 'em married."

ANN PLATZ

To Have and to Hold

What greater thing is there for two human souls
than to feel that they are joined…
to strengthen each other…
to be at one with each other in silent
unspeakable memories
GEORGE ELIOT

ONE OF YOUR PRIMARY HUMAN NEEDS IS INTIMACY. NOT
JUST TO HAVE, BUT TO HOLD.

THE WORD INTIMACY IS ALMOST ALWAYS AUTOMATICALLY
EQUATED WITH THE ACT OF PHYSICAL UNION. IN MARRIAGE,
THAT IS A BEAUTIFUL PART OF THE DEFINITION, BUT A
HUSBAND AND WIFE ARE MORE THAN LOVERS IN THE SEXUAL
SENSE. THEY ARE—FOR EACH OTHER—THE PRIMARY SOURCE
OF EMOTIONAL, MENTAL, AND SPIRITUAL "KNOWING."

GOD'S DESIGN WAS FOR MAN AND WOMAN NOT JUST TO BE
LEGALLY JOINED FOR PRACTICAL REASONS, BUT TO BE
PRESENT WITH EACH OTHER IN A DEEP AND PASSIONATE WAY,
JOINING SOUL TO SOUL AS BODY TO BODY. WHEN THEY
STAND AT THE ALTAR AND PLEDGE TO KEEP THEMSELVES ONLY
FOR ONE ANOTHER, EACH IS SAYING BEFORE GOD AND

WITNESSES: "I WILL MEET YOUR NEEDS FOR AFFECTION, COMMUNION, COMMUNICATION, AND AFFIRMATION. I WILL SEEK THOSE SAME THINGS FROM NO ONE ELSE BUT YOU."

"TO HAVE" IS THE FLOUR AND SALT OF YOUR WEDDING VOW.

"TO HOLD" IS THE SUGAR AND SPICE.

ISAAC AND REBEKAH, REVISITED

𝒢

You can't reason with the heart; it has its own laws,
And thinks about things which the intellect scorns.

MARK TWAIN

While I would never presume to compare my love life with that of Isaac and Rebekah, I have experienced parallels to the way they found one another. All of us had to rely upon God to present a perfect mate, and in the end our stories were ones only God could have written.

Tom was ordained in 1978 but chose to go into business instead of the ministry. Over the years his secular pursuits began to gradually chip away at his faith. A hurtful relationship deepened the damage. By summer of 1993, Tom's father died and Tom found himself struggling emotionally and spiritually. At this crossroads he realized that he had lost his simple faith. He began to pray that God would guide him as he attempted to piece together their relationship. And he asked God to bring a woman into his life who would love both God and himself.

Over time Tom reasoned that teaching children in Sunday school might help him regain the basics of his beliefs. The Sunday before he was to meet the children, he met his coteacher—me!

I was divorced, and like Tom, hoping to meet someone who would bless my life emotionally and spiritually. I felt God had assured me this would happen. About five years before I met Tom, God had directed me during prayer to Genesis 24. In this story Abraham sent his servant to find a bride for his son Isaac. The servant found Rebekah, and one of the gifts he gave her as a promise of her forthcoming marriage was a bracelet.

As I read I understood that God was telling me these details would be repeated in my life: I would marry, and my husband-to-be would come bearing a bracelet. So I watched and prayed, and cherished this promise in my heart.

The church Tom and I attended had ten thousand members, so we had never met before we were teamed for Sunday school. Initially we weren't romantically interested in each other, but over the next few months we developed a good friendship. We both loved being with, teaching, and planning activities for the ten-year-old children we taught. Even during Tom's two-month business trip out of town, we talked almost every day to plan for our class.

Slowly our friendship grew, and five months after we met, we had our first date. We got together to celebrate Tom's birthday. All was well until I gave him a casual peck on the cheek and wished him a happy birthday. You would have thought I had just dropped a rock on his toe! I was hurt and confused by his negative reaction.

As Tom drove me home, we talked. He shared his hurts and fears from that earlier relationship and his spiritual and emotional struggles from the previous summer. Then we prayed together. Tom asked God to help him see his plan for us. After the prayer, Tom said he felt God directing us to continue our relationship.

As we dated, though, our relationship became a battle between Tom's fear of a committed relationship and my frustration with his indecision. Even though he sensed God was opening a new chapter in his life, Tom repeatedly tried to pull away from our growing closeness. I tried, sometimes unsuccessfully, not to react with anger. Yet through it all we prayed, alone and together, and God spoke to each of us. God urged Tom to keep seeing me, and he encouraged me to be patient with Tom.

As time passed I saw that Tom was beginning to fall in love with the Lord. And I realized that I was falling in love with Tom.

God continued to work on both of us. I knew God had freed Tom to love again when one day he told me I was his "wondrous gift from above"—the very woman he had prayed for the previous summer. Within that week, Tom was on his knees in my living room proposing marriage. The engagement present? *A bracelet!*

We were married in a small historical country church in my hometown. Tom planned the wedding and wrote the vows, including the Genesis 24 story in a congregational responsive reading.

No, we weren't Isaac and Rebekah, but Tom and Linda were just as happy.

LINDA TERRY

It is the man and woman united
that makes the complete human being.
Separate she lacks his force of body
and strength of reason;
he her softness, sensibility
and acute discernment.
Together they are most likely
to succeed in the world.

BENJAMIN FRANKLIN

GUITAR LOVE

*If music be the food of love
then play on!*

SHAKESPEARE

When I went away to college, I met and fell in love with the most wonderful man in the world. But upon meeting him, my father described him as "every parent's nightmare."

Admittedly, Wayne was unemployed. And his hair was shoulder-length. And he had dropped out of college. And his only and most treasured possession was a guitar.

But I loved him!

Near the end of my senior year, I received a great job offer back in California. Now that I think about it, the job was probably arranged by my father. On graduation day, Wayne told me that he planned to follow me to California and that he wanted to marry me. I was so happy I cried tears of joy—until he told me he was going to ask my father's permission.

When my father and Wayne disappeared at my graduation dinner, I knew Father would ask Wayne all the pertinent questions like, "How do you plan to support her?" "Where are you going to live?" and maybe "What are you going to eat?"

When they reappeared, Father spoke for both of them. "We have decided," he said, "that if Wayne wants to marry you, he needs to go back to college. We'll talk about marriage after he graduates."

Wayne and I cried as we parted. We knew that both my parents were secretly hoping that I would meet someone else.

No one was more surprised than my parents when eventually Wayne graduated from college and landed a great job in California. "Are you sure you want to marry Wayne?" they grilled me.

"I want your blessing," I assured them, "but forsaking all others, I will marry Wayne!"

Eventually my father reluctantly gave us his permission. Wayne and I were officially engaged.

There was just one big problem. "I can't afford an engagement ring yet," Wayne apologized. "But I can promise that we will always make beautiful music together forever!" I assured my romantic fiancé all that mattered was that we were together. Secretly, however, I was concerned. What would my parents think if Wayne couldn't even buy me a ring?

A few weeks later when we were celebrating Valentine's Day, Wayne presented me with a box of chocolates and in it was a beautiful diamond engagement ring. "Are you sure that you can afford this?" I asked. "You've only been working a couple of weeks."

Wayne just smiled and winked as he said, "God just dropped it down from heaven!"

Later, I discovered that he sold his beloved guitar to pay for my ring. His incredible sacrifice made the ring even more special to me, and it helped my parents see what a great heart Wayne possessed.

Those first few years we were married weren't easy. We ate a lot of beans as we struggled in the music industry. Eventually, however, Wayne became a successful businessman with closely cropped hair, a three piece suit, and a mortgage. He provided me with everything I could ever want or need.

One day, as we searched a music store, Wayne lamented that he wished he still had his old guitar. Instantly I decided what I would get him for our anniversary—a new guitar. Why hadn't I thought of that earlier?

A couple of months before our anniversary, I ran into an old college friend of Wayne's. We reminisced for a while, but as we were parting, he said offhandedly, "Oh, tell Wayne that I met an old acquaintance of his last week at the gym."

"Who?" I asked, assuming I'd probably know him, too.

"Oh, you wouldn't know him. He just got to know Wayne when Wayne sold him his guitar."

Needless to say, my heart skipped a beat. But what were the odds that this guy still owned the guitar after all these years? *Lord, let it be!* I prayed.

I quickly jotted down the acquaintance's name and said good-bye and raced home to dial information, quietly breathing prayers. A few minutes later, I introduced myself to the stranger on the phone. Excitedly I told my story while he listened politely.

"Yes," he said. "I remember Wayne. And I still have that guitar."

On the night of our anniversary, I gave my husband one of the greatest surprises of his life. He was so astonished when he saw the guitar he could hardly speak. "How did you ever find this?" he asked.

"Let's just say that God dropped it down from heaven," I answered.

Wayne and I are still making beautiful music together. And my parents agree I couldn't have found a better guy had I looked the whole world over.

KITTY AND WAYNE, AS TOLD TO SUSAN WALES

DREAMING ON
THE FAIRWAY

There can be no true love
even on your own side, without devotion;
devotion is the exercise of love, by which it grows.
ROBERT LEWIS STEVENSON

I don't know if it was love at first sight or not, but something pulled John and me together. We met. We laughed. We started to date. And almost right away, we began dreaming about the future.

John was tall, athletic, outgoing, and he wanted to become a golf pro. I couldn't imagine anything more marvelous than being married to a golf pro. We both felt certain that God had brought us together—to share both our dreams and our lives. We met in April, got engaged in August, and were married in December.

For our honeymoon we went to Sea Island, Georgia. Even while we were on our honeymoon, John was studying for the Professional Golf Association school he would begin attending as soon as we returned.

When he scored number one in his class and in the state, it seemed to both of us that our dreams were well on their way to becoming reality.

From the beginning of our marriage, I had envisioned John coming home for lunch in the afternoons. We would have a fun life that centered around his activities at the country club.

Yet that dream was not to be. A few years into our marriage, John realized that he needed to leave his current golf job to become a consultant in the golfing industry. That way he could make more money and have more control and leverage in developing his career as a pro.

His first consulting job took him to Wisconsin—as it turned out, to stay. This wasn't the dream we had had in mind either. John wanted me to quit my own job and join him. But the request left me stunned. I loved my job. If I quit, I would miss both the work and the people. Besides, I didn't know a soul in Wisconsin. All I could imagine were cows upon cows. I hadn't realized they even golfed there.

But a decision had to be made. And the decision was based on my answer to a question: *How much was I willing to help John pursue his dreams?*

Trembling with uncertainty, I said yes, and we moved to Wisconsin with our firstborn. Starting over wasn't easy. I had made my decision out of love for my husband. But I was still uncertain whether or not we'd done the right thing. And I kept wondering where my own dreams fit in to all of this.

As time passed, we struggled to carve out a life together. Nothing seemed to come together. I'll admit, I felt vindicated—we'd followed John's half of the dream, and it seemed to have taken us nowhere. Finally we arrived at a breaking point. I prayed and prayed for God to give me guidance. After all, hadn't God given us a dream to share? Wasn't it God's dream, too?

One day we were driving through the city. For some reason, I leaned over to John and asked, "If you could do anything you wanted professionally, what would you do?"

His brow furrowed for a moment. "I'd like to run golf tournaments with Legacy Ministries—tournaments like the one I did for Crawford-Limits," he replied. "My business would be benefit fund-raisers out there on the greens."

And with barely a hesitation, I replied, "We could call it Golf for Goodness Sake."

We looked at each other and smiled. Immediately, an entire plan seemed to tumble out, and a feeling of rejuvenation stirred within us. During the next hour, it was as if a light shined down upon us—and our dreams became one again.

The company, founded in 1992, now produces over one hundred tournaments a year to raise money for nonprofit organizations and important causes. We're both convinced that this work is important. Much of the money that John has helped to raise has gone to charities for juvenile diabetes, Downs syndrome, Alzheimer's dsisease, and cancer. This has allowed John to really make a difference in the lives of others while doing what he loves most.

Today I am busy with our two small daughters. John and I love and support each other in both our work and marriage. We take the vows of our marriage very seriously—to love, to honor, to cherish. And we've added one of our own...to dream.

SUZANNE WHITE

Oh, hasten not this loving act,
Rapture where self and not-self meet;
My life has been awaiting you,
Your footfall was my own heart's beat.
PAUL VALERY

THE BIRTHDAY CARD

When I am dead my dearest,
Sing no sad songs for me;
Plant thou no roses at my head,
Nor shady cypress tree.
Be the green grass above me
With showers, and dewdrops;
And if thou wilt remember
And if thou will forget.

CHRISTINA ROSETTI

A lot of people feel disappointed, even cheated, when retailers display merchandise for upcoming holidays back-to-back, blurring the lines of distinction between Thanksgiving, Christmas, and New Year's. Greeting card stores seem especially guilty of promoting one holiday ever so early, then crashing it into the next. And so it was that spring with the usual holiday pileup. All at once Mother's Day cards and Father's Day cards were fighting for shelf space before Easter cards were even cleared away.

But in my family it's a real convenience. In one fell swoop, I can gather not only my parents' Mother's and Father's Day cards, but also my husband's, my niece's and my best friend's birthday cards.

This particular May I found myself in my usual rush-rush, hurry-hurry mode, scurrying from work to home with a pit stop at the Hallmark store just before hitting the Chinese food drive-through. My mind was racing, as is normal for most lifestyles these days, forty thoughts zipping around in the brain at once. But my number-one priority was getting my mom's Mother's Day card in the mail by tomorrow morning at the latest. I was convinced that disaster would strike if that card arrived a day or two late. Timing was everything.

The next card I needed in a hurry was my husband's birthday card. "Nothing mushy, gushy," I could hear him say. I scanned the rows for the humor section. That made me think about asking his advice about that rattle in my car engine, although I already knew all too well what I'd hear. "Sweetie," he'd say. "If God wanted your dear sweet husband to give you advice all the time, he'd have made me a psychiatrist!"

My hubby was a real tease. Probably the most important thing he taught me was to laugh…a lot. "It's the only thing that'll keep you young," he'd rib.

I paid the cashier, and just as I exited the store, it began to rain. We greatly needed the precipitation, but if you've ever been in an Atlanta rush hour in a rainstorm, you know your drive will be total torture. Pulling out onto I-75 was just as I had predicted. So I pressed the autodial on my cell phone and called the Chinese restaurant, pleading for a delay of at least forty-five minutes on the to-go order. A little frustrated, and not totally satisfied that I had communicated very well, I decided to try to get my neck and shoulders to relax.

I took deep breaths and inched up into a crowded lane. I took more deep breaths. After ten minutes, no cars in any of the four lanes had moved more than a yard. I tried stretching my fingers, ankles, and toes. Still no traffic relief.

After idling for twenty minutes, I noticed that I was just about the only one with my car still running. So I too gave up hope and turned my car key to OFF.

Then the rain started beating down so hard that I couldn't see the car's bumper directly in front of me. It was rather deafening. But I cracked my window just a hair because the smell of rain has always been one of my favorite things. That staved off the boredom for a few minutes, but soon I started looking around inside the car for something to do.

My greeting cards! Perfect! I could spend the time filling out all my greeting cards. I had my Daytimer with all the addresses I needed and even managed to dig out a pen from the bottom of my purse.

My mom's Mother's Day card was easy. I wrote lots of "I Love Yous" and such. The ooey-gooier the better. I knew if I didn't say something to bring tears to her eyes, then I'd not done my job well.

"Enough of that!" I said aloud as I reached for my husband, Stephen's, card, complete with his preference: a joke and a zinger. I giggled as I thought how terribly different my mom's and husband's personalities were. Were. But from the very first time I brought Stephen home—for the big interview, as my husband coined it—they were teasing each other unmercifully.

Were.

And then I felt my heart kind of sag. It was one of those times with all your might you try NOT to think about something. But the harder you push it away, the faster it lands in your lap. I glanced down at the "Happy Birthday, Hubby" card and sighed sadly. I couldn't believe it. After nine years of my husband's passing, I had bought him a birthday card.

You would think between the rain, the traffic jam, and the now sure-to-be-cold Chinese food, I'd be a writhing blob of Jell-O. But much to my great surprise, a comforting feeling came over me. It was kind of like a warm chill, if you can imagine, wrapped around my shoulders—like a hug.

Out of the blue, God had sent me a little gift from heaven. On a really rotten day where virtually everything had gone awry, God stepped in. For just a couple of hours, he let me forget the burden and sadness of widowhood. At the same time, he gave me a hefty kick in the pants to remind me that my Stephen was still with me. His spirit, wisdom, and even his silly humor were all right here, even nine years after God called my dear sweet husband home.

Especially on a day like that day, I thought this was a generous and awesome gift from my Lord. And right there on I-75 I told him so. I thanked him also for his unique ways of getting our attention.

Happily, I was stuck in that rainy metal logjam for another thirty minutes, all the while enveloped in happy memories of my lovable, often laughable husband and the life we shared for such a short time.

DEE ANN GRAND

Thy love is such I can no way repay,
The heavens reward thee manifold I pray.
Then while we live, in love let's so persever,
That when we live no more, we may live ever.

ANNE BRADSTREET

A PERFECT DAY

For memory has painted this perfect day
with colors that never fade.

CARRIE JACOBS BOND

When I first met David Wilson at college, I was suspicious of his impeccable manners and the respect he showered on me. I'd been accustomed to guys who were too cool to be concerned about my comfort or my feelings. He just seemed like *too* much of a gentleman. I assumed he must be a phony, since nobody could be that perfect.

How wrong I was!

As time wore on, I became accustomed to David's treating me like a lady, and I realized the value of being with such a loving and sensitive man. I realized that I had found someone very special, and as our relationship progressed I knew I wanted to spend the rest of my life with David.

I shouldn't have been surprised that David's proposal was such a special one, but even he surpassed my expectations.

My birthday was only days away when David showed up at my office with a dozen red roses. "I'm going to kidnap you for the day," he announced.

I glanced over at Stella, my boss, and she was smiling and nodding. David had planned this out, making all the arrangements for me to have the day off.

We drove along the coast down to Corona Del Mar, our favorite beach. We settled on a nice spot, and David spread out a blanket, opened the umbrella, and put the picnic basket down. We ate delicious strawberries and sipped sparkling cider. It seemed like a perfect day…but it was only the beginning.

David suggested that we go for a walk along the ocean's edge. We walked hand-in-hand for about an hour, and when we returned, I noticed roses on the sand marking the path back to our blanket. Because this was typical of David, I knew he had them placed there. *Pretty special for a birthday,* I thought. But then I remembered who I was with.

But there was more…much more.

When we got back to the spot where our blanket had been, there was a big beautiful white tent, palm trees, and a table laid with starch white linens, china, crystal, a hurricane lamp, and a buffet table with giant shell ornaments. A server welcomed us and said, "Welcome to your ocean view reservations. Your table is waiting."

The waiter handed me a personalized menu that included all my favorite dishes. After our salads were served she brought out a very special bottle of wine that David and I had purchased while wine tasting in the Santa Inez Valley on a special date he had planned for me two years before.

This is it! He's going to propose! I thought. My palms began to sweat and my heart raced. But no sooner had this thought occurred to me, the server said, "I understand you're celebrating your birthday…Happy birthday!"

Suddenly a wave of disappointment washed over me, but when I realized that this was not going to be a proposal, I was no longer nervous and relaxed to enjoy my birthday dinner with David.

Afterward, David suggested that we walk to our favorite spot on the beach. Suddenly David fell to one knee and spoke the most beautiful words I have ever heard as he asked me to be his wife, promising me that he would make every effort to see that my life with him was as close to perfect as possible. Knowing he would live up to that promise, I said yes as he slipped the most gorgeous pear-shaped diamond ring on my finger. We hugged and cried as onlookers cheered and applauded.

Reminiscing about the past when we'd first met and all the special times we'd shared, we then talked excitedly about our future and what was ahead. David then escorted me back to the tent where the candlelight was flickering and the moon was rising over the water. He took me in his arms and we danced until the last glimmer of the rays of the sun disappeared. It had been a *perfect* day and a *perfect* proposal.

David and I were married a year later. As we live out the days of our marriage, I've realized that although David is not perfect (nor am I!), his thoughtfulness fills even those imperfect days with love.

I will forever carry the memories of that *perfect* day at the ocean when it all began.

RUBRIA PORRAS WILSON

Two happy lovers make one single breath,
one single drop of moonlight in the grass.
When they walk, they leave two shadows that merge,
and they leave one single sun blazing in their bed.
PABLO NERUD

PETALS OF LOVE

Love adds a precious seeing to the eye.
WILLIAM SHAKESPEARE

My mother, Margaret Williams, was nearing her seventieth birthday and we knew she was expecting a celebration. As a matter of fact, she had hinted strongly to her four children, individually of course, what lovely parties her friends' children had given them. She also declared that they had not spared any time or expense in their planning. I got the message loud and clear!

After a quick call to my sister, Mary Ashley, I soon discovered that as her gift Mother wanted cherry trees.

"Cherry trees? Why?" I asked.

It seems that when Mother was growing up in her hometown of Orangeburg, South Carolina, the most gorgeous Yoshino cherry trees grew along the river bank at the Edisto Gardens. Mother told Mary Ashley that upon her death she wanted the family to plant these trees in honor of her.

We certainly didn't have to wait until she died to plant the cherry trees. We decided to do it for her birthday. We got busy and planned a tea at the Arts Center, located out in the gardens. About five hundred people attended the birthday party and over $17,000 was raised to purchase Yoshino cherry trees. Over a thousand trees were planted. That was nine years ago and hundreds more have been planted since to honor someone or commemorate the passing of another birthday in our family. It's become quite the tradition. This family tradition has made all of my family passionate about Yoshino cherry trees. I can spot them in the dead of winter. When I see one in full bloom, in all its glory, it thrills me to no end.

I am a true romantic and I love flowers! My husband, John, knowing of my love for flowers, filled my bed with pink rose petals on our tenth anniversary. This was his way to remind me of his love for me and also of the promise he made to me the night before we married.

Knowing that I had been hurt by a previous divorce, John took my hands and kissed my fingertips and then gently said, "I vow and declare that my love will erase from your memory every tear you ever cried. Your life with me will be a bed of roses." His expression of love was so powerful and healing to me. What did I do to ever deserve a husband like John? His love and sensitivity had opened a locked portion of my heart.

As our nineteenth anniversary approached this year, I smiled and with a twinkle in my eye inquired as to what Mr. Rose Petals was up to this year in honor of our anniversary. He laughed and taunted me. "You'll see." What could he do to ever top the bed filled with roses?

The day before our anniversary, we found a house we wanted to buy. The evening of our anniversary, John and I headed out to our favorite anniversary restaurant, The Ritz Carlton. We discovered that we were an hour early so we drove by the new house. As we drove in the circular drive, I noticed the trunks of the trees. "John look what's all around us! Yoshino cherry trees!"

"One, two, three, four, five, six, seven, eight!" John counted out loud.

They were large, mature cherry trees. They must have been at least twenty-five years old.

"Eight," I said triumphantly, "means new beginnings."

Just about that time the wind began to blow causing the trees to swing back and forth. Cherry blossoms instantly filled the air and rained down upon us, carpeting the driveway with soft pink petals. Here we were again on our anniversary blessed with a visual sign of our love. This time it was a gift for both of us and we knew right away who the messenger of this dear message was!

ANN PLATZ

From This Day Forward

Childhood wonder upon her face
Visions of flowers, cake, and lace
White horses, picket fences, and blue skies
Long ago dreams in a little girl's eyes.
SUSAN WALES

THERE'S SOMETHING BEAUTIFUL—ALMOST MAGICAL—ABOUT THE WORDS *THIS DAY.*

THIS DAY, YOUR WEDDING DAY, IS THE FULFILLMENT OF CHILDHOOD DREAMS. YOU WEAR THE GLISTENING WHITE GOWN, DRINK IN THE FRAGRANCE OF A CHURCH FILLED WITH FLOWERS AND OF BEST FRIENDS SHEDDING JOYFUL TEARS AS YOU PLEDGE A LIFETIME OF LOVE TO THE ONE YOU HAVE CHOSEN. YOU AND HE ARE THE CENTER OF ATTENTION.

THIS DAY IS YOUR DAY!

BUT THERE IS MORE TO *THIS DAY* THAN THE MUSIC, MISTY EYES, AND CELEBRATION. *THIS DAY* IS A MILESTONE THAT MARKS A TURNING POINT. FROM *THIS DAY* AS A HUSBAND AND WIFE, YOU WILL WALK TOGETHER INTO THE GREAT UNKNOWN. YOUR VOWS ARE THE MOMENTUM, AND THE

TRIMMINGS—RIBBONS, CAKE, AND YARDS OF WHITE TULLE—
ALL PART OF THE RITUAL TO UNFURL YOUR SAILS IN THE
OPEN SEA.

THOUGH YOU MAY NEVER WANT *THIS DAY* TO END, IT WILL
END...CALLING YOU TO NEW BEGINNINGS.

THIS DAY IS A NEW DIRECTION IN GOD'S DIVINE DESIGN. IT IS
YOUR DAY. IT IS HIS DAY. AND GOD, ALONGSIDE YOU AND
YOUR BELOVED, IS LOVING EVERY MINUTE OF IT!

THE BLUE SCARF

The setting sun, and music at the close,

As the last taste of sweets, is sweetest last,

Writ in remembrance more than things long past.

SHAKESPEARE, *KING RICHARD*

When Meredith, Ed White's wife of twenty-five years, was killed in an auto accident, Ed was sure his life had ended too. He would have given all he owned to have just one day, even one hour, to tell his Meredith good-bye.

But life went on for Ed. In fact, he quickly learned that responsible, single, middle-aged men were in great demand. Every one of his friends seemed to have a widow or divorcée that they couldn't wait to introduce to Ed. But he ignored the avalanche of invitations that began to appear shortly after Meredith's death.

It was three years later that Ed finally accepted a social invitation to a large gathering at the home of friends. As guests crowded around the buffet, Ed still ached with a feeling of incompleteness. *Meredith should be by my side,* he thought. Somehow, he survived until the end of the evening.

But as he was leaving, he caught sight of a beautiful silk scarf across the room. The scarf brought back a flood of other memories. He studied the face of the woman who wore it. *It couldn't be her…or could it?* he wondered.

The woman was preparing to leave, too, and he followed her out.

Catching up with her, he said, "That's a beautiful scarf you're wearing."

She muttered a quick thank you and began to walk faster.

"I guess I'm not very good at this," he told her, trying to keep up. "I'm Ed. And you are…?"

"Sunny," she answered without a trace of enthusiasm.

It is her. It must be her, he thought to himself, but the woman with the scarf seemed to share no such recognition. He worked hard to persuade her to join him for a late-night coffee, and finally succeeded.

As they sat across from one another in the booth, she barely looked at him. But he tried again. "That scarf you're wearing…"

She interrupted him. "I don't mean to appear rude but I should have never worn this scarf."

"And why not?" he asked. "It matches your blue eyes perfectly."

Definitely the same eyes, he thought. But how much they had changed, hidden by what seemed to be a veil of sadness. When she began to cry, he offered her his handkerchief.

"I'm sorry, I was rude," she said appearing to soften, but still keeping her eyes looking downcast. "This scarf just reminds me of all the mistakes I've made in my life. All the bad choices. What might have been. You see, I haven't had a very happy life. Things could have been different if I had only followed my heart instead of my ambitions."

"Don't you believe in second chances?" he asked.

"Why, I…yes, I suppose I do," she said, raising her eyes to meet his for the first time. "But I've already had plenty. It's too late for me now…was it Ed, did you say?"

"Yes, Ed. Ed White." Now as she looked at him, her countenance began to change. A smile of recognition spread across her face.

"So where did you get that scarf, Sunny?" he asked gently.

"From…you!" she said, and they both burst out laughing.

You see, nearly three decades earlier, Sunny had been Ed's first love, but she had refused his proposal, choosing instead to go to California to pursue her career. At first devastated over his loss, Ed had eventually met and fallen in love with Meredith.

Life had not been as kind to Sunny. A failed marriage had found her once again living alone in a tiny apartment, struggling to make ends meet in New York. But lately Sunny had begun to talk to God about her past, praying for forgiveness and another chance. As for the scarf, she had searched it out just this evening to wear to the party as a sign of faith that—though she never expected to see Ed White again—God had graciously heard her prayer.

That very evening, he did!

When Ed and Sunny were married later that year, Ed was swept away with gratitude that his beaming bride, Sunny, was by his side—right where she belonged. And the blue scarf she wore reminded them both that God does indeed give second chances—and third and fourth ones, too.

SUNNY AND ED WHITE,
AS TOLD TO SUSAN WALES

Love gives naught but itself
and takes naught but from itself.
Love possesses not nor would it be possessed
for love is sufficient unto love.
KAHIL GIBRAN

LET THERE BE LIGHT

Lovers alone wear sunlight.

E. E. CUMMINGS

It had all the makings of a disaster. First off, I wasn't even home when my favorite niece, Paige, called to announce her engagement…and to say that she wanted to be married before she left for school. Oh, and one more thing: She wanted to be married at *my house* in three weeks.

From a pay phone at the golf camp I was attending, I gasped. Not only was I away from home then, but a long-planned visit to Ireland loomed. The trip meant I would be away from home for the crucial ten days before the wedding was to take place.

I stuttered that sure, we could pull off a formal wedding in a few weeks, even with my immediate and imminent absences. I hung up the phone wondering what I'd just done. I sorely wanted to make Paige's dreams come true, but could we really plan and present a wedding in the time, and with the distractions, we had? I determined to try my best.

Once I returned from camp, Paige and I talked and planned and then talked and planned some more. In the days before I left the country, we got the tent, tables, chairs, flowers, music, food, and everything else that goes into making the perfect wedding. She arranged for her aunt and cousin to cater the wedding breakfast at the eleven o'clock ceremony for seventy-five guests. We handled as many of the details as possible before I left for my trip.

I returned from Ireland on Thursday night. By Friday morning, the tent was erected and all of the tables were set up. Beautiful garlands draped the courtyard, fish pool, and columns. The linens were pressed and starched and the china set out with care. The silverware had been polished till it shined. I was impressed! We worked hard all day and by Friday night, we were exhausted but we went to bed thinking, with great pride, *Everything is done. Everything will be perfect.*

Then came the horrible storm. We awoke at four o'clock Saturday morning to clouds dumping so much water so quickly on the tent that it was in danger of collapsing. The electricity was out. Frantic questions filled the soggy air: "How are we going to cook the wedding breakfast?" Even worse, "How are we going to dry the bridesmaids' hair?"

By ten o'clock we had relaxed a little. The rain had stopped. The tent company reerected the tent. The power was back on. Aunt Janet and Cousin Mary Ellen had all sorts of things simmering in the kitchen and the guests were arriving.

We served coffee and punch in the rose garden. The air was still misty. *That could be a problem,* I thought. Then I noticed that Paige was nowhere to be found. "Where's the bride? Does anyone know where the bride is?" These were not the kind of questions I wanted to be asking less than an hour before the wedding was supposed to start.

Paige burst in a few minutes later. Apparently she had had traffic problems in the fifty-five-mile trip from her home to mine. And in the moments between my asking where Paige was and her arriving, the sky had darkened and the clouds hung ominously low above our heads.

Once again, our frenzied yet loving plans were threatened. With a strained smile, I invited the guests into the house a bit early and treated them to the quartet's calming music. I needed calming music myself right about then. Inside, I gave up. Discouragement consumed me. *What a complete mess,* I thought gloomily. *What a terrible day to be married.*

The ceremony was finally set to begin. We directed the guests to where the two wings of the house met in the middle of the open oval foyer. Above our heads was a large skylight. Unfortunately, there was no light that day, just shades of dark gray. It was so dark that I hoped the bride would be able to see her way down the "aisle."

Then Paige and her betrothed, Tim, appeared. Paige entered from the left, the groom from the right. When I saw their beaming faces, I smiled. They were indeed a lovely couple. I could see the love in their eyes. No exterior light could brighten the room more than their smiles did.

And as they joined hands underneath the skylight, the gray clouds parted and the sun broke through triumphantly. Bright sunlight shined directly on the couple. All of us watching uttered an audible gasp.

I finally understood that regardless of how disastrously the day began, the beauty of a wedding wasn't in the details of decor or weather. It was in the love of a man and a woman, and that illumination was matchless.

BETH JONES, AS TOLD TO ANN PLATZ

LEGACY OF LOVE

But oh, she dances such a way!
No sun upon an Easter-day
Is half so fine a sight.
SIR JOHN SUCKLING

My mother, the late Eleanor Powell, was starstruck almost from birth. She loved acting, dancing, and any form of showbiz. As a young teenager she spent her summers working as a dancer in Atlantic City. Gus Edwards discovered her and signed her for his revue in New York City. Billed as the World's Greatest Tap Dancer, Mother danced her way to Broadway in such hits as *Fine and Dandy, Hot Cha,* and *Scandals.*

Then Hollywood called and Mother went on to star in several films including Cole Porter's *Born to Dance, Rosalie* with Nelson Eddy, *Honolulu* with Burns and Allen, *Ship Ahoy,* and *Lady Be Good* with Red Skelton. MGM cast Mother with Fred Astaire in *Broadway Melody of 1940.* She was a smashing success and finally people were starstruck over her!

During World War II, Mother was asked to accompany the famous actor Pat O'Brien of *Boys Town* fame and the beautiful actress Merle Oberon on a warbond tour. As the congenial group traveled all over the country by train, Mr. O'Brien developed a fatherly interest in my mother.

"I'd like to introduce you to that talented young actor, Glenn Ford," Mr. O'Brien told her. "Glenn needs to meet a pretty, nice young woman like you!" Mr. O'Brien had recently worked with the young actor in the popular

191

movie, *Flight Lieutenant.* "Mark my words," he said emphatically, "this young fellow is going to be the top leading man day soon!"

Mother listened politely, but she wasn't really interested. She already had a special someone in her life. Besides, some well-meaning friend was always trying to fix her up with a dashing new star and they were all the same. She thought she was past being starstruck and could no longer be impressed.

Since moving to California, my mother lived quietly in Beverly Hills with her mother. Grandmother made sure her daughter was properly chaperoned around Hollywood. She often accompanied Ellie to social events, movies, and church. The life of a young starlet in Hollywood could be very lonely at times, so mother and daughter grew very close. Ellie was also devoted to her faith.

It was a beautiful summer night when mother and daughter happened to see *The Adventures of Martin in Eden,* starring none other than Glenn Ford. Mother was immediately mesmerized by the movie. Like millions of other young women across America, she fell in love with the handsome young actor she was watching on the big screen.

She was starstruck!

When Mother phoned Pat O'Brien to take him up on his offer to introduce her to Glenn Ford, Mr. O'Brien was amused and honored to play the role of matchmaker. He arranged a lovely dinner party at his home to introduce the popular young couple. My father was on leave and when he showed up in his uniform, he captured my mother's heart forever! For his part, Father was attracted to mother's sweet spirit and her values. They were both dating other actors, but following that enchanted evening at the O'Brien home, they only had eyes for each other.

Eleanor Powell and Glenn Ford were a real item in Hollywood. The gossip columns buzzed with the exciting details of their wholesome romance. Mother and Father fell deeply in love. My grandmother had raised her daughter to be an old-fashioned girl, so it was only appropriate that my father popped the question over an ice-cream soda. She accepted immediately!

Eleanor Powell and Glenn Ford were married in 1943 during the war, and I was born a few years later.

Just as Pat O'Brien had predicted, my father's film career soared. Father starred as the leading man in many hit films such as *Gilda* with Rita Hayworth; *A Stolen Life* with Bette Davis; *The Blackboard Jungle; Teahouse of the August Moon; Imitation General* with Red Buttons; *Torpedo Run* with Ernest Borgnine; *The Gazebo; It Started with a Kiss* with Debbie Reynolds; and *The Rounders* with Henry Fonda.

Despite all the fame and fortune my parents enjoyed, they taught me that the most important things in life were faith and values. In the fifties, while my father's star grew brighter, my mother dedicated herself to being a wife and mother. She also created the Emmy-Award-winning television series, *Faith of Our Children,* and my father became a regular participant on her show.

Both of my parents gave me a great legacy of love by teaching me the importance of loving God and others, and I have passed this legacy to my own children. What started as a simple case of stargazing ended in a Christian family whose values endure generation after generation.

AS TOLD TO SUSAN WALES BY PETER FORD

Peter Ford and his wife Lynda, the proud parents of three children, recently celebrated thirty years of wedded bliss. They reside in Beverly Hills with their father, actor Glenn Ford.

IT HAPPENED ON THE BROOKLYN SUBWAY

Great loves were almost always great tragedies.
Perhaps it was because love was never truly great
until the element of sacrifice entered into it.

MARY ROBERTS RINEHART

The car was crowded, and there seemed to be no chance of a seat. But as I entered, a man sitting by the door suddenly jumped up to leave, and I slipped into the empty seat.

I've been living in New York long enough not to start conversations with strangers. But, being a photographer, I have the peculiar habit of analyzing people's faces, and I was struck by the features of the passenger on my left. He was probably in his late 30s, and when he glanced up, his eyes seemed to have a hurt expression in them. He was reading a Hungarian-language newspaper and something prompted me to say in Hungarian, "I hope you don't mind if I glance at your paper."

The man seemed surprised to be addressed in his native language. But he only answered politely, "You may read it now. I'll have time later on."

During the half-hour ride to town, we had quite a conversation. He said his name was Bela Paskin. A law student when World War II started, he had been put into a German labor battalion and sent to the Ukraine. Later he was captured by the Russians and put to work burying the German dead. After the war, he covered hundreds of miles on foot until he reached his home in Debrecen, a large city in eastern Hungary.

I myself knew Debrecen quite well, and we talked about it for a while.

Then he told me the rest of his story. When he went to the apartment once occupied by his father, mother, brothers, and sisters, he found strangers living there. Then he went upstairs to the apartment that he and his wife once had. It was also occupied by strangers. None of them had ever heard of his family.

As he was leaving, full of sadness, a boy ran after him, calling, "Paskin bacsi! Paskin bacsi!" That means "Uncle Paskin." The child was the son of some old neighbors of his. He went to the boy's home and talked to his parents. "Your whole family is dead," they told him. "The Nazis took them and your wife to Auschwitz."

Auschwitz was one of the worst Nazi concentration camps. Paskin gave up all hope. A few days later, too heartsick to remain any longer in Hungary, he set out on foot again, stealing across border after border until he reached Paris. He managed to immigrate to the United States in October 1947, just three months before I met him.

All the time he had been talking, I kept thinking that somehow his story seemed familiar. A young woman whom I met recently at the home of friends had also been from Debrecen; she had been sent to Auschwitz; from there she had been transferred to work in a German munitions factory. Her relatives had been killed in the gas chambers. Later, she was liberated by the Americans and was brought here in the first boatload of displaced persons in 1946.

Her story had moved me so much that I had written down her address and phone number, intending to invite her to meet my family and thus help relieve the terrible emptiness in her life.

It seemed impossible that there could be any connection between these two people, but as I neared my station, I fumbled anxiously in my address book. I asked in what I hoped was a casual voice, "Was your wife's name Marya?"

He turned pale. "Yes!" he answered. "How did you know?"

He looked as if he were about to faint.

I said, "Let's get off the train." I took him by the arm at the next station and led him to a phone booth. He stood there like a man in a trance while I dialed her phone number.

It seemed hours before Marya Paskin answered. Later I learned her room was alongside the telephone, but she was in the habit of never answering it because she had so few friends and the calls were always for someone else. This time, however, there was no one else at home, and, after letting it ring for a while, she responded.

When I heard her voice at last, I told her who I was and asked her to describe her husband. She seemed surprised at the question, but gave me a description. Then I asked her where she had lived in Debrecen, and she told me the address.

Asking her to hold the line, I turned to Paskin and said, "Did you and your wife live on such-and-such a street?"

"Yes!" Bela exclaimed. He was white as a sheet and trembling.

"Try to be calm," I urged him. "Something miraculous is about to happen to you. Here, take this telephone and talk to your wife!"

He nodded his head in mute bewilderment, his eyes bright with tears. He took the receiver, listened a moment to his wife's voice, then cried suddenly. "This is Bela! This is Bela!" and he began to mumble hysterically. Seeing that the poor fellow was so excited he couldn't talk coherently, I took the receiver from his shaking hands.

"Stay where you are," I told Marya, who also sounded hysterical. "I am sending your husband to you. We will be there in a few minutes."

Bela was crying like a baby and saying over and over again, "It is my wife, I go to my wife!"

At first I thought I had better accompany Paskin, lest the man should faint from excitement, but I decided that this was a moment in which no strangers should intrude. Putting Paskin into a taxicab, I directed the driver to take him to Marya's address, paid the fare and said good-bye.

Bela Paskin's reunion with his wife was a moment so poignant, so electric with suddenly released emotion, that afterward neither he nor Marya could recall much about it.

"I remember only that when I left the phone, I walked to the mirror like in a dream to see if maybe my hair had turned gray," she said later. "The next thing I know, a taxi stops in front of the house, and it is my husband who comes toward me. Details I cannot remember; only this I know—that I was happy for the first time in many years.

"Even now it is difficult to believe that it happened. We have both suffered so much; I have almost lost the capability to not be afraid. Each time my husband goes from the house, I say to myself, 'Will anything happen to take him from me again?'"

Her husband is confident that no horrible misfortune will ever befall them. "Providence has brought us together," he says simply. "It was meant to be."

PAUL DEUTSCHMAN

Reprinted from the May 1949 Reader's Digest. Copyright 1949 by Paul Deutschman. Reprinted with permission of The Reader's Digest and Regina Ryan Publishing Enterprises, Inc., 251 Central Park West, New York 10024

TOGETHER...AT LAST!

❧

Two such as you
With such a master speed
Cannot be parted nor be swept away
From one another
Once you are agreed
That life is only life forevermore
Together wing to wing and oar to oar.

ROBERT FROST

osemary was the only child of a Yorba Linda rancher and an eighth-generation Castilian Spanish beauty. She had a happy childhood, her life full of love, adventure, and activities around the ranch. Their doors were always open to family and friends, who were guests of great meals and joyous fiestas hosted by Rosemary's family.

John was the son of a close-knit, civic-minded family. He was the high school football hero and track star. He was nineteen and Rosemary was fifteen. The beautiful teenager fell deeply in love with her high school idol, John Raitt. The feelings were quite mutual, and they were allowed to see one another, properly chaperoned.

Alarmed that the two youths were becoming too serious, their families convened. Aside from being too young to get so serious, the families believed there were many differences between the two. She was a Catholic and he was Presbyterian. Rosemary's mother also wondered aloud what kind of future John, who aspired to be a football coach, would have. "He can't possibly provide the life that Rosemary is accustomed to having," she said. Both families agreed it was for the best that the two separate.

Their love forbidden, Rosemary and John were forced to go their separate ways. John went to the University of Southern California, where he starred on the Trojans' track and field team. He also began what would be a wonderful singing career. His magical tenor voice propelled him up the ladder of success in the world of theater and music.

The pain of Rosemary and John's separation was, for a time, unbearable. But, in order to please their families, they eventually married others and had families of their own.

John became a great success in the theater and on Broadway. Rosemary watched him perform in *Oklahoma, Showboat, Carousel,* and *Annie Get Your Gun*. She remembered the days of their youth, when she had been his girl.

Eventually, the two lost touch and only faded memories of the other and their first love lingered.

Years later, the hometown boy came back home to perform in the local theater. Afterward, Rosemary's mother came backstage to tell him she was sorry. She had been wrong about John's success. But it was too late, for John and Rosemary were both happily married.

The years passed. John was divorced, and Rosemary widowed. One day, John's manager told him he had seen Rosemary. "I met someone at a party that knew you...said she was your first love," his manager told him.

"Who?" John begged to know.

"My neighbor, Rosemary. She's a widow now."

John had the phone in his hand, and he silently prayed that Rosemary would answer as he dialed her number. She did.

"Do you know who this is?" John's voice rang out.

"No," came Rosemary's reply.

"It's your first love!" he announced.

"John!" she squealed with delight. Suddenly there was silence at the other end of the line. It had been fifty-eight years.

"Would you like to have dinner tonight?" he asked her.

"My hair's in curlers and I have a baked potato in the oven," she told him.

"I can't take no for an answer," he told her. "We've waited too long for this moment."

When John walked through the gates of her home, he saw Rosemary waiting at the door. He remembered seeing the same vibrant blue eyes he had gazed into fifty-eight years earlier.

It was as though nothing had changed between them. They talked until four the next morning. It seemed that they knew one another on a deep spiritual level and neither of their hearts had changed after all these years.

The young lovers, who had by now grown old, took up right where they'd left off as teenagers and began courting again. It wasn't long before John proposed. They were married at Rosemary's home in the gardens under the magnolia tree surrounded by their blended families, serenaded by John's daughter, singer Bonnie Raitt. It was a magnificent family celebration of love.

Always the hopeless romantic, on their wedding day John presented Rosemary with a gift for every year they'd been apart...fifty-eight presents in all!

Today, they count each day as a gift as they celebrate their golden years together.

At last, the young lovers were reunited.

Editor's note: The great Broadway singer, John Raitt, still performs his music for all his fans. Rosemary is on the board of Regents at Pepperdine University, which she helped found. Pepperdine named their musical theater in honor of the couple, THE JOHN AND ROSEMARY RAITT CENTER FOR THE PERFORMING ARTS.

I KNOW WHO YOU ARE!

Grow old with me! The best is yet to be,
The last of life, for which the first was made:
Our times are in his hand who saith,
"A whole I planned,
Youth shows but half trust God:
see all, nor be afraid!"

ROBERT BROWNING

It was a spontaneous trip home to Savannah for the Thanksgiving weekend. Charlotte decided just in time to get the last seat on the last flight from Atlanta to Savannah. It would be fun to surprise her mother, her sister, and all the nieces and nephews around the holiday table.

The next day Charlotte happened to meet her friend Betty at the supermarket. Betty, delighted to see her, invited Charlotte to attend a party she was giving that night.

Charlotte demurred, saying, "Nobody will remember me after all these years. Besides, I never go to parties unescorted." Betty persisted, though, and at last, Charlotte agreed. "Okay—I could drop in for an hour," she said.

The weather was warm and glorious, Betty's house was beautiful with candlelight and flowers, and Charlotte felt glad she had chosen a becoming red dress for the occasion. As she mingled with the other quests, enjoying herself, she nevertheless watched the time. *I'll leave before it gets late*, she told herself.

After the hour was up, Charlotte moved toward the door only to be intercepted by an attractive, smiling gentleman. "Excuse me. I'm Norris Pindar," he said, "and I understand that you write."

"I know who you are—" Charlotte began.

"No, you don't," the gentleman corrected her, sure he had never met her before in his life.

"Don't you sing in the Christ Church choir? Baritone? Don't you solo every Christmas in *The Messiah*? And at Easter, don't you sing 'Were You There When They Crucified My Lord?'" *There. He stands corrected,* she thought.

"You do know who I am!" he replied, sounding amazed.

"Do you write, also?" Charlotte asked, smiling.

"No, but my wife does. She has written several books."

"Where is your wife? Maybe I know her." Charlotte searched the room with her eyes, thinking she might spot a former newspaper colleague.

"She's dead," he said.

The wedding band on his hand...speaking of his wife in present tense...suddenly she comprehended the situation. "When did it happen?" she asked. He named the date, even the time of day—just six and a half weeks before—and she immediately understood. "This is your first time out since...?"

"Yes."

"I had a sadness also. It was not as terrible as yours, but my world seemed to fall apart. My friends brought me through it," Charlotte told him. "You are doing the right thing, coming to this party. These people have loved you all your life. Let them help you now."

He seized her hand. "Please talk to me," he begged. Leading her to a sofa, he engaged her in lively conversation as others in the room took note of the woman in the red dress who was allowing the widower to hold her hand. When he let out a big laugh, full and free, one woman looked distinctly disapproving.

The next day Charlotte flew back to Atlanta, still thinking of that honest, hurting man with the good face and gentle ways. He would telephone, she felt sure. *Tomorrow, after church, after lunch,* she surmised.

Then he'd wait because perhaps I'd want a nap. He will call at four o'clock, Charlotte concluded.

The telephone rang at exactly four. As the days went by, other long-distance calls escalated their friendship. Over long conversations they explored music, poetry, and politics—everything that mattered. They fell in love.

Two weeks after Thanksgiving, Charlotte's telephone rang and Nell, an old friend, was on the line. "I have something important to tell you," Nell began. "I had to be rushed to the hospital on Thanksgiving Day. They placed me in intensive care. I was alone, unable to talk, very sick, and I began to pray for friends. Your face came to my mind, and I prayed for you for a long time.

"Charlotte, you are going to meet someone soon who you will marry. You are to begin praying for him right now, because he needs prayers. He is recovering from a deep hurt, a terrible grief."

Charlotte felt amazed. "Nell, I think perhaps I met him," she said, slowly. "I went to Savannah for Thanksgiving and someone was there—someone wonderful."

"I prayed for you on Thanksgiving, but even more intensely the next day," Nell said. "There was no telephone in my room, so I couldn't get in touch with you. This is the first moment I've been well enough to call."

She was praying for me at the very moment that I was meeting Norris, Charlotte realized. Suddenly another memory jolted her. A couple of months before she had received two telephone calls in one hour. Both Eliza and Ann had called to give her that same message: she would soon meet a man she would marry. "Pray for him," they told her. "He needs your prayers right now." Neither woman had been aware that the other called; yet both gave the same message. Charlotte had prayed that day, of course, but only once. Since meeting Norris, she had been much too happy to think of her friends' advice.

When Charlotte checked her date book she realized, stunned, that those two earlier telephone calls had arrived on Saturday. Norris's wife had died on Monday. "He needs prayer right now," she remembered her friend saying.

Coincidence? Neither Norris nor Charlotte would call it that. Consider Charlotte's last-minute decision to visit Savannah on Thanksgiving Day; her taking the last seat on the last flight from Atlanta; the party invitation she hadn't wanted to accept; her hospitalized friend's prayer the day she and Norris met; two other friends' telephone calls in which they advised her to pray for a man she would eventually meet and marry; her own prayer for that unknown man, uttered just two days before his world was shattered.

"An unseen hand guided you," Norris later said.

"A divine appointment," Charlotte agreed.

Six months after they met, Norris and Charlotte were married. Twelve years later, they are still living happily ever after, certain they came together by divine appointment.

CHARLOTTE AND NORRIS PINDAR

And I will make thee beds of roses,
And a thousand fragrant posies.
CHRISTOPHER MARLOWE

To Love, Honor, and Cherish

How many times do I love thee, dear?
Tell me how many thoughts there be
In the atmosphere
Of a newfallen year,
Whose white and sable hours appear
The latest flake of Eternity:
So many times do I love thee, dear.

ELIZABETH BARRETT BROWNING

IN A WORLD WHERE LOVE IS TOO OFTEN DETERMINED BY HOW SOMEONE MEETS YOUR NEEDS OR MAKES YOU FEEL, WEDDING VOWS SEEM ALMOST NAIVE. YOU PROMISE TO LOVE, HONOR, AND CHERISH BECAUSE GOD HAS BROUGHT YOU TOGETHER WITH SOMEONE IN HIS PLAN. YOU ARE SEEKING TO GIVE YOURSELF WHOLEHEARTEDLY.

LOVE IS NOT MERELY AN EMOTION. LOVE IS A DECISION. YOU OPEN YOUR HEART A LITTLE. LOVE BEGINS TO FILL IT. YOU CHOOSE TO OPEN IT WIDER. YOU RISK HURT. SOMETIMES YOU LET GO. LOVE FLOWS LIKE THE TIDES. SOMETIMES FEELINGS SWELL. SOMETIMES THEY RECEDE. BUT THE POWER OF THE SEA REMAINS. THIS IS ALL IN THE DIVINE DESIGN.

To HONOR IS ALSO A CONSCIOUS CHOICE YOU ARE
MAKING. IT MEANS TO OFFER ESTEEM, RESPECT, AND
COURTESY. YOU PROMISE TO THINK FIRST OF YOUR BELOVED
AND HIS OR HER WELFARE. HONOR GIVES GLORY TO GOD
BECAUSE IT IS ENTIRELY UNSELFISH. HONOR DOES NOT GRASP.
IT BOLDLY OFFERS PRESENCE, NOT PRESENTS, TO THE LOVED
ONE.

To CHERISH IS AN INTIMATE CARING, AND RESOLUTELY
HOLDING DEAR. IT DOTES ON ANOTHER, CARRYING DEEP
IMPULSES TO GIVE AND SHARE AND PROTECT. TO CHERISH IS
TO EMBRACE LIKE A SOFT, STRONG SQUEEZE. IT MAY ALSO
BARELY TOUCH THE LOVED ONE LIKE A BREEZE TICKLES THE
FACE OF PRAIRIE GRASS.

WHEN YOU MAKE YOUR WEDDING VOWS TO LOVE, HONOR,
AND CHERISH, YOU ARE TELLING YOUR SOON-TO-BE SPOUSE,
"YOU ARE GOD'S GIFT TO ME. I WILL BE THERE FOR YOU.
NOTHING IN HEAVEN AND EARTH CAN CHANGE THAT."

THE GREEN DRESS

Oft in the still night
Ere Slumber's chain has bound me,
Fond Memory brings the light
Of other days around me;
The smiles, the tears,
Of boyhood's years
The words of love then spoken.

THOMAS MOORE

Spring had come late that year, which may have been why it hit them both so hard. Typically Meredith and Ben had reacted to the season in opposite fashions. With fresh awakenings of a youthful nostalgia, Meredith had fallen in love with her husband all over again. Ben, on the other hand, had fended off her romantic overtures, instead spending all of his free time locked up in the sunroom of their country home. Inspired by the sights and sounds that also stirred his wife's heart, Ben was painting again.

It was well into May, with tulips and daffodils adding patches of brilliance to their yard, before Meredith finally dared to venture inside the room to peek at his completed canvases. It was loneliness that pulled her more than curiosity. She was looking only for a way to connect with the husband she missed. Ben with his stubborn artistic temperament had always insisted that she not see his work until he chose to present it. Wary of his quick temper, she had learned early to comply. As she hesitated on the threshold, she reassured herself that twenty-four years of marriage carried with it some liberties. Anyway, today he was giving a seminar in a neighboring town and would not be back until evening.

The paintings were propped against the baseboards below the windows. From the doorway she could see the soft pastels of the drifting watercolors that were his trademark. But as she walked closer, she noted with surprise that the first pastoral background also included a human figure—a novelty for Ben. As Meredith examined these recent pieces she realized instantly that the same female figure was in each canvas. Her face was always hidden from view and her hairstyle, even hair color, varied from print to print. But in every scene the pale, spring-green dress she wore caught the viewer's eye like a beacon.

It was a sleeveless sundress with wide, tie-back ribbons falling in a loose, feminine bow at the small of her back. In some poses, the wind that swept the grasses into undulating waves molded the green dress against her figure. In the forest scenes, a shaft of sunlight caught her among the shadowy evergreens and her skin seemed to glow beneath it. Although the girl was never in the foreground and was often only an ethereal suggestion amid springtime greenery, Ben had managed to make her the center of attention.

Meredith envied the slim, youthful figure and gorgeous long hair, so opposite her own short, graying brown curls and the forty-five-year-old shape that had widened with the birth of each of her three sons. When she had complained about gravity and age conspiring against her, Ben had always insisted that she was as attractive as ever. Her bedroom mirror told her otherwise.

For a few days Meredith allowed her suspicions to simmer. Was the woman someone Ben had recently met and fallen in love with? Or was she a fantasy he had conjured out of marital boredom? One was almost as bad as the other. Ben still favored her with his kisses and his brown-eyed smile each morning and curved his solid warmth around her every night, but Meredith would not be deceived. Somehow they had grown apart; they had let complacency replace passion. When was the last time they had talked about their relationship, their dreams? When was the last time they had said "I love you"?

She held it in until Saturday. The morning had dawned warm and sunny and the two of them had brought their coffee onto the patio. Meredith was flipping halfheartedly through a gardening magazine and Ben was reading the paper when they were both distracted by a familiar sound. It was the honking of geese and they stood and scanned the skies. Suddenly, there they were, streaming toward them in a trembling, black skein as they flew over the southern horizon.

A rush of joy pounded through her. There was always hope, as eternal as the cycle of the seasons and the return of the geese. Impulsively, she turned to Ben. "Let's take the day off, hon, and hike down to the river. I'll pack us a lunch. We can just relax and dangle our feet and talk. It'll be like old times. What do you say?"

Ben's unshaven face creased in a weak smile of apology. "Sorry, Mer. I planned to paint today. You know what they say...."

No, Meredith did not know what "they" said. Make hay while the sun shines? Idle hands do the devil's work? The wife's always the last to know?

Her jealousy boiled over. Unable to bite back the words, she confronted him. "Ben, I looked at your paintings this week." She watched his face sober and knew she had hit a nerve. Her bones were melting and her heart hurt, but the words kept coming. "You...you've never put people in your pictures before. Who's the girl in the green dress?"

When he turned away from her to look down over the fields, she lost her ability to breathe. He was her life. She could not bear this. Her mouth tasted like copper and her vision was blurred like the watercolors that had brought them to this moment. When he finally turned to answer her, she was stumbling across the patio to the house. His quiet response carried across the yard and stabbed her before she could close the glass door between them.

"An old girlfriend, Mer. Just an old girlfriend."

Meredith had often used housework as an outlet for frustration and anger. Today she used it to distract her from panic. She knew she should have met Ben's statement with a frontal attack, but her reeling mind had become incapable of coherent argument.

It was the closets that bore the brunt of her frenetic activity. She had finished the boys' bedrooms and was now attacking the one she shared with Ben. Lifting out their clothes and thinking that she soon might be packing one set of them into suitcases brought on a wave of nausea so great that she was forced to drop them on the floor and sit on the edge of the bed with her head between her knees. As the sickness subsided, she lay down slowly on the bed—the bed they might never share again. Thoughts of finality continued to ambush her. She rolled onto her side and stared into the open closet beside the bed.

When her eyes fell upon the stack of old photo albums, her breathing quickened. Second from the bottom was the worn brown binder that held Ben's premarriage photos. It wasn't that she wanted to know. They were past that hurdle. It was simply that she had to see—had to put a face to her rival. But as Meredith slowly turned the plastic pages, she realized she had no way of knowing which girl was being immortalized in her husband's faceless portraits. She was more than halfway through the book and had just made up her mind to stop this foolishness when she found her.

Actually, there were two prints of the same woman. Her brown hair tumbled loose in waves in one of them and trailed down her back in a thick braid in the second. But the dress was unmistakable. In reality it was more blue than green, closer to aqua in a print of cornflowers and daisies. But Meredith recognized the squared neckline that set off the smooth, tanned skin, and the ties that were looped in an old-fashioned bow at the back. There was one of the girl seated in a field on a blanket. An open picnic basket gaped invitingly beside her. In the last frame, she stood atop a sand dune, face turned to the wind that was blowing fog in across the sea, plastering her damp dress to her young figure.

In both photographs, the beautiful girl had worn the dress of Ben's paintings; the garment of his dreams and his inspiration. Meredith knew it well. During that wonderful summer it had been her favorite.

CATHY MILLER

THE SECRET OF LOVE

The face is the mirror of the mind,
and eyes without speaking
confess the secrets of the heart.
SAINT JEROME

These words are ancient jewels minced from the quarry of life. Read them only if you dare treasure them. For it would be better to never know than to know and not obey.

The hand that writes them is now old, wrinkled from the sun and labor. But the hand that guides them is wise—wise from years, wise from failures, wise from heartache.

I travel from city to city. I buy jewels from the diggers in one land and sell them to the buyers in another. I have weathered nights on stormy waters. I have walked days through desert heat. My hands have held the finest rubies and stroked the deepest furs. But I would trade it all for the one jewel I never knew.

It was not for lack of opportunity that I never held it. It was for lack of wisdom. The jewel was in my hand, but I exchanged it for an imitation.

I have never known true love.

I have known embraces. I have seen beauty. But I have never known love. If only I'd learned to recognize love as I have learned to recognize stones.

My father taught me about stones. He was a jewel cutter. He would seat me at a table before a dozen emeralds.

"One is true," he would tell me. "The others are false. Find the true jewel."

I would ponder—studying each one after the other. Finally, I would choose. I was always wrong.

"The secret," he would say, "is not on the surface of the stone; it is inside the stone. A true jewel has a glow. Deep within the gem there is a flame. The surface can always be polished to shine, but with time the sparkle fades. However, the stone that shines from within will never fade."

With years, my eyes learned to spot true stones. I am never fooled. I have learned to see the light within.

If only I'd learned the same about love.

But I've spent my life in places I shouldn't have been looking only for someone with beautiful hair, a dazzling smile, and fancy clothes. I've searched for a woman with outer beauty but no true value. And now I am left with emptiness.

Once I almost found her. Many years ago in Madrid I met the daughter of a farmer. Her ways were simple. Her love was pure. Her eyes were honest. But her looks were plain. She would have loved me. She would have held me through every season. Within her was a glow of devotion the likes of which I've never seen since.

But I continued looking for someone whose beauty would outshine the rest.

How many times since have I longed for that farm girl's kind heart? If only I'd known that true beauty is found inside, not outside. If only I'd known, how many tears would I have saved?

True love glows from within and grows stronger with the passage of time.

Heed my caution. Look for the purest gem. Look deep within the heart to find the greatest beauty of all. And when you find the gem, hold onto her and never let her go.

For in her you have been granted a treasure worth far more than rubies.

Seek beauty and miss love.

But seek love and find both.

MAX LUCADO
TELL ME THE SECRETS, MAX LUCADO,
© 1993, CROSSWAY BOOKS, WHEATON, ILLINOIS

TWELVE RULES FOR A HAPPY MARRIAGE

Love seeth not itself to please,
Nor for itself hath any care,
But for another gives its ease,
And builds a Heaven in Hell's despair.

WILLIAM BLAKE

♥ Never both be angry at once.

♥ Never yell at each other unless the house is on fire.

♥ Yield to the wishes of the other as an exercise in self-discipline if you can't think of a better reason.

♥ If you have a choice between making yourself or your mate look good, choose your mate.

♥ If you must criticize, do so lovingly.

♥ Never bring up a mistake of the past. Your silence will be greatly appreciated.

♥ Neglect the whole world rather than each other.

♥ Never let the day end without saying at least one complimentary thing to your life's partner.

♥ Never meet without an affectionate greeting.

♥ When you've said or done something hurtful, acknowledge it and ask for forgiveness.

♥ Remember, it takes two to get an argument going. Invariably the one who is wrong is the one who will be doing most of the talking.

♥ Never go to bed mad.

ANN LANDERS

WHAT BECAME OF JESSIE?

Though upon life's sea you wander,

in my heart you're ne'er forgot.

I shall hope with loves allegiance

That you too forget me not?

SAYING FROM A ROMANTIC TREASURY OF LOVE

She was waiting for me at the insurance office where she worked in the little Missouri town of Bolivar. It had been half a century since we'd last met—in high school—although we had never gone out. It was my abiding shyness, her looks, and chicken pox that had kept us apart.

Her name was Jessie. In the spring of '42, I had planned to ask her to the high school dance, except I got chicken pox. She went instead with a boy named Milos. I had liked him, but now I wasn't sure. After the dance, due to my limited social skills, I could find no ready reason to ask her for a date.

When school ended, my family moved to St. Louis, but I never forgot her. At the University of Missouri, I met and married a girl named Sylvia. We had a son and a good marriage that lasted forty-one years until her death.

During my marriage, I sometimes thought of Jessie. Once at Thanksgiving, her image made me feel sad about what might have been, and once on a train I thought I heard the conductor call out Bolivar, and I wondered what she was doing.

A year after my wife's death, I attended a family reunion and ran into my cousin Anna, who still lived in Bolivar. "Whatever happened to that girl named Jessie?" I asked.

"Oh, she's still there," she answered. "Been a widow for ten years." Jessie had married a boy in our class named Charles. They had two sons, then separated. He died in the mid-'80s.

Anna gave me Jessie's telephone number and I called her. The conversation lasted almost an hour. Jessie told me that she had become old, gray, and fat, but I didn't believe it for a moment. We agreed to meet.

Missouri in late summer looked somnolent, the growing season all but over, touches of autumn color appearing in the maples that stood in clumps along Interstate 44. I rolled off the interstate a few miles east of Bolivar and before I knew it, her office came into view. I parked outside and walked in.

Her hair was neither gray nor the blonde of my remembrance, and she was tall and slender. Her eyes were bluer than I remembered, and her nose still tilted prettily upward.

"Well hello," she said with a dazzling smile. "Is there someone you wanted to see?" I hadn't known about her teasing side. Her hands, I noticed, were shaking.

During lunch, we found out much about each other. The next day we went to Branson, Missouri, and stayed the night—in separate rooms. "I'll visit you in Connecticut," she promised when I left a couple of days later. Within a month, she appeared at the airport.

A whirlwind of letters and phone calls followed the next year, which culminated in my selling my house and moving back where I began, within miles of her door. One evening, as we were looking at housing tracts, I asked, "Why are we doing this?" for she had always demurred at talk of marriage.

"Just in case," she said.

Robert and Jessie were married on January 26, 1995—fifty-three years, four months, and eighteen days after he first saw her in Miss Williams's English class. He's been an AARP member for ten years.

ROBERT G. BEASON,
REPRINTED FROM MODERN MATURITY, MARCH–APRIL 1999.
BY PERMISSION OF ROBERT G. BEASON

NORMA'S RIBS

*The way to a man's heart
is through his stomach.*

FANNY FERN

When I was a young woman, I worked as a secretary for the navy in London. Occasionally I joined my friends and coworkers at a local club after work for a night of dancing and fun. Later each evening a group of American G.I.s, who were stationed nearby, drove over to London and joined us at our table.

The first night the Americans came over, William, an attractive soldier in the group, caught my eye. He had the cutest dimples I'd ever seen! As I watched him, I knew somehow that he was exactly the kind of man that I wanted to marry. I felt a special attraction to him—I just couldn't explain it.

The only problem was, no matter how hard I tried to get his attention, William hardly noticed me. It was as though I was invisible. Every time I tried to start a conversation with him, he gave me a friendly nod and then walked away. Other times he put his head down on the table and fell sound asleep.

"What do you want with a man like that?" my girlfriends chided me. "He's a bore! Get out on the dance floor and meet some *fun* guys."

I always shook my head and said, "I've found the man I want."

"You're wasting your time, girl!" they'd say in unison. "He doesn't even know you're alive."

I knew they were right, but I just couldn't tear myself away from the idea that William was the man for me. I just kept praying that he would notice me one day.

A few months later two of my friends married and I volunteered to prepare their wedding dinner. I am from Barbados, so I cooked up a batch of barbecued ribs, our island specialty, using my family's spicy recipe.

As I was putting the finishes on the table, one of my friends squealed, "Well, look who's here!"

My heart leapt when I saw William at the door.

After the wedding, when everyone was gathering around the dinner table, you can imagine my delight when William took the empty seat beside me. We exchanged pleasantries, but once more, he turned away and began talking to someone else. I told myself not to be discouraged, at least he was sitting beside me.

I noticed that William's plate was piled high with my ribs. I kept my eyes on him as he bit into them. After some thoughtful chewing, he announced, "These ribs are the best things I've ever put in my mouth!"

I swelled with pride. Nothing pleases a cook more than seeing someone enjoy her food. As William took another bite, his face burst into a wide grin and he declared to everyone, "I'm going to marry the woman who cooked these ribs."

I almost fell out of my chair. Then one of my friends yelled out, "She's sitting right beside you!"

Suddenly he turned around and for the very first time, William really noticed me. He looked into my eyes like he'd never seen me before. "Why haven't I gotten to know you sooner?" he asked.

I told him I'd been in front of him for months but he hadn't noticed. William and I spent the evening getting to know one another and when we were throwing rice at the departing newlyweds, he asked me out. We dated for a year and really enjoyed one another's company. I fell in love with William and suspected that he loved me too, but he never made any mention of his intentions. I kept thinking, *This man sure takes his time!*

On the one-year anniversary of our first date William saw me to my door. I decided to drop a bombshell and see what happened. I said,

"Good-bye, William. It looks like I won't be seeing you anymore!"

"Wh—what do you mean?" he stammered.

"I don't date anyone for more than a year," I told him. "That's my limit."

Immediately he proposed, and we've been happily married for thirty-six years!

Am I still cooking those ribs? I confess I haven't made that dish since that fateful night when William finally noticed me. That night should have made a believer out of me: The way to a man's heart *is* through his stomach. But oddly enough, William fell in love with *me*, not just my cooking! To prove it, William has cooked our ribs ever since.

NORMA McKINNEY

LOVE ACROSS THE MILES

His house she enters, there to be a light,
Shining within, when all without is night;
A guardian angel o'er his life presiding,
Doubling his pleasure and his cares dividing.

SAMUEL ROGERS

My son Trevor was a confirmed bachelor. At twenty-five he was working hard at a promising career and savoring his freedom. Being a fun-loving and outgoing person, he has always been a party animal. He loves a good time as well as the next Generation Xer. And he was enjoying being single.

Girls have always been drawn to Trevor, and despite his carefree, not-interested-in-long-term-commitment demeanor, his dates often heard wedding bells after just a few evenings. He seriously considered marriage only once. The girl was a wonderful person, beautiful, and crazy about Trevor. But after a time, he realized he was not ready for marriage and did not want to lead her on. He told her he was not "good marriage material" and broke off the relationship.

Shortly after this decision, he met Rentia (pronounced Ren-sha). If the name sounds a bit exotic, it is because Rentia is a Dutch Afrikaner from South Africa. She and Trevor met when she was working as an au pair for a family in a Chicago suburb and attending college as an exchange student. Trevor and my older son, Jeffrey, had gone out for a night on the town to celebrate Jeff's visit for spring break. Though they were in a crowded restaurant, Jeff and Trevor noticed Rentia's accent right away. Our family had had the marvelous opportunity to visit South Africa several years ago and became familiar with the Afrikaners' distinctive and charming way of speaking.

Trevor and Jeff found the source of the accent and introduced themselves to her. (The fact that she was a tall, gorgeous, hazel-eyed blond gave them the incentive they needed to make the first move.) Trevor and Rentia had an immediate rapport and talked nonstop about her beautiful country.

After their first date, Trevor told his father and me that he had met a girl he really liked. After a few dates, he told us he thought he had found the girl he wanted to marry. This sounded strange indeed coming from our confirmed bachelor who, a few months before, had said he "just wasn't ready for marriage." But when we met Rentia we could see why Trevor was so smitten. She was not only attractive but warm, sophisticated, and wonderful with our grandchildren.

Weeks passed and in spite of our skepticism, Trevor spoke more and more about marriage. And with unconcealed dread, he discussed Rentia's upcoming departure. Her visa expired in June. They had met in March. After a short courtship, Rentia left this country—and the man she had come to love.

For Trevor and Rentia to be married, they learned she would have to acquire a K-1 or "intent to marry" visa. These are not easy to get. The immigration red tape is unbelievable. And it is very expensive. But Trevor and Rentia, from separate countries, persevered, and after spending a fortune on long-distance phone calls and preparing a mountain of paperwork, they had done everything they could to make the visa possible. Then they had to wait.

And wait they did—for months. It was as though the paperwork had been sucked into a black hole somewhere. Rentia and her father could get no definite answers to their inquiries. Their phone calls were not returned. They often encountered voice mail instead of a real person—it was a classic example of bureaucracy at its worst.

This was especially frustrating for Rentia and her family as they were trying to plan a wedding in South Africa for her family and friends. After that ceremony, the couple would return to the United States to be married here. But how could she plan a wedding when she could not set a date?

In October, Trevor made the long trip to visit Rentia, meet her parents, and take her an engagement ring. It was a joyous week for the couple to renew their love and commitment to each other. Rentia loved the diamond ring, her family loved Trevor, and he loved them. After the visit, they were more determined than ever to see the wedding take place. But still no visa arrived.

Toward the end of the year, Trevor and Rentia set a date late in February. They thought that surely by then she would have her visa. January passed; February came and went, but no visa. My husband and I made plans to fly with Trevor to South Africa for the wedding. Trevor and Rentia resigned themselves to the possibility that he might have to return to America without his bride until the visa department took action. They did not even buy a plane ticket for Rentia. But I kept praying for a miracle. I could not believe after all this young couple had gone through that Trevor would have to come home alone.

In desperation, just before we left the country, my husband suggested that Trevor call a senator who is an old friend of ours, and his office had been helpful in the early stages of the process. When Trevor called, the senator's staff could not believe that he and Rentia had waited more than seven months for a visa. They were appalled and even suggested they might introduce legislation to prevent these kinds of delays. They proceeded to write a letter to the South African embassy to see what the problem was.

The day before the wedding was to take place, Rentia got a call from the embassy. They said they had gotten a letter from the United States Congress and that they had to "bring this situation to a close." Though Rentia's wedding day was planned out to the minute, the officials insisted she come to Johannesburg the next morning for the final interview for her visa. This meant four hours just driving. But she knew she had to do it, and she agreed.

Bright and early the morning of her wedding day, Rentia, her father, and my husband went to Johannesburg. I stayed home with Rentia's mom and we prayed. And finally, at the very last minute, the visa was granted. We were so thankful!

Then we faced the fact that we had no plane ticket for Rentia's return to America after the honeymoon. The couple's resources were gone, and they knew a ticket bought at that late date would be terribly expensive. So we began to pray again. After we had exhausted all our ideas, Rentia's cousin found a student fare for $500! Rentia even was able to get a reservation on the same flight as Trevor.

Two weeks later, after a fabulous honeymoon in Cape Town (a gift from the bride's aunt and uncle), the couple came home to a joyous welcome from Trevor's "old" parents and Rentia's new ones. They were married in this country soon afterward, and we gave them a beautiful reception for friends and family who had missed the first wedding.

I have often heard that anything you get for free, you don't really appreciate. But if something is gained through much adversity and hardship, it is not only appreciated, but treasured. Perhaps this is why Trevor and Rentia are so happy, even though they live the simple, frugal lives of newlyweds in a small apartment. It is a joy to see them together. They revel in each other's company.

I chuckle when I see how totally devoted my son is to Rentia—not bad for someone who was not "good marriage material."

SHIRLEY ROSE

LASTING LOVE

❧

So we grew together,
Like to a double cherry, seeming parted,
But yet an union in parturition;
Two lovely berries molded on one stem.

WILLIAM SHAKESPEARE

The courting rituals of the young Billy Graham were not conventionally romantic, to say the least. Instead of sending 20-year-old Ruth Bell bouquets of roses, he brought her bottles of vitamin pills. Instead of taking her dancing under the stars, he insisted that she do jumping jacks and toe-touches. The Wheaton College Bible student, who had skipped a semester due to fatigue, was more than flattered. "When I came back from our first date," Ruth, now 75, recalled, "I remember telling the Lord, 'If you let me spend my life with that man, it would be the greatest privilege I could think of.'"

Her prayers were answered. In Montreat Presbyterian Church in North Carolina, on August 13, 1943, the daughter of missionaries wed the 24-year-old Baptist pastor she had met at Wheaton. The next morning, Ruth awoke to find her new husband asleep on the floor. "Daddy thought the bed was too soft or something," says their daughter Gigi Tchividjian-Graham, 50, "but Mom was devastated." Over the next five decades, Ruth would spend many more nights alone in bed, often sleeping with her husband's tweed jacket, while Rev. Billy Graham, now 77, took his spiritual message around the world.

After the wedding, the couple started a ministry in the town of Western Springs outside Chicago. They were so poor that a piece of red satin over a lightbulb served as a fireplace. As Graham's fame and mission grew, so did his travel schedule, leaving Ruth mostly alone to raise their five children. "I'd rather have a little of Bill than a lot of any other man," she said.

Intent upon making a home for her husband, Ruth built a log house on 150 wooded acres in Montreat in 1954. Graham returned there to his wife and family after each crusade. "Every time they got back together, it was like a honeymoon," says Gigi. "They shared a lot of physical love. That was very reassuring to me." Their commitment was apparent to everyone. "He would stand up whenever she came in the room," says Graham biographer William Martin, adding that a 69-year-old Graham told him, "You know, we're still lovers." Today their intimacy has been hindered by the complications of old age. He is fighting Parkinson's disease; she, a chronic lower-back problem. They spend their time at home, in twin armchairs, in front of a real fireplace. "They don't like to be separated by a lot of miles," says Gigi. "They just like knowing the other one's right there."

"What you're looking at is one person with two heads," says their friend, singer Pat Boone, of the Grahams. "They share commitment."

USED BY PERMISSION OF *PEOPLE* WEEKLY
© 1996 TIME INC.

LOVE STORY

❧

Two souls with but a single thought,
Two hearts that beat as one.

FREDRICH HALM

grew up in New Orleans, Louisiana. Jerry and his family loved New Orleans. They vacationed there often. And Jerry had almost married a girl from my church. They had dated for years, but finally Jerry realized that he just wasn't ready for marriage. He ended the relationship, much to her disappointment. His mother was also very disappointed.

People in his family were beginning to think Jerry would be a bachelor forever; there were several men in the family who had never married. And, after all, he was twenty-six. That was old to be unmarried in 1967.

Even after ending the relationship with Jackette, he remained friendly with her family and still loved New Orleans. He belonged to the U.S. Coast Guard Reserve at the time and requested his two weeks active duty in New Orleans. When he was granted this request, he immediately called the sister and brother-in-law of his old girlfriend to let them know he would be in New Orleans for two weeks. In fact, he would come in a few days early if they would fix him up with a date. This couple led the youth group in my church. So they asked me if I would like to go out with this guy.

Like everyone else, I didn't really get excited about blind dates, and I told them as much. But they assured me that this guy was different. He had almost become a part of their family. He was very nice, from a great family, a Christian, and cute. "And," they told me, "he can always relocate if anything should come of this."

I agreed to go out with him. We double-dated with our mutual friends. They drove Jerry up to my house, but he did not come to the door.

There was a Beware of Dog sign on the gate. So Jerry stood in the street yelling for me. I was not used to being treated this way, especially on a first date. I finally walked out on the porch and asked why he wasn't coming in. He said it was because of the sign. About that time, my tiny Chihuahua ran out barking. The friends in the car were in hysterics and my mom and I thought it was pretty funny, too. Jerry was the only one not laughing. That was our first meeting.

I did not think he was terribly good looking, but he did have pretty blue eyes, and I liked him from the start. He asked me out the next night. We were going to a Mardi Gras parade. When he picked me up, I was wearing a beret. It was cold for New Orleans in February. Besides, I thought I looked very chic. He asked me why I was wearing the hat. I said to keep me warm. Then he said, "Well, let's do something inside, then." I countered with, "Well, my hair looks a mess now." He said, "Take it off and let me see." I did, and he assured me I looked better without the beret. What a feisty Texan he was! I did not wear the hat, but he has often said that if he knew me then like he does now, he would never have asked. It was the first and last argument he ever won.

After those first two dates, we were both smitten. He began his Coast Guard duty and did not have leave every evening. But the evenings he was off, we were together. My church had a Valentine's banquet during that week, and I asked him to come with me. He, unfortunately, had duty that night. So I went alone. When I walked into the church, Jerry stepped from behind the door and surprised me. I couldn't have been more thrilled if it had been Harrison Ford standing there. He told the amusing story of how he was able to get leave.

He asked his CEO if he could get off. The officer asked what was so important. He sheepishly said he wanted to go to a Valentine's banquet with a girl. (This guy had guts, you must admit.) Much to his surprise, the officer grinned and said, "Well, if you are crazy enough to ask, I am just crazy enough to say Yes."

That night was very significant in our lives. Jerry shared his dreams and his calling into Christian television with me. We bared our hearts as if we had always known each other and we became forever connected. That night, Valentine's Day, 1967, we fell in love. We had only had a few dates, but we both knew we were meant to be together. We were married six months later.

That was thirty-two years ago, and today I think he is very handsome. He was much too skinny back then. And he still has those incredible blue eyes. Nowadays, I feel fortunate to be able to visit New Orleans once or twice a year. Guess who relocated!

SHIRLEY ROSE

To get the full value of joy,
you must have someone to divide it with.
MARK TWAIN

For Better, for Worse

Fair or foul—on land or sea—
Come the wind or weather,
Best or worst, whate'er they be,
We shall share together.
WINTHROP MACKWORTH PRAED

MARRIAGE, LIKE LIFE—EVEN A LIFE SUBMITTED TO THE WILL OF THE HEAVENLY FATHER—CARRIES NO GUARANTEES.

MARRIAGE, LIKE LIFE, BRINGS UNEXPECTED AND UNPREDICTABLE EVENTS.

WE ALL GROW AND CHANGE EVEN AFTER WE SAY, "I DO."

CHANGE USUALLY ISN'T EASY, NOR IS IT WELCOMED. CHANGE DOESN'T NECESSARILY BRING OUT THE BEST IN PEOPLE; SOMETIMES IT BRINGS OUT THE WORST, IF ONLY FOR A SEASON. BUT EVEN CHANGE FOR THE WORSE CAN MAKE YOU BETTER—IF YOU ALLOW IT.

WHEN YOU PROMISE "FOR BETTER OR FOR WORSE," YOU ARE ANTICIPATING THE FACT THAT CHANGE WILL COME. IT MAY APPEAR IN MANY DIFFERENT SHAPES AND SIZES AND TEXTURES. YOU ALLOW FOR THAT. YOU SAY TO YOUR

SPOUSE, "WHATEVER COMES, I WILL STAND BY YOU, SUPPORT YOU, AND OFFER YOU ANY ASSISTANCE I CAN TO HELP YOU THROUGH THIS JOURNEY CALLED LIFE. I WILL BE WITH YOU IN YOUR GOOD TIMES AND IN YOUR TOUGH TIMES, TOO. NO MATTER WHAT, I'LL BE THERE FOR YOU."

THERE ARE NO GUARANTEES. BUT THE MOST IMPORTANT WORD TO DESCRIBE THE JOURNEY THROUGH LIFE TOGETHER IS THE WORD THROUGH. YOU CAN'T FLOAT ABOVE CHANGES. YOU CAN'T FLY AWAY FROM DANGERS. YOU DARE NOT GO AROUND THE THINGS YOU DO NOT LIKE. JUST PREPARE TO GO THROUGH THE WORST. YOU WILL FIND THAT IS THE WAY TO DISCOVER WHAT BETTER REALLY MEANS.

WRAPPED IN
FORGIVENESS

Nobody has ever measured,
even the poets,
how much a heart can hold.

ZELDA FITZGERALD

The home where my brother, Bob, and I grew up was filled with all the acts of rebellion and destruction: drinking, cursing, smoking, and parties. Our father was often involved in petty thievery and our mother, who worked at the local diner as a waitress, we suspected of having a drug habit. In spite of this we managed to survive. There was always enough to eat and we had clean clothes and a warm place to sleep.

Bob chose to rise above his circumstances and got involved in a youth group at our church. Our parents teased him unmercifully and I called him several choice names myself: *Jesus Freak, Mr. Clean, Bible Thumper.* The people at Bob's church took good care of him and helped him go to a Christian college when he graduated.

I was too cool to go to church. I figured, *If you can't lick 'em...join 'em.* By high school I was a drinker, a drug user, and a drug dealer. I spent some time in jail.

It was during my senior year in high school that Bob rescued me from the gutter and took me to his church. I was so low that I was ready to find God. With the help of the church members I turned my life around. I entered a treatment program and found a good job.

I soon met a lovely Christian girl, Donna, at church and she became my wife. She didn't care about my past and neither did her family. They were very forgiving people who admired me for making something out my life. Donna loved me for who I had become. I was a blessed man.

After a couple of years of marriage, I received a promotion at my job and began to go to night school. My life with Donna was going along beautifully. We were soon able to afford a little home with a picket fence in a nice neighborhood and then had our first child. Donna was the best wife a man could have. She was very good with money, could turn hamburger into a feast, and transformed our little cottage into a castle with her creativity.

Shortly after our second child was born, our dream life slowly unraveled into a nightmare. I was laid off at my job and because of my criminal record, I was unable to find employment. Everyone at church tried to help, but our lives began to fall to pieces. Donna was forced to take a secretarial job. At home alone, I began drinking again.

Donna insisted I get help but I wouldn't listen. She finally enlisted the help of our pastor and my brother, but I refused to give up drinking and even started taking drugs again.

"I love you," Donna tearfully admitted, "but it's the drugs or me."

I was shocked but because of my pride, I walked away, leaving my beautiful wife and children behind.

Initially I enjoyed being on my own without responsibility and anyone around to make me feel guilty. When I called home occasionally, Donna always said, "I love you, Ted, and you're welcome to come home when you stop drinking."

I always laughed and hung up. My brother and several men from the church tried to talk to me but I didn't want help; I wanted to be left alone.

After six months of isolation and unemployment, and in great need of cash, I got involved in a major drug deal. Right after the buyer handed me the money, he pulled out a pair of handcuffs. He was an undercover cop.

Because of my previous record and the seriousness of the crime, I was sent to a federal penitentiary in another state. I had brought such disgrace to our little family that when Donna wrote me with news and pictures of our children, I expected that she would soon ask for a divorce.

Life in prison looked pretty hopeless. Like so many other men there I feared I was losing my family. "It won't be long until the letters will stop coming," my cellmate warned me. I cried myself to sleep that night.

Bob wrote to me and insisted that I get involved with the prison fellowship. Once again it was men of faith who helped me turn my life around. The next few years in prison, the men in prison fellowship even helped me finish my college degree.

I kept in touch with Donna to let her know about the changes I was making in my life. I wrote that I knew God had forgiven me and I prayed that she would also. Her letters came frequently and were friendly, but she never made any mention of us—she just said that she was proud of me for turning my life around. When I asked if we had any hope of putting our lives back together, she wrote that we would have to wait and see.

Because the prison was such a great distance from our home, Donna was able to bring the children to see me only one time, when our church took up a collection. I was even more depressed when they left. Donna had appeared warm and loving, but she refused to talk about our future. I also felt ashamed that my young children had seen me behind bars.

I was amazed at how Donna held our home together. As a single mother, she did it all: worked, maintained the house and yard, cooked all the meals, and attended to the children. I told her in a letter how much I appreciated her and how sorry I was to have placed such a heavy burden on her shoulders.

When I was paroled, I wrote to Donna to tell her I was coming to see the children. I desperately wanted to know if she would take me back. Remembering a famous song, I wrote, "If there is any hope for the two of us to put our lives back together again, please tie a yellow ribbon around the tree in the front yard."

Bob picked me up at the bus station to drive me over to our house. As we turned into our street, I told Bob I couldn't look. I shut my eyes and covered them with my hands. I asked Bob if would he look for me. Then the car came to a stop. Bob was silent.

"Bob," I insisted, "tell me!"

Hardly able to speak, my brother whispered, "Open your eyes, little brother. You've got to see this."

Donna had wrapped our entire house in a giant yellow ribbon with a great big bow, and she and the children were waiting with open arms at the front door.

When I walked through that door of forgiveness, all the rebellion of my past melted away. I knew that my life would never be the same—and it wasn't.

AS TOLD TO SUSAN WALES

I wish I could remember the first day,
First hour, first moment of your meeting me;
If bright or dim the season, it might be
Summer or winter for aught I can say.
So unrecorded did it slip away,
So blind was I to see and to foresee,
So dull to mark the budding of my tree
That would not blossom yet for many a May.
If only I could recollect it! Such
A day of days! I let it come and go
As traceless as a thaw of bygone snow.
It seemed to mean so little, meant so much!
If only now I could recall that touch,
First touch of hand in hand! Did one but know!
CHRISTINA ROSSETTI

AN EMPTY PLACE

&

Where we love is home
Home that our feet may leave
But not our hearts.
OLIVER WENDELL HOLMES

Helen always thought that when Harry left her, it would be in a pine box. Instead he departed in a late-model Porsche with a late-model product manager in his company.

For a year Helen's moods rode from happy high (when anyone told her that Harry was miserable with the new woman) to desperate low (when Harry called about speeding up the divorce so that he might be free to marry again).

It was the advice of her attorney to remain unemployed ("You get a good job, and it will affect your settlement") that left Helen so much time and so little activity.

Her married friends were busy choosing up sides, and it seemed to her that they were all on Harry's side. Well, why not? He had the social life, and she had—what did she have? She had a bitter lump where there used to be a heart. She had an empty place at the table, an empty place in her bed, and as she looked around there was no way to fill the empty places.

Her married daughter and her son, who was in law school, were not much help. "Get out, Mom," they both said when they called. What did they expect her to do? Hang out in bars? Invite men to take her out? How did they think a woman who still considered herself married could go out and look for the next man? Why wasn't it easy for women the way it was for men? Why couldn't a woman just meet a younger man and take up with him the way men did with younger women? Didn't anyone understand that men between the ages of fifty and sixty were not out looking for women the same age?

And then one day Helen picked up a magazine, and there at the back in the Personals section was a series of ads she'd always glanced at but never read. Here were ads from single white males (conveniently shortened to "SWM") looking for women. Of course, for every ad from a man there were thirteen or fourteen from women. Still...

The one that caught her eye read, "California man wants to meet sophisticated New York woman 25–34 who knows books, theater, fine dining. Object: fun. Photo a must." There was a box number for replies.

In the era of AIDS and herpes, in the world of gay men and bisexuals, in the swamp out there that awaited newly single women, could Helen afford to risk answering?

On second thought, she counseled herself, what did she have to lose? You couldn't get AIDS in the mail, and besides she wasn't 25-34. So, once he saw her, all would be lost anyway.

Helen went through her box of old pictures. Here was one from 1957 in a bathing suit. She could send that. Of course, in that picture she had long hair. Now her hair was short. Maybe she could get a fall....

For three days she looked through old pictures, and just as she was ready to call a photographer, a letter came from her daughter. Inside were four sweet pictures of Helen with her two-year-old granddaughter Mavis.

Why not? she thought.

Helen went right to her desk and answered the man in California. She wrote:

Dear California Man,

If you want a truly sophisticated New York woman, please be advised that I know theater from the plays of Shakespeare to the musicals of Sondheim. I know restaurants from Soho to Harlem, and I know books from the Bible to this week's bestsellers.

So why am I writing to you?

Because despite the fact that I'm loving, blond, and thin, despite the fact that I'm articulate and supportive, I couldn't hold on to my husband of thirty years.

There must be something wrong with me, and I want to know what it is.

You want a woman 25–34. My instincts tell me that only a man over fifty would want a woman 25–34. Well, I'm not 25–34. I am 25 plus 34. I am 59. Further, I am a grandmother.

Proof is this enclosed picture. The little girl is my granddaughter.

If all of this does not horrify you, please respond, and let's see if we can help one another.

I'll show you the New York you want to see, and you can show me where I went wrong after thirty years.

You see, I lost my husband to a woman 25–34 who doesn't know what I know. But she does know one thing I don't know. She knows how to get my husband and keep him.

The answer came back the following week.

A message was left on Helen's answering machine. "Helen," the voice said. "Until I read that letter, I didn't know what a dummy I'd really been. I'm the California man from the ad. I guess you know by now it's me, Harry. I'm ready to come back home. You see, you're wrong. That woman knew how to get me, but she couldn't keep me. I'm so tired of explaining who Keats is, and I'm tired of hearing that anyone who lived through World War II must be in a retirement home. I think fifty-nine is a wonderful age to begin again. Besides, that picture really tore me apart. After all, I'm that little girl's grandfather."

Excerpted from *Funny, You Don't Look Like a Grandmother,* by Lois Wyse. © 1989 by Lois Wyse. Reprinted by permission of Crown Publishers, Inc., a division of Random House, Inc.

THE CRUCIAL
INGREDIENT

*Life in common among people who
love each other is the ideal of happiness.*
GEORGE SAND

As a writer, a dispenser of information and opinion, if not wisdom, I could never subscribe to the "ignorance is bliss" theory. We need to know things. Knowledge is good—very good. However, as far as marriage is concerned, as good as it is, knowledge is not the crucial ingredient. Commitment trumps knowledge every time. Without commitment, the knowledge necessary to make a marriage work is unattainable. Knowledge and commitment are certainly not mutually exclusive: In the best of marriages, commitment leads to knowledge. Commitment must be the foundation, however.

When Marty and I got married, we knew *nothing*. No one told us anything. There was no premarital counseling, "Engagement Encounter," or "Marriage Encounter." Marriage seminars, books, and video series were still in the distant future. We didn't know such things existed, because they didn't. In our day, after you finished college, you got married. That was the thing to do. No one told you how to do marriage; you were expected to learn on the job.

Certainly, no one told *me*. Even if people in the know had planned to teach me about marriage, they couldn't. They were too dumbstruck. Here was a crude, academically challenged basketball player from Texas about to marry an urbane, straight-A homecoming queen from Pennsylvania. All they could do was to shake their heads in awe and roll their eyes heavenward in amazement. Knowledgeable people would have issued stern warnings against this unlikely match.

Even though Marty's father was a minister and had married many couples from his parish, he did not give her any premarital counseling. All her family and friends did was to ask her over and over again, "Are you *sure* you want to do this? Are you really sure?" Certainly, we never had counseling together.

So, we got married. We did it without a course, a video series, or even a book. We just got married. Almost all our friends and classmates did the same thing in the same way.

Well, let me tell you, ignorance did not produce bliss. Marriage was hard. Learning while doing was hard. We made it only because commitment prevailed. Commitment overcame ignorance and was the glue that helped us stick together. As we learned, often the hard way, it slowly got better and better. Now, it is so good we can hardly stand it. Knowledge *and* commitment have produced a sort of bliss better described as joy. Without the commitment, we would never have lasted long enough to learn anything. Commitment always trumps knowledge.

As far as I know, all our friends and classmates did it the same way we did—just got married and learned how to be married as they went. The strange thing is that divorce has been so uncommon among this group that it is statistically inconsequential. None of us knew what we were doing. We had not been counseled, taught, or tested. The wedding vows themselves were our basic instructions: *To have and to hold from this day forward, for better for worse, for richer, for poorer, in sickness and in health, to love, to honor and to cherish, forsaking all others until death do us part.* Marty and I have the blessing of living near many couples who went to school together and married in abject ignorance just like we did. We see them on almost a daily basis. It is a joy to report that these marriages have not only endured for forty years or more, they have triumphed. They are beautiful to see, wonderful to revel in as only friends of long standing can do.

These days it is so different. Young people have access to so much marriage information. Experts teach, tutor, and test them, yet so many of their marriages end tragically in divorce. They have the knowledge. The missing ingredient is commitment, and, in marriage, commitment trumps knowledge every time.

Thanks be to God for teaching us commitment, which led to knowledge, which produced a lifetime of joy!

BOB BRINER

Popular author Bob Briner wrote this to honor his bride, Marty, and their long marriage before succumbing to cancer earlier this year.

PERFECT LOVE

*The supreme happiness of life
is the conviction that we are loved.*
VICTOR HUGO

I have always faced partings from loved ones with pain and fear, probably because I have experienced so many of them. My mother died when I was only thirteen months old. My father and I went to live with his mother, who raised me with a lot of love and nurturing. Twelve years later, my grandmother died and her death devastated me. That's when I started to become introverted and fearful.

Then my father remarried and I went to live with his new family. It was a difficult transition. I never felt accepted and the loneliness was chilling. I cried a lot. I remember vividly the melancholy that rose in me when I'd stare out the window at night. I felt like there was a giant piece missing from my heart. I didn't understand my emotions and neither did my father, which created distance between us. Throughout my growing-up years I missed our closeness and the feeling we'd once had as family.

Once an adult, I met Andrew quite by accident one day through a mutual business acquaintance. Our connection was immediate. I wanted to know as much as possible about Andrew, and as quickly as possible. Our first date was two weeks later and we both knew quickly that there was something special between us.

At the same time, Andrew was building his business five hundred miles away from home. He was gone eleven days out of fourteen and it was a real test for us. We both knew that our relationship, even in its fledgling days, was well worth the effort, but it was still hard. When Andrew was in town, his time was split between me, his two sons, and my young son. Some weekends were incredibly wonderful and others—well, others were harried, confused, and chaotic.

At the end of the weekend, when it was time for Andrew to return to the business world, I experienced terrible depression. I loved him so much and it hurt so deeply that he couldn't stay.

All the old pain I associated with people leaving resurfaced. Every Sunday I feared that Andrew would never return. I expected, deep down, that like my mother and grandmother, he'd eventually leave me altogether.

Even as I struggled with these feelings, I knew this was no way to begin a relationship. I was driving myself crazy fearing the future and distressing Andrew even more in the present. I desperately wanted to come to terms with my emotions. Throughout my life I had heard, "You shall know the truth, and the truth will set you free." I knew that discovering and embracing the truth would be an important key to unlocking my closet of fears.

Then a wise minister told me that I was experiencing an "orphan issue." Now I had a name for my feelings. Every time Andrew left, I felt like an orphan—like all my security and hope left with him. When I was finally able to identify what was going on inside me, I was able to do something about it. With a pastor's help, I applied the truth of God's love to my life and learned to accept the truth of Andrew's love and commitment as well. Meanwhile Andrew and I prayed for guidance and patience and asked God to bless our relationship with strength and courage.

By releasing my past, I opened my heart to my future. The change, which occurred over time and with much prayer, was miraculous. Andrew and I married and God gave us great happiness. The person I am today is the person I always wanted to be: confident, secure, and full of faith in God and in my husband.

The Bible says that "perfect love drives out fear" (1 John 4:18). God's perfect love certainly did that for me.

AS TOLD TO ANN PLATZ

A NEW LOVE

God is our refuge and strength,
a very present help in trouble.
PSALMS 46:1 (KJV)

The memories of my childhood are deeply riddled with insecurities, fear, and pain. Following the death of my alcoholic father, my mother found herself in ill health with few resources to care for her children and herself. Unable to work, Mother had to rely on family members. My brother, sister, and I were shuttled from one relative's home to the next. I often felt abandoned and grew terrified of being left all alone with no one to care for me.

One day I overhead my aunts and uncles speaking quietly behind closed doors in the next room. "What shall become of the children?" one relative wondered. Someone else mentioned sending Mother away to a hospital. Another spoke up and suggested, "Perhaps an orphanage will take the children."

Fear gripped my heart. I had no one and nowhere to turn. I could not possibly burden my sick mother. Then I remembered my heavenly Father—the one we had learned about from Mother and at Sunday school. Perhaps he would help me. "Dear God," I begged, "please don't let them take my mother away!'

God miraculously touched my life at this early age. The next night I knew that God had heard my prayers when I heard my mother speaking the words of the Twenty-third Psalm. Again I prayed to God and thanked him because I knew without a doubt that he was beginning to heal my mother. And he did. We survived those difficult circumstances, and along the way, God met our every need.

By the time I became an adult, I had slowly drifted away from God. At twenty-one, I met a divorced man ten years my senior who did not share my faith. I had read the Scripture, "Do not be unequally yoked," but hardly gave it a second thought. Blindly, I just breathed a sigh of relief that I would no longer be lonely and would have someone to care for me for the rest of my life. We were married, but we divorced after only three and a half years. Yet even in our failure, God blessed the marriage with our beautiful daughter, Stephanie.

Again, I was lonely and rejected, this time with a young daughter of my own to care for. Those old childhood fears began to resurface. In the years that separated me from that scared little girl listening outside the closed door, I had forgotten the power of prayer and God's love. Remembering how God had come to my rescue, I became determined to find him again. He was closer than I thought possible.

God's healing touched my life, and six months later, I met and fell in love with Bob, who exhibited all the traits I so desired in a husband. We were married soon after. I knew that the Lord had sent this wonderful man who encouraged me in all areas of my life, from family to business. It was Bob who suggested that I enter the real estate field, where I quickly became a success. Soon we were blessed with our daughter Susan, and I felt sure God had answered all of my prayers.

A few years into our marriage, again, things became rocky. Bob and I were moving in separate directions. I had become wrapped up in my career and Bob was working ninety miles away. We were becoming emotionally as well as physically distant. I felt that old emptiness forming in my heart and I panicked. Success and money weren't the answer. I didn't want to be alone and without love. I felt like that little girl again—scared, anxious, afraid to be alone, and uncertain about which way to turn.

Even with all my successes, I hadn't managed to find the balance and stability that I had always longed for. Then it hit me. I wasn't paying attention to God's will or to his presence. I wasn't being the wife that God had called me to be. As I sat in my chair, I suddenly noticed the light shining through the bay window: streams of light—a beacon to show me which way to turn. Before I realized it I was on my knees praying, drawing close to God once again.

The first thing I asked God to do for me was to give me a new love and a new heart for my husband. I knew I still loved him and that he still loved me, but I just needed to find that love again. God did just that. I felt waves of love wash over me. I felt rejuvenated and peaceful. I began to realize what a gift my husband was and that gift had come straight from God.

Although I had grown close to God in the past, I hadn't fully surrendered. Turning over my life and heart to God's will was the greatest decision I ever made. He drew my husband to him. Together, we discovered a deeper and greater love than either of us had ever known or thought possible. Our daughters benefited from our love and faith. Today both they and their families love and serve the Lord.

In addition, Bob and I decided to become partners in business as well as marriage. With God's blessings and Bob's support and expertise, the company has grown and flourished to become one of the top real estate offices in the country.

Bob and I grew as a couple in God's grace, and that has made all the difference in the world. We face the joys and sorrows of our life together. After years of pain, God washed it all away and replaced it instead with peace, comfort, happiness, and most importantly, a newfound love for God, for life, and for my beloved husband.

JENNY AND BOB PRUITT

PRINCE CHARMING
FELL OFF HIS HORSE

⚮

Child of the pure, unclouded brow
And dreaming eyes of wonder!
Though time be fleet and I and thou
Are half a life asunder,
Thy loving smile will surely hail
The love-gift of a fairy tale.
LEWIS CARROLL

That fateful day in May, I was fifteen years old and working in the local root beer stand. It was a hangout for some of the cool kids in the area. It had everything I could want: pinball machines, a jukebox, hamburgers, friends, malts, and lots of guys to flirt with. That early summer day a guy came roaring up on a motorcycle, wearing the requisite black leather jacket and sideburns. I recognized him as Jerry Schreur, age nineteen, the most notorious guy in town, and suddenly I knew he was the guy I'd been waiting for: Prince Charming on a Triumph.

On our first real date we put the top down in his Pontiac convertible and went riding around the Ottawa Beach State Park on Lake Michigan. After that weekend, I never dated another person. I lived for Jerry Schreur. He seemed to be the answer to all my needs. Being his girlfriend gave me an enormous sense of power.

Needless to say, my mother was not thrilled that her daughter was dating the town criminal. People either loved Jerry or hated him. They felt either very safe with him or completely threatened. Jerry was easily the most exciting man in town, and I was dating him!

But that wasn't enough. In my dream the princess always married Prince Charming. In my fairy tale Jerry drove up, I jumped behind him on the bike, and we rode off into the sunset. I didn't worry about what happened after that—I would simply be with him all the time and he would never let me go. "Happily ever after" would take care of itself.

Sure enough, the prince and princess married on February 28, 1964. I was eighteen and pregnant and my groom was twenty-two, a convicted felon who had been out of work for several months. We had no money for a honeymoon and lots of debt, but I was still excited. We moved into our castle—a drafty, old, one-bedroom house in the middle of a field—and I waited for the perfect life to begin.

Two years later, I was pretty convinced I had picked the wrong leading man. I had two baby boys and a husband whose mysterious silence—which I had once found so intriguing—now drove me to distraction. I needed someone to talk to. No fairy tale had prepared me for the isolation, not to mention overtime at the factory, two crying babies, no money, and a house that was falling part. I was twenty, disillusioned, and disappointed. And I didn't see any way out.

Skip to three decades later. The prince and the princess are, surprisingly, still together, and a happy ending is actually within reach. How? In a word, God. God has washed our marriage in his grace and mercy. Without an everyday grace that enables us to forgive and love each other, I know I would have quit a long time ago.

Looking back, we never should have made it. We got married for the wrong reasons: need, anger, pain, difficulty, lust, and yes, even love. We had very little faith in God or each other. I went into marriage looking for someone to take my dead father's place, cherishing me and telling me I was valuable. I married a man who expected me to take care of myself and wasn't very good at expressing his feelings. Anyone could have predicted the problems that lay ahead.

No one could have predicted how God would save us, though. The first thing we had to do was let go of the fairy tale. You can't fix a fairy tale—it doesn't really exist. And you can't fix reality—until you face it. When I found myself questioning my marriage and my choice of mate, I finally looked at both for what they were. It was only a first step, but it was an essential one.

The next step was finding something that could hold us together, and we did. We found Jesus. A friend introduced us to God's love and revealed that he had a plan for our lives. By then I was ready to exchange my script for God's—anyone's plan had to be better than mine! Jerry and I worked on forgiveness, and when we couldn't do that, we worked on prayer.

While Jerry and I struggled to learn to commit and communicate, I found myself daily strengthening my relationship with Jesus. And inherent in that relationship was obedience, which meant I would stick to the vows I'd taken that giddy day with Jerry. In his hunger for answers, Jerry followed a similar path. In obedience we both found freedom because we were doing what God wanted us to do. And in freedom we found love.

Was it worth it? Yes, for we have discovered that God can make a glue no one can dissolve. Today Jerry and I are partners who have created a life that brings us no small measure of joy and even delight. Jerry and I left the fairy tale behind a long time ago. But we believe that it is possible to keep the "happily" in "ever after." My Prince Charming got back on his horse—his convertible—and we still drive around Ottawa Beach. Only now Jerry's sideburns are gray; proving our marriage has stood the test of time.

JUDY SCHREUR

Jerry Schreur, Ph.D., is a minister and counselor in Grand Rapids where he and his wife Judy, a humorist and healthcare professional, are popular writers and speakers.

FINDING PEACE
AT HOME

*One word frees us all
From the weight and pain of life:
That word is love.*

SOPHOCLES

One of my best gifts to Rosalynn was to resolve a recurring argument. I was very busy at the time, putting the final touches on a book. I went into my study early one morning, turned on my computer, and hit a button that automatically put the date on the screen. There it was: August 18, her birthday, and I hadn't gotten her a present! Rosalynn was still in bed. So I started wondering what I could give her that I didn't have to go down to my cousin Hugh's antiques store to buy. In desperation, I tried to analyze the things that caused trouble in our marriage—in addition to my forgetting anniversaries and birthdays.

One of the things that had created a problem for us for thirty-five years or more was punctuality. I was affected by my training in the navy and, I think, inherited the trait from my father. Whether to meet a train, to attend a baseball game, or to keep an appointment, he was always there long ahead of time. If someone kept him waiting, he had no patience. He would stalk out of a doctor's office if his appointment was delayed for more than ten minutes. Unfortunately, I, too, am uncomfortable if someone keeps me waiting and if I'm late and inconvenience someone else, I get even more uptight. To the surprise of my campaign workers and some audiences, I even kept to a strict schedule during my political campaigns, in the governor's office, and in the White House.

And so Rosalynn and I had a lot of arguments about being on time. She always claimed that she was never late, and this would be true if judged by the standards of a reasonable person. What should two or three minutes matter between a husband and wife preparing to go to a movie or a party? But I was not reasonable, holding Rosalynn to a standard of absolute precision. Even before our appointed time for departure, I would remind her of the need to leave and would often produce at least a dirty look if I had to wait at the door.

So, reflecting on all this on that morning of her birthday, I wrote a note to her: "Rosalynn, I promise you that for the rest of our marriage, I will never make an unfavorable remark about tardiness." I signed it and gave it to her for a present. So far I've pretty well kept my promise, and she still agrees that it was the best birthday present I ever gave her.

PRESIDENT JIMMY CARTER.
LIVING FAITH BY JIMMY CARTER, © 1995 BY JIMMY CARTER.
REPRINTED BY PERMISSION OF TIMES BOOKS,
A DIVISION OF RANDOM HOUSE, INC.

For Richer, for Poorer

*Man's greatest riches is
to live on a little with contented mind;
for little is never lacking.*

LUCRETIUS

IT'S AN OLD SAYING, BUT TRUE: MONEY CAN'T BUY
HAPPINESS.

THAT'S CERTAINLY THE CASE IN A MARRIAGE RELATIONSHIP.
IT'S NOT HARD TO FIND WEALTHY PEOPLE—SOME EXTREMELY
SO—WHO ARE ALSO EXTREMELY UNHAPPY IN MARRIAGE.
OTHER COUPLES HAVE ALMOST NOTHING, YET ARE
BLISSFULLY CONTENT WITH EACH OTHER AND THE WORLD.
WHETHER YOU HAVE LITTLE OR MUCH, IT'S HOW MUCH YOU
APPRECIATE THE THINGS YOU HAVE AND THE LOVE YOU
SHARE, NOT HOW MANY THINGS YOU HAVE TO APPRECIATE
OR LOVE, THAT MAKES THE DIFFERENCE.

THE SECRET IS GRATITUDE.

WHEN YOU TAKE TO HEART THE WORDS FOR RICHER, FOR
POORER IN YOUR WEDDING VOWS, YOU ARE REALIZING THE
KEY TO A SUCCESSFUL MARRIAGE IS COMMITMENT TO GOD
FIRST, AND THEN TO EACH OTHER. THEN, WHATEVER

COMES—POVERTY OR WEALTH—YOU CAN HANDLE THE
STRESS THAT GOES ALONG WITH IT. YOU WILL BE TIED INTO
THE ATTITUDE OF GRATITUDE. PRAISE AND THANKSGIVING
FLOW FROM THAT, THE MOST FERTILE SOIL FOR LOVE TO
GROW.

A MAN AND A WOMAN WHO BELIEVE IN, TRUST IN, AND
ARE SUPREMELY THANKFUL FOR ONE ANOTHER AND THEIR
LORD ARE TRULY THE RICHEST PEOPLE ON EARTH.

THE UNMATCHED GIFT

*The fragrance always remains
in the hand that gives the rose.*

HEDA BEJAR

Iremember Dad going off to speak in a tiny church and coming home ten days later. My mother greeted him warmly and asked how the revival had gone. He was always excited about that subject. Eventually, in moments like this she would get around to asking him about the offering. Women have a way of worrying about things like that.

"How much did they pay you?" she asked.

I can still see my father's face as he smiled and looked at the floor. "Aw..." he stammered. My mother stepped back and looked into his eyes.

"Oh, I get it," she said. "You gave the money away again, didn't you?"

"Myrt," he said. "The pastor there is going through a hard time. His kids are so needy. It just broke my heart. They have holes in their shoes and one of them is going to school on these cold mornings without a coat. I felt I should give the entire fifty dollars to them."

My good mother looked intently at him for a moment and then she smiled, "You know, if God told you to do it, it's okay with me."

Then a few days later the inevitable happened. The Dobsons ran completely out of money. There was no reserve to tide us over. That's when my father gathered us in the bedroom for a time of prayer. I remember that day as though it were yesterday. He prayed first.

"Oh, Lord, you promised that if we would be faithful with you and your people in our good times, then you would not forget us in our times of need. We have tried to be generous with what you have given us, and now we are calling on you for help."

A very impressionable ten-year-old boy named Jimmy was watching and listening very carefully that day. *What will happen?* he wondered. *Did God hear Dad's prayer?*

The next day an unexpected check for $1200 came for us in the mail. Honestly! That's the way it happened, not just this once but many times. I saw the Lord match my Dad's giving stride for stride. No, God never made us wealthy, but my young faith grew by leaps and bounds. I learned that you cannot outgive God!

My father continued to give generously through the mid-life years and into his sixties. I used to worry about how he and Mom would fund their retirement years because they were able to save very little money. If Dad did get many dollars ahead, he'd give them away. I wondered how in the world they would live on the pittance paid to retired ministers by their denomination. (As a widow, my mother received just $80.50 per month after Dad spent forty-four years in the church.) It is disgraceful how poorly we take care of our retired ministers and their widows.

One day my father was lying on the bed and Mom was getting dressed. She turned to look at him and he was crying.

"What's the matter?" she asked.

"The Lord just spoke to me," he replied.

"Do you want to tell me about it?" she prodded.

"He told me something about you," Dad said.

She then demanded that he tell her what the Lord had communicated to him.

My father said, "It was a strange experience. I was just lying here thinking about many things. I wasn't praying or even thinking about you when the Lord spoke to me and said, 'I'm going to take care of Myrtle.'"

Neither of them understood the message, but simply filed it away in the catalog of imponderables. But five days later my dad had a massive heart attack, and three months after that he was gone. At sixty-six years of age, this good man whose name I share went out to meet the Christ whom he had loved and served for all those years.

It was thrilling to witness the way God fulfilled His promise to take care of my mother. Even when she was suffering from end-stage Parkinson's disease and required constant care at an astronomical cost, God provided. The small inheritance that Dad left to his wife multiplied in the years after his departure. It was sufficient to pay for everything she needed, including marvelous and loving care. God was with her in every other way, too, tenderly cradling her in His secure arms until He took her home. In the end, my Dad never came close to out-giving God.

DR. JAMES DOBSON FROM *LOVE FOR A LIFETIME*. USED BY PERMISSION OF MULTNOMAH PUBLISHERS.

LET'S MAKE BEAUTIFUL MUSIC TOGETHER

O, my luve is like a red, red rose,
That's newly sprung in June.
O, my luve is like a melodie,
That's sweetly played in tune.
ROBERT BURNS

I had just moved from New York to Los Angeles to begin my singing career in film, television, and theater. Like many struggling young performers, I had to find a second job to support myself until I became a star. As a Christian, I believed that singing with a church choir would suit me perfectly. I was also single, and my Southern Baptist mother had often told me that the best place to meet a nice man was at church.

After I landed a theatrical role in *Camelot,* I told everyone I was looking for a soloist position in a church choir. I finally found a suitable position at a Presbyterian church near Pasadena. My first big assignment was to be the soprano soloist for the Christmas program. The church had hired an orchestra for the performance, and we began practicing early in December.

At our dress rehearsal, I personally stopped to thank each orchestra member for a practice session well done. When I stopped to thank one of the cellists, a friend who knew that I wanted to meet some eligible men played matchmaker. "I want to introduce you to the flutist, Bobby Shulgold," he said. "He looks exactly like Bruce Willis."

"Yeah, sure," I replied. "I just ran into Bruce Willis a couple of nights ago, so we'll see about that." When my friend led me over to Bobby, my first reaction was one of utter shock! There stood a very hip young man with long hair and an earring in his ear. "Definitely not my type," I whispered to my friend. "But I have to admit this guy's even cuter than Bruce Willis!" I mumbled, "So much for matchmaking."

As I turned to leave, several members of the orchestra insisted that I join them for coffee across the street. Although I was exhausted from the rehearsal, I could hardly refuse. I felt greatly obliged to show my appreciation for all their long practice sessions and hard work.

When we arrived at the restaurant, Bobby grabbed the seat beside me and began to entertain me with magic tricks. *What talent,* I thought. *He not only plays a flute; he's a magician, too!* Even though I was amused by the magic tricks, I was extremely tired and thought the night would never end.

When the evening finally came to a close, Bobby insisted on walking me to my car, and we exchanged cards. I knew this guy would never be anything but a friend—he was definitely not husband material in my book—so I tried to give him the brush-off as politely as possible.

I had to admit I was flattered the next day when Bobby called, but I was still not interested. When he invited me to his house for dinner and a movie, I began to make up all sorts of excuses. To my surprise, by the time I hung up the phone, he had convinced me to go to the movie with him. I was furious that I had let this gentle man persuade me to go out with him when I had had no intention of doing so.

When the day of our first date arrived, Bobby phoned to tell me that he had been offered a gig. This was a perfectly acceptable excuse to break a date because opportunities for musicians to work are often few and far between. Frankly, I was relieved. Then Bobby took me by surprise when he asked, "Will you come to my performance?"

I hadn't planned on this, but I was backed into a corner. "Of course," I replied weakly. *I'll show him*, I thought. *I'll take a girlfriend along so he'll clearly understand that I'm not the least bit interested in him.* Bobby just was not my type.

When my girlfriend and I arrived, I made her promise not to leave me under any circumstances. "I don't want to lead the poor guy on...he's really a nice guy."

"You have my word," my friend assured me.

As the jazz ensemble began to play, Bobby's talent and good looks began to cast their spell on me. By the end of the performance I could hardly wait for my girlfriend to leave. When Bobby asked the two of us to go to dinner, I shot her a look that could kill. Luckily she caught on.

"Gee," she said, "I'm sorry to disappoint you, but I suddenly remembered that I have a report to prepare for tomorrow." Bobby and I went on to have a great dinner.

On our next date we went to a movie. When Bobby reached for my hand, no one was more surprised than me that my stomach did flip-flops. "This must be love," I happily told myself. I was right about that...before I knew it, we were madly in love. Three years later we decided to marry.

When we counseled with the minister, we discussed with him the fact that we were both musicians without steady paychecks. We were professionals and our services were in demand; even so, as anyone in the entertainment business knows, it can be feast of famine. We considered the true meaning of the wedding vows—for richer, for poorer. We knew we had to support each other in every way and that would mean both of us would have to make significant sacrifices. Bobby had been so excited about our first date, yet he had to break it. He needed to make himself available when called and he had to have an income. We knew that more such times lay ahead of us.

The minister told us that being married changes everything—that something spiritual happens when you become man and wife. Bobby said, "It couldn't possibly change anything for me! I love Renee and couldn't possibly have any stronger feelings for her than I do this very moment!" The minister smiled knowingly.

Our wedding ceremony was beautiful. Each of us was very close to a grandmother, so we exchanged our grandmothers' wedding bands. After we were married and heading toward our honeymoon destination, Bobby held my hand and looked me in the eyes. "You know," he said, "the minister was right—there is something so incredible about marriage. I love being married to you." I cried tears of joy because we both felt such a spiritual bond after our ceremony. It's almost impossible to put into words until you experience it yourself. It was all part of God's perfect plan.

Remember the vow, "for richer, for poorer"? We were tested at the onset. On our wedding night, my talented musician husband was called to do a very important recording job. These opportunities don't occur that often, and I insisted that he take advantage of his big break. Can you believe that we spent our honeymoon night in a recording studio? My understanding and concern for my husband's career and our future really touched Bobby's heart. Although we had a wonderful time in the recording studio that night, I warned Bobby that a girl has to draw the line somewhere. I told him I expected him to be by my side when our first baby arrived. "No career break or any amount of money will tear me away," he promised.

My advice to singles is "Don't judge the book by its cover. The Lord has unexpected plans for us, and his plans are greater than any we could ever concoct for ourselves." My advice to married couples is to support each other as you make beautiful music together and apart.

RENÉE BURKETT SHULGOLD, AS TOLD TO SUSAN WALES

REAL RICHES

For thy sweet love remember'd such wealth brings
That then I scorn to change my state with kings.
But if the while I think on thee, dear friend,
All losses are restor'd and sorrows end.

WILLIAM SHAKESPEARE

In the year 1141 A.D., the Weinberg Castle in Germany held unimaginable riches: gold, silver, jewels, and treasures of every kind. The residents of the castle lived happily and peaceably for years while enjoying their good fortune.

The day came when the kingdom was threatened. Several of the watchmen came down from the towers to confer with the king and his knights inside the castle. They reported that the castle was surrounded on all sides by a massive enemy army far outnumbering their own. The king met with the knights and they mournfully concurred that the enemy would surely take over the castle, kill its occupants, and confiscate all the riches for their own.

Inside, the men of the castle sadly admitted defeat to their subjects. They not only were aware that the life they enjoyed was about to come to an end, but they would most likely lose their lives as they fought to defend their castle.

The lead of the great army surrounding the castle sent a message to the gate announcing that all the women and children would be released before the battle began. However, the wives of Weinberg sent word back to the enemy leader with their own demand: As they fled the castle, the opposing army must allow them to carry out their most prized posses-sions. Aware that the women could only carry so much, the leader agreed to their terms.

When the drawbridge was lowered and the massive gates were opened, the attackers were move to tears by the sight before them. Each woman carried her greatest possession in her arms…her husband.

When the residents were safely at a distance, the army charged the castle, taking it over and claiming all the riches for their own. The women of Weinberg shed not one tear over the loss of their fortune because they had carried with them the only riches that really mattered—the men they loved.

These women knew the true meaning of riches.

RETOLD BY MEGAN CHRANE

THE GIFT

*Love's looking together
in the same direction.*
ANTOINE DE SAINTE-EXUPÉRY

Though I haven't been married long, I have already begun to understand why Solomon wrote praises of companionship in Ecclesiastes: "Two are better than one, because they have a good return for their work: If one falls down, his friend can help him up. But pity the man who falls and has no one to help him up!" (Ecclesiastes 4:9–10, NIV) One Christmas brought home the truth of this passage to me and my wife.

Christmas had always been a special time in my family. Each year when I was growing up, my family would drive to the small Georgia town where my grandparents lived. As a young boy, I looked forward to taking baskets of ham, turkey, and pies to the less fortunate families in my grandparents' town. What I remember most about these Christmases are the looks of joy and appreciation on the faces of the families with whom we could share. I am so thankful that my family taught me the true meaning of Christmas and how much greater it is to give than receive.

When I married, I decided I wanted to continue this tradition in some way. My wife, Heather Whitestone, a former Miss America, certainly cared for others as much as I did. Heather, who is deaf, has a real sensitivity to the needs of others.

We spent our first Christmas mostly receiving blessings, though, instead of giving them. We had an opportunity to go to the Holy Land with the pastor and other members of the Fort Lauderdale Baptist Church. It was the adventure of a lifetime that we will always cherish. What better place to celebrate our Savior's birth than his birthplace?

The next Christmas, we planned to return to the Holy Land, but at the last minute a speaking engagement caused us to cancel our plans. Disappointed, we accepted an invitation from Fort Lauderdale Baptist Church to attend their Christmas pageant. While it wasn't the Holy Land, Heather and I were still able to recall the warm memories of our trip from the year before as we joined the pastor and other members of our group at the pageant. It was during the service that the Lord placed it in our hearts to give a special love offering.

We asked the pastor if he would select a couple who could not afford, but would benefit from, this inspirational tour of the Holy Land. He chose a young minister and his wife. Heather and I found ourselves blessed through the cards and letters the young couple sent from the Holy Land. We were able to see and experience our original trip through the eyes and words of the couple. It was as though we were on the trip sharing every precious moment with them. A new tradition of giving, one we would fulfill as a couple, was born.

When the next Christmas arrived, Heather and I asked, "How can we top the blessings and pleasure that we received from our gift of last Christmas?" We had a very busy few months and before we realized it, Christmas was just around the corner. I prayed that God would again reveal to us how to share our blessings. When Christmas morning arrived, I awoke feeling very disappointed with myself. I got down on my knees and prayed, "Forgive me, Lord, for my poor planning. Would you show us someone to bless this Christmas?"

Later that morning, we loaded our car with packages and headed to my grandmother's house. We had just stopped for gas when a car sputtered into the station. I saw the attendant shaking his head. The family's radiator had overheated and the car had broken hoses, but there was no mechanic on duty anywhere on Christmas Day, the station manager sadly explained.

"Is there anything I can do?" I asked the young driver. He explained that he was driving his aunt and uncle and their family to Mississippi to spend Christmas. "But it looks like we won't make it," he said sadly. I wished there was a way I could help, but I knew absolutely nothing about car mechanics.

Back in the car, Heather asked what was happening. When I explained the situation, she said without hesitation, "John, we have two cars in our garage at home! Why don't we lend the family our car?" This had never occurred to me. I was suddenly awed by the power of two—God's purpose for marriage. I had the desire to help someone, but alone I hadn't known how. God used my precious wife to show me.

The family gratefully accepted our offer and celebrated Christmas dinner with their family in Mississippi. When the young driver returned the car, he thanked me profusely for rescuing his family's Christmas.

"Don't thank me," I insisted, "thank God." I then told him about my prayer. I had asked God for someone to help. He looked at me incredulously.

"You were an answer to my prayer, too!" he exclaimed. "I woke up Christmas morning knowing there wasn't any money and that there wouldn't be any presents. When I prayed, I told the Lord that it didn't bother me about not getting any presents, but could he please provide a safe journey for my family to Mississippi. He gave us you and your generosity," he said and smiled.

God answered two prayers that Christmas Day, and I learned in a fresh way the value of marriage. Heather and I can hardly wait to see what next Christmas brings!

HEATHER WHITESTONE AND JOHN MCCALLUM

MONEY CAN'T BUY YOU LOVE

He who has conquered doubt and fear has conquered failure.

JAMES LANE ALLEN

It's hard to meet people in a big city like Atlanta. I decided to enroll in a French class both to find folks of similar interests as well as to improve my French.

I was a little late for my first class and it had already started when I arrived. When I rushed into the room, I immediately noticed a very attractive girl in a seat close to the front of the class. We traded nods and smiles as I made my way to a seat.

I was late for the next class as well. I had been Rollerblading with some friends and had ripped my clothes. I didn't have time to go back home and change, so I arrived at French class looking like I had just been in a fight. I was afraid the pretty girl wouldn't smile or look my way. Instead she moved her books from the seat next to her and motioned for me to sit down.

I immediately found Joan friendly and intimidating at the same time. In retrospect, I have to laugh. There I was, an entrepreneur, a businessman. I worked with big names and numbers in my real-estate business—I could ask a banker for five million dollars without flinching, yet I couldn't get up enough nerve to ask this lovely lady out. Months passed before I managed one day to invite her to study French with me at a nearby coffeehouse. Then finally, after three months of this "study-dating," she asked *me* out on our first official date!

From there our relationship grew and grew. I think that somewhere in the back of my mind, I knew from the beginning that I would ask Joan to marry me. I just didn't know how or when. I finally gathered my resolve to propose. I confess I hadn't really thought my plan through. I didn't even have a ring. But what I feared most was that by proposing, I would be asking this beautiful girl I loved into a difficult and unpredictable life. The real-estate market fluctuated so rapidly that I never knew from one moment to the next whether I would make my bills or collapse in bankruptcy. It seemed almost selfish to ask Joan to share such a life with me, but I had to try.

I rented a small boat and we sailed out to this little cove on an island. We decided to go for a swim. Because we were in the water, I couldn't get down on one knee. So I just blurted out, "Will you marry me?"

"Oh, Rick, you're so funny," she replied.

I nearly sank to the bottom. This wasn't the response I had expected. She thought I was joking.

"Joan, I'm serious. I'm asking you to marry me," I repeated. I could see that she believed me the second time. Her eyes clouded with tears.

In my lack of planning I hadn't organized my thoughts, but I wanted to be completely honest with her. "Joan," I stuttered, "my career is so volatile. One day the real-estate market's up, the next it might plummet. No one can ever tell. The market can either be a feast or famine. I want you to know what you'll be getting into if you marry me. There are a thousand ways we could go bankrupt. We could be destitute."

Joan just shook her head at me. "First you want me to marry you and now you're trying to talk me out of it. Make up your mind!" She laughed.

"I just want you to know what could possibly happen, that's all," I assured her.

"Listen to yourself. 'Could possibly happen'—do you think any of that matters to me?" she asked. "'For richer, for poorer'—that's in the marriage vows for a reason. Marriage isn't about how much money you make. It's about how much love we have. Don't worry over what may never happen. Worry if I'm going to say yes or no," she announced with a grin.

Fortunately for me, she said yes. We got married in a beautiful ceremony filled with friends and family. When Joan left her corporate job and joined me in real estate, she made her personal philosophy her business one as well: Don't worry about the future; just concentrate on today.

Over the last five years she's taught me to find great joy in today and trust that together, we can handle whatever comes our way. Not a day passes that I don't admire her serenity and thank my lucky stars that even though I underestimated her, she more than believed in love—and in me.

RICK SKELTON

Friendship is the union of spirits,
a marriage of hearts,
and the bond of virtue.
WILLIAM PENN

BEHIND EVERY GREAT MAN IS A GREAT WOMAN

A woman reasons by telegraph,
And his (a man's) stage-coach reasoning
cannot keep pace with hers.
MARY WALKER

Thomas Wheeler, CEO of the Massachusetts Mutual Life Insurance Company, and his wife were driving along an interstate highway when he noticed that their car was low on gas. Wheeler got off the highway at the next exit and soon found a rundown gas station with just one gas pump. He asked the lone attendant to fill the tank and check the oil, then went for a little walk around the station to stretch his legs.

As he was returning to the car, he noticed the attendant and his wife were engaged in a animated conversation. The conversation stopped as he paid the attendant. But as he was getting back into the car, he saw the attendant wave and heard him say, "It was great talking to you."

As they drove out of the station, Wheeler asked his wife if she knew the man. She readily admitted she did. They had gone to high school together and had dated steadily for about a year.

"Boy, were you lucky that I came along," bragged Wheeler. "If you had married him, you'd be the wife of a gas station attendant instead of the wife of a chief executive officer."

"My dear," replied his wife, "if I had married him, he'd be the chief executive officer and you'd be the gas station attendant."

Reprinted by permission from *The Best of Bits and Pieces*. Arthur J. Lenehan, Editor, © 1994, The Economics Press, Inc. 1-800-526-2554.

In Sickness and in Health

*In marriage, one cannot do anything
alone—not even suffer.*
MARY ADAMS

JIM WAS ANYTHING BUT A GIVING HUSBAND. IN FACT, HE WAS THE MOST NEEDY MAN THAT LOIS HAD EVER KNOWN. IT'S NOT THAT JIM DIDN'T LOVE HIS WIFE; HE LOVED HER MORE THAN LIFE ITSELF. BUT JIM WAS A BEDRIDDEN INVALID.

DESPITE ALL THAT—AND MAYBE, IN SOME WAYS, BECAUSE OF IT—LOIS'S LOVE FOR JIM BURNED HOTTER AND BRIGHTER THAN THE DAY THEY WERE FIRST MARRIED. NO ONE WHO KNEW THEM WOULD SUGGEST THAT LOIS PLACE HIM IN A NURSING HOME.

"I LOVE HIM NOW MORE THAN EVER," LOIS TOLD A FRIEND, "AND I WOULDN'T WANT HIM ANYWHERE BUT WITH ME."

WHEN YOU STAND AT THE ALTAR, GLOWING WITH VITALITY, VIGOR, AND PASSION, VOWING TO LOVE IN SICKNESS AS IN HEALTH, YOU CANNOT SEE WHAT THAT MAY MEAN. YOU MAY HAVE YEARS OR DECADES TO PRACTICE LOVE IN HEALTH BEFORE SICKNESS FALLS. YOU MAY HAVE ONLY DAYS OR HOURS. SICKNESS IS SCARY, AND NEVER

CONVENIENT, BUT LOVE AND COMMITMENT WILL CAUSE YOU TO LOOK BEYOND THE FRAILTIES OF AN EARTHLY SHELL INTO THE SOUL OF YOUR BELOVED.

WHEN YOU VOW, "IN SICKNESS OR IN HEALTH," YOU ARE TELLING YOURSELF THE TRUTH ABOUT LIFE. YOU ARE PREPARING YOUR HEART FOR THE DAY, OR MANY DAYS, OF WATCHING THE ONE YOU LOVE SUFFER. YOU ARE GIVING YOURSELF A REALITY CHECK. THIS, TOO, IS ONE OF THE GLORIES OF LOVE: YOU TAKE THE BITTER WITH THE SWEET. AND YOU WATCH GOD MAKE EVEN THAT GOOD.

THE HEALING POWER
OF LOVE

We are each of us angels
With only one wing
And we can only fly
Embracing each other.
LUCIANO DE CRESCENZO

I didn't know if I would make it to my fiftieth birthday or not. Charles and I had been married for twenty-five years when I discovered a lump in my breast that was later diagnosed as malignant. This began a devastating and frightening time for the entire family. From the beginning, I decided I wasn't going to quit. I would fight my best fight—for my family and for myself.

I did everything the doctors instructed me to do. I underwent the chemotherapy and radiation treatments. I watched as my hair fell out, slowly at first, and then by the handful, until I was completely bald. My scalp wasn't the only part of my body that suffered: The illness robbed me of all energy and strength.

Through it all, Charles was so strong. He hardly left my bedside. Whenever I opened my eyes, he would be there, having fallen asleep at the foot of the hospital bed, his hand still holding tightly onto mine. He was my angel watching over me, refusing to let anything take me away from him. Charles would rub my bald head and massage my back and arms. He'd tell me how much he loved me and how beautiful I was to him.

When he said he understood my pain, I believed he truly meant it.

The cancer had ravaged my body—this was evident to everyone—but if you looked into Charles's eyes you would think he was the one battling cancer. He felt everything I felt.

After two years of chemo and radiation, I was cancer free. But damage from both the disease and its treatment still clung to my body. I felt weak and empty. It was a sense of exhaustion that went beyond the physical. It was a weariness in heart and spirit that seemed irreparable.

Yet after those two long, hard years, I did make it to my fiftieth birthday. For all of us, this was a time of celebration. Charles wanted to do something that commemorated my life and my survival. He started brainstorming. With the help of our children, he put his plan into action. Unbeknownst to me, he had the children pack some clothes for me. They then drove me to the base of Kennesaw Mountain where, long before the cancer, Charles and I used to jog together.

"Honey, we are going to climb this mountain!" Charles announced. As I looked at his huge grin, I suspected that my beloved husband had lost his senses.

"Charles, I can't climb this mountain. I'm wearing a skirt, and besides, I don't have the energy to do this. It's too much." I shook my head.

Charles took my hand and pointed to the mountain. "Maybe you can't. We can. We can do this together. Just like always," he said. I could see the love and patience in his eyes. I nodded my agreement and we left the children at the base of the mountain.

We huffed and puffed. Charles kept encouraging me, saying words to keep me going and when I couldn't anymore, he almost carried me to the top. He was right. Maybe I couldn't have made it to the top alone, but together we did and it was glorious.

Climbing down the mountain was much easier, as it always is. I felt so exhilarated by the time we reached the car. Energy and life coursed within me. I had to thank both God and Charles for their amazing gift. Charles opened the trunk of the car and pulled out the sweetest and coldest watermelon I had ever tasted. While we climbed, the watermelon had been on ice in the trunk—Charles had thought of everything. I think it was the best-tasting food I ever ate.

Without my knowledge, Charles had also made reservations at a bed and breakfast that served good old Southern cooking: fried chicken, butter beans, rice, and sweet potato casserole, just like my grandmother made. I felt like I hadn't eaten in years. I'm sure I made quite a spectacle.

The next night Charles presented tickets to see the Four Tops and the Temptations at an outdoor concert. I felt like a teenager again, like we were just starting to date. I felt the years and the cancer fall away. We even danced on the lawn to our favorite song. Charles had yet another surprise: a candlelit picnic on the grass while the music played. Everything was so romantic and there I was, alive with my dear husband, spending the perfect weekend.

Late that night, Charles broke down and cried. He admitted that there had been a point when I was so sick and so weak that he had almost given up hope. "I thought I had lost you, but then I remembered God was in charge, not me," Charles whispered. "I had to keep faith that you would recover. I had to keep faith in him. Even if you had died I knew everything would be okay. God has a reason for all that he does. I'm just thankful he chose to keep us together."

As my husband confessed his fears and faith, I looked deep into his eyes and felt the love coming from them touch my soul. I knew that I was the one who should be thankful for this wonderful man God had given to keep me safe and to always make me feel the healing power of love. I hope I have many more birthdays with this man.

MELDA COLLINS

AMAZING GRACE

Love is...born with the pleasure
of looking at each other,
It is fed with the necessity
of seeing each other,
It is concluded with the
impossibility of separation!

JOSÉ MAERTÍ

At the age of nine, young Judy Taylor found darkness closing around her. Specialists confirmed to her distraught family that nothing could be done to save her sight. As time passed and Judy's vision faded, she didn't waste time feeling sorry for herself; she made the best of a sad situation by attending a high school for the blind. She triumphed there, graduating and then moved on to a mainstream college where she earned a degree in education.

Basking in her independence, Judy moved into her own apartment, which was located over an electrical shop. Judy often sat in the yard facing the shop, and when a new radio and television engineer began working there, Judy apparently caught his eye. He never failed to greet the young woman cheerfully or to tease her gently. One day when she took out the garbage, Judy discovered the workshop "voice" sitting on her bin sunning himself. "Do you mind moving?" she scolded him with smile. "This is not a garden seat!" He obliged with easy charm and introduced himself as Ian Taylor (no relation).

Ian never seemed bothered by Judy's blindness. Their encounters became more frequent and a friendship grew. Eventually the two became inseparable. It was Ian who introduced Judy to her first oak apples, pulling the tree branches low enough for her to touch them, and Ian who guided her fingers around the beautifully formed nest of a jenny wren. Judy came to rely upon Ian's companionship and his comfort—it was his shoulder that she cried on when her beloved seeing-eye dog passed away.

Judy was falling in love with Ian, but she stubbornly denied her feelings. *After all,* she thought, *who would want to take on a blind woman?* To her, it seemed impossible for their relationship to develop into anything more than a friendship.

Still, the couple's relationship deepened. And although Ian and Judy were constant companions, six years passed before he proposed. He took his time, he said, because "I wanted to be certain that what I felt for Judy was love—not pity for her blindness or admiration for the way she coped with it."

Once Ian was sure, Judy acknowledged her feelings as well. The couple set a date. On their wedding day, as the beautiful song, "See That You Love One Another," rang out in the church, Judy felt buoyant with happiness.

Judy and Ian were eventually blessed with two healthy and active sons, and the family enjoyed busy and meaningful lives. The years passed. When Judy was fifty-two, one evening a health scare sent her to the emergency room. After tests showed Judy was fine, the doctor touched her arm and casually asked, "How long have you had that squint?"

Judy's right eye had always tended to wander, but this was the first time anyone had referred to it as a squint. On their ride home, Judy told Ian, "I'd like to have my 'squint' repaired."

Judy went to an eye specialist who explained that a simple operation would correct her squint. Then the doctor softly broached the subject of Judy's blindness; he said that since both her optic nerves appeared healthy, she might be able to regain part of her vision by simply removing her cataracts. He promised no miracles but said, "You have nothing to lose."

Stunned, Judy returned home to tell Ian the news. After more than forty years in the darkness, she was being offered a glimmer of hope—the tiniest chance of regaining some sight. The thought was so overwhelming that she burst into tears. With Ian's encouragement, Judy decided to have the operation. The family tried desperately not to get their hopes up.

The half-dreaded day after the surgery finally arrived. When the dressing was peeled away, Judy slowly lifted her head. "What can you see?" a nurse asked tentatively.

"A bright horizontal light," Judy replied. As she turned her head she said, "More bright lights." Then she realized what was happening. She shouted, "I can see! I can see!"

Judy describes what her first sight of Ian, her husband of almost twenty years, was like: "That afternoon, I heard Ian's footsteps. So many times, I had listened for those steps. Then his hand took mine. And I was looking at him—my husband—for the very first time!"

This time, Ian caught Judy's eye. "I had always thought about him with his dark hair and dark eyes, and somehow knew what he would look like," Judy says. "I wasn't surprised until suddenly I became aware I was looking straight into his eyes. I shall never forget it—the first time, as an adult, I caught someone's eye. I am glad it was the eye of someone I loved."

CONDENSED BY SUSAN WALES FROM THE BOOK, *AS I SEE IT* BY JUDY TAYLOR. USED BY PERMISSION OF THE AUTHOR.

THE ONE WHO DIDN'T EVEN TRY TO GET AWAY

Just as there comes a warm
sunbeam into every cottage window
so comes love born of God's Care
for every separate need.

NATHANIEL HAWTHORNE

I was invited to a party for chefs and concierges. Tired from the week's activities, I almost didn't go. At the last minute, though, I decided I would. As a restaurant critic, I knew I would see many friends and colleagues there. It sounded like a nice way to cap a busy week.

So I went. That's where I saw him for the first time. Standing across from my table with dark brown eyes and a slight smile, he nodded at me. He worked his way around the table and we struck up a conversation. Our connection was immediate and wonderful. It seemed like all the other people in the room evaporated.

I remember that I had food in my hand and that I was trying to talk and eat at the same time. It didn't exactly work. He asked me what profession I was—chef? concierge? I told him first that I was a food critic, but also that I was a new author. I had just published my first book, *No More Bad Hair Days*, which chronicled my fight with ovarian cancer.

This is usually the point in conversation when people, especially men, grow uneasy, make an excuse, and flee. The "*c* word" makes people extremely uncomfortable. I had grown used to this reaction, but this man surprised me. Instead of excusing himself, he stayed. He asked, with a sincerely concerned look, if I was all right.

I smiled. I leveled with him—no use hiding the relevant facts. I used words like "few short months," "not expected to," and "doctors have done everything, but...." Not only did he not flinch, he asked to see me again. This was a man of *many* surprises.

On our first date, time flew as we talked and laughed together. When I stood to go, he asked, "When will I see you again?"

"I'll be out of town on a tour to promote the book for five days," I said, grinning. He called the night I got home. He asked me on a date for the following Sunday and I eagerly accepted.

The weather turned cold and rainy on Sunday. Lou and I agreed to meet after church for a meal and a movie. From our first date, he remembered the name of my favorite restaurant, so he made reservations for brunch. As soon as we walked in, I saw two friends waving at me. Lou graciously invited them to join us. I liked the way he wanted to get to know my friends.

After a wonderful brunch, we went to the Atlanta History Center, which turned out to be a favorite place of both of us. The more we talked, the more we discovered we had in common. It was like we were cut from the same cloth. After the Atlanta History Center, we went to see the movie *Washington Square*. It was so romantic we stayed in our seats afterward, savoring the story and watching the credits roll.

On our way home from this perfect afternoon, Lou suggested we grab some dinner. I couldn't believe that all of this was happening. I enjoyed his company so much, it was like a piece of my life had fallen into place. I happily agreed to dinner. I wasn't ready for our date to end yet either.

Afterward, we went to my house and finished that cold and rainy Sunday with a card game and conversation in front of a glowing fire. That night, we both experienced an incredible meeting of minds and souls. We absolutely hated to say good-bye.

A friend was coming to town to help me repair some things. He'd be in town for five days. Lou asked if he could call me after the visit was over. True to form, five days later Lou telephoned. "Did you miss me?" was his first question. I laughed and said yes. I invited him over for dinner that night. I wanted to cook for him and sit in front of the fireplace again. It felt so wonderful to have him around. I felt like I had been waiting for this my entire life.

Six weeks later, on the Tuesday before Thanksgiving, Lou came over for dinner. He stood up and very confidently stated that he wanted me to call my attorney. "I want this in writing," he said. "I don't want anything you have. I don't want you to be my girlfriend. I want you to be my wife."

We were both crying, and of course I said yes. There was nothing in the entire world that I wanted more than to be Lou's wife.

I didn't realize there were holes in my life until I met Lou. For a long time, I had been preparing to die. Lou reminded me that no matter what happens you have to continue to live and find all the blessings in each day. He is the biggest one of all.

SUSAN HYDE

There is nothing more nobler
or more admirable than when
two people who see eye to eye
keep house man and wife,
confounding their enemies
and delighting their friends.
HOMER

ARVELLA'S LOVE LETTERS

Thanks to the human heart by which we live,
Thanks to the tenderness, its joys, and fears,
To me the meanest flower that blows can give
Thoughts that do often lie too deep for tears.
WILLIAM WORDSWORTH

In his book, *Goliath, The Life of Robert Schuller,* Schuller's son-in-law, Jim Penner, describes the night that they received the news that Dr. Schuller was clinging to his life, and undergoing emergency brain surgery. Penner was reading Arvella's forty-year-old love letters from Dr. Schuller when she joined him in the library.

"He wrote that to me the fall after we met."

Arvella's voice startled me. I was so engrossed in the letter that I hadn't heard her come in. She stood in the doorway with a sweet smile I needed so much.

"When does your plane leave?" I asked her.

"I can't get a flight out until the afternoon," she said. "All I can do is sit and wait for any news."

She crossed over to where I was and gently took the letter from my hand. She swept the skirt of her housecoat under her legs and settled herself in the easy chair. Her eyes beckoned me to sit across from her. I was mesmerized by the mood of it all and sat near the edge of my seat. She read the letter.

My darling Arvella, she read. *The days seem longer and longer now that*

we are farther and farther apart. I watch the rain outside the classroom win-
dow and I think of you. I sit at night alone in the darkness and I think of you.

I shiver when I remember the warm and glowing times we shared
together. The gathered memories, like chimes, flood my soul with melody. It is
a tune of thrills, deeper than any symphony. Yet, like a hymn, it stills all worry,
all foolish fears, because it hums in future years. Now, it echoes a duet. The
harmony high, the melody low. And may the great Musician let it swell, some
day, in fortissimo.

She laid her hand over the letter and smiled at me. I knew she wasn't
in the library anymore. She was seventeen again, an innocent, young
schoolgirl back in that little town in northeastern Iowa, lying alone on her
bed. She read on.

Reflections on a Rainy Day
by Robert Harold Schuller
Raindrops—
Those moody little raindrops
Seem to smother my window-pane.
They haunt my mind with something;
But I search for the thought in vain.
I'm sure they rest serenely
As they snooze on the fallen leaves.
Their trip has made them lazy,
And they hang on the shingled eaves.
Perhaps they're a wee bit lonesome
For their cozy bed of sky.
And now they've made their journey
They can breathe a contented sigh.
Lonesome—
Lonesome, that's all
If she were here
I'd say, "My dear,
Let's take a moonlight walk."
I'd squeeze her hand
Its warmth is grand

And off we'd stroll and talk.
She'd smile a bit.
I love her wit.
Then reach some spot of bliss.
And there we'd stop.
Her arms would drop
Around me. (It's she I miss.)
—R. H. S.

"He was so exciting when I first met him. He was so sure of himself," Arvella said. "He loved the spotlight. When we were in high school, he was a senior and I was a freshman. He was in the school play." Arvella smiled as she talked. "The other actors got so upset with him because he would improvise in the middle of a performance and steal the show."

She looked up at me and said, "You know why I fell in love with him, Jim?"

I didn't have the answer.

"Because he had bigger dreams," she said. "He had bigger dreams than anyone I had ever met in my life. He used to talk about the things he was going to do. The places he was going to see, the people he was going to meet. I remember on one date, we were driving along in his car and he started telling me about the power of radio. He was fascinated by the number of people it could reach. He talked about what a great tool it could be to help people. He was…entrancing."

She looked back down at the letters in her lap. "What was so attractive about him were his dreams. He had bigger dreams. He was the most attractive man I had ever met." She paused and then smiled to herself, "He still is."

Arvella sifted through the stack of letters. She came upon an envelope that was the smallest of all. She opened the tiny flap and removed a small card. It was about the size of a thank-you note.

"This is my favorite one," she whispered. "He said he kept it in his drawer for a year before he sent it to me. This isn't really a love letter to me. It was a prayer he wrote to God."

She took a long pause. I think she wanted to be very careful that she read the words just right. She looked the letter over and said:

> You be the breeze, I'll be the cloud
> You be the wave, I'll be the sand
> You be the wind, I'll be the feather
> You be the arm, I'll be the hand.
> You be the sun, I'll be the shadow
> You be the hope, I'll be the dream
> You be the light, I'll be the window
> You be the love and I'll be the faith.
>
> —R. H. S

I had to catch myself, because those words caught my heart. My eyes started to mist up.

Arvella's face showed the anguish she was feeling. In the forty-one years they had been married, this was the only time he hadn't called her before going to bed. Now he was lying in an operating room halfway across the world and she was waiting to hear if he was alive or not.

Editor's note: Dr. Schuller eventually recovered from his surgery and continues his ministry at The Crystal Cathedral today.

SOMEONE TO COUNT ON

&

One knows what one has lost,
but not what one may find.

GEORGE SAND

Just the other day, a young lady pushing a man in a wheelchair came to the front of the church. His body was twisted and his face was permanently contorted into a sneer. Slumped over in his wheelchair, the man seemed oblivious to his surroundings.

I walked down the steps of our pulpit to speak with her, so that I could ascertain what their needs were. I was sure that she was an attendant assigned to care for the poor, unfortunate soul whose condition left him helpless and disfigured. I leaned down near her ear and whispered, "What may I do to assist you?" I was almost sure that she wanted prayer for her patient. I was taken aback when she introduced the man as her husband. With a strong chin and a stiff upper lip, she said that she and her husband wanted to join the church. She spoke with pride, as if he were standing beside her in a three-piece suit. I stumbled for words, embarrassed by my assumption yet sorry for their predicament. As I searched for words to answer her, she reached down to catch a stream of saliva that was extending from her husband's lips like single strand of spaghetti. She wiped him lovingly and stood back up to continue her request. She explained that her husband had been in a terrible accident that left him almost completely incapacitated. One day he was a healthy, vibrant, virile man; the next he was as he sat before me. I had to swallow to hide my tears, as I was filled first with admiration and then with awe at this woman who could love this man and treat him with great affection. I knew that she was with a man who could no longer hold her, touch her, or whisper in her ear. I knew that he had not lovingly patted her while they dressed for church or given her a sly look of promised love and fulfillment. I knew that he had not dried her neck when she slipped out of the shower with beads of moisture kissing her skin. I knew that she had the task of taking care of him while no one took care of her.

I tell this story to underscore that life does bring changes. When we stand before a congregation, a preacher, and God, we make vows in a few minutes that we may have to keep for the next fifty years or more. We make those vows and walk into the future, an abyss of unexpected adventure that can lead to peril without warning. The vows are a blank check that destiny will write as we walk through life together. It is altogether possible that we might have to keep those vows, the ones that say for better or for worse, for richer or for poorer, in sickness and in health. Will we be able to keep those promises in the face of calamity, poverty, and infirmity?

We all want someone we can count on to stand by us through thick or thin. This is the lover who matters. Most people think being a good lover is about being able to perform sexual feats with great skill and sensitivity. That would be fine if we spent all of our lives in bed. But the truth of the matter is a good lover doesn't start or end in the bedroom. A good lover is the one who stays when all others have walked away. It does not matter if he is as agile as a cat and as sensitive as a frayed nerve ending. If he does not love you with his heart, stroking your body and teasing your senses will soon become meaningless. Loving the body is not enough. Your mind and your spirit need to be cared for too. Who cares if your man is built like an Adonis if he doesn't stand by you in a storm? His twinkling eyes mean nothing if he does not prove to be reliable in a crisis. Oh, my friend, being a good lover is more than hips, lips, and fingertips. It is the ability to hold the cold wind of life in your hot hands until the wind warms under your loving touch. It is standing by the bed until the light goes out in my eyes and you kiss my face one final time. It is the ability to stay with me until the machine stops and the ventilator ceases to pump air into my lungs, and I speak one last time or squeeze your hand. If you ever have to fight a real storm, you will need a lover, but not the kind you might normally seek. This is a lover of the day, not just the night. Lovers that deal with the day are more difficult to find than the kind that grope you in the night. If a tragedy occurs economically or, worse still, physically, will he still be your lover? I know these are sobering thoughts that people seldom consider, but they are the realities of life.

T. D. JAKES "EMBRACING SOMEONE ELSE," FROM *THE LADY, HER LOVER, AND HER LORD* BY T. D. JAKES, © 1998 BY BISHOP T. D. JAKES. USED BY PERMISSION OF G. P. PUTNAM'S SONS, A DIVISION OF PENGUIN PUTNAM INC.

BASEBALL BILL

G

*I live with those who love me
whose hearts are kind and true.*

GEORGE LINNAEUS BANKS

*B*ill and Marlene were married right out of college and had a brilliant baseball career ahead of them. Bill was the star third baseman for a pennant-winning team and had one of the best earned run averages in his second professional year.

The year after, Bill was in an automobile accident and suffered an injury that put him out of baseball and more. His neck was broken by the collision, and he was confined to a wheelchair for the rest of his life.

Marlene was accustomed to baseball fame and a high style of living in the fast lane of celebrity. With the injury came enormous medical bills, experimental therapies, and round-the-clock nursing care. Their insurance did not cover the extensive medical treatments needed for Bill's recovery.

Marlene and Bill always enjoyed an energetic romance, but after the injury their love burned brighter even though they had little privacy during the recovery. Their intellectual conversations became the most attractive part of the day. Marlene looked forward to getting to know her husband on a deeper level and Bill was touched and strengthened by Marlene's commitment to him during this trial. During this time of physical challenge, dwindling finances, and heartbreaking disappointment, their love soared to new

289

heights and they understood that one's greatest need is to be loved uncon-ditionally. A tragedy simply polished the gold in their marriage to a new bril-liance.

AS TOLD TO FRAN BEAVER AND DOROTHY ALTMAN

Go seek her out all courteously,
And say I come,
Wind of species whose song is ever
Epithalamium.
O hurry over the dark lands
And run upon the sea
For seas and land shall not divide us
My love and me.
Now, wind of your good courtesy
I pray you go,
And come into her little garden
And sing at her window;
Singing: The bridal wind is blowing
For Love is at his noon;
And soon will your true love be with you,
Soon, O soon.

JAMES JOYCE

THE WALK THROUGH
THE VALLEY

There is in every true woman's heart
a spark of heavenly fire,
which lies dormant in the broad
daylight of prosperity;
but which kindles up, and beams and
blazes in the dark hour of adversity.

WASHINGTON IRVING

*L*ee and Doug were the perfect match—her weaknesses were his strengths, and vice versa. He was methodical and organized; she creative and daring. While she was given to strong emotions, he was calm. While he liked to plan everything, she loved spontaneous decisions and flights of fancy. One of the things they held in common was gratitude—they were thankful God had brought them together.

They were both also single working parents. Lee had a successful interior design business in Los Angeles, but marriage to Doug meant relocating with her young children to Canada.

It looked as if the pair of opposites would blend beautifully and enjoy a smooth life together—until they received shattering news only weeks before their wedding.

Doug was house-hunting in Toronto for their expanded family while Lee remained in Los Angeles to plan their wedding. One weekend Lee decided to take a break from her hectic schedule to get a little sun—then she wouldn't have to worry about sunburn when they were on their honeymoon in Hawaii. She also figured a little color would also look nice when she walked down the aisle in a few weeks. As she stretched out on her towel by the pool, Lee discovered a lump the size of a golf ball on her right side.

Fear gripped her as she ran to call Doug. One of the things Lee loved about Doug was that where she was fearful, he was unflappable. "It's probably nothing," he assured her. "Don't worry unless a doctor tells you to worry."

The doctors were less comforting. They told Lee bluntly but gently that she had advanced cancer of the colon and just a 20 percent chance of survival. Lee was stunned, but she was not afraid. As she sat in the doctor's office, she knew it just didn't make any sense that she would finally fall in love, plan to marry, and then die before her new life began. She determined to see the challenge through. Though self-pity tried to creep in, Lee replaced it with thanksgiving for Doug—someone so special to walk with her through this valley of the shadow of death. Lee felt a surge of faith, knowing God had a plan for her and Doug.

When Doug heard the news, he called his family physician for some reassurance. Instead, the doctor advised Doug not to marry Lee. "There's little chance that she will survive," he said as kindly as he could. "At least wait and see."

Doug felt a surprising well of hope. He left immediately to be with Lee during surgery. He told his wife-to-be, "We're going to beat this!"

The surgery went well, but Lee's doctor still gave a negative prognosis. Lee and Doug stayed strong: They wrote their wedding vows while Lee recovered! "Our wedding is only weeks away," they told the dubious hospital staff with determination, "and we're going to be married."

Lee had to begin chemotherapy immediately. Between wedding showers and parties, she attended her treatments. As the poison liquid dripped into her veins, she thought of Doug and their future together. And she thanked God.

Lee experienced a little queasiness and lost some weight but otherwise felt fine. Hope kept her buoyant, and the cloud she floated on carried her down the aisle into Doug's supportive and loving arms. Doug told her she was a beautiful bride: "No one would ever know you're ill," he said tenderly.

When the minister reached the words in the vow, "in sickness and in health," the wedding guests sobbed openly. Doug and Lee smiled knowingly and squeezed each other's hand.

The couple enjoyed a wonderful honeymoon. The only sad part was a bleak moment when Lee was brushing her hair and much of it came out in the brush. It reminded the couple of the reality of her illness, but it didn't dissuade them from joy. Doug reminded Lee that all that mattered was that they were together.

For the next two years Lee received the powerful chemo treatments. After seven years the doctors finally gave a new prognosis: Lee was cancer free and hopefully would remain so!

Eighteen years later, as Lee and Doug celebrated their anniversary in their California home, they looked back on their saga with—what else?—gratitude. Their greatest common bond sustained them during the fight of their lives, and it remains their source of strength and joy today.

LEE MINK AND DOUG BARR

TEAMWORK

✍

Two are better than one
For they have good return for their work.

ECCLESIASTES 4:9

When I was growing up, my parents imparted a great example to my sister, brother, and me about teamwork. My father was a "liberated man" who helped my mother with her duties. He was never ashamed of pitching in to help around the house. He'd mop the floor, vacuum, and even don an apron if Mother needed his help.

Mother did her part as well. She helped Daddy with the traditional "men's work." Together they would paint the house, wallpaper a bathroom, wash the cars, and plant the garden. One time the two of them even added a screened porch to the back of the house. As far as they were concerned, every duty was gender indifferent.

Duties were also age indifferent—my parents included us children in their projects at every opportunity, teaching us how to work as a team.

Just as Mother and Daddy entered their golden years, I married and sadly moved 2,000 miles away from them. Fortunately they are very healthy and I have had little cause for concern. My parents are enjoying their retirement. Both have boundless energy and are always involved in some new project. Recently they built a new home—quite a task for a couple their age! Daddy supervised every nail the builders hammered into their dream home and Mother enjoyed decorating when it was finished.

It gives me great peace of mind to know that they are enjoying one another's company to the fullest, still sharing their duties. And they are still teaching me about teamwork. They gave me a most poignant lesson recently when Daddy had to have surgery.

When the doctor told my father that he would have to undergo carpel tunnel surgery, my father tried to postpone it because it was the season for some serious gardening. The doctor insisted that the surgery couldn't wait.

When Mother phoned me with the news, she insisted that it wasn't necessary for me to come. "Your father won't even stay overnight at the hospital."

So I stayed in close touch by telephone. Mother called to tell me that the surgery had gone smoothly and Daddy was resting well, although in pain. Mother herself had a cold and wasn't feeling well. I wished I had gone home.

When I awoke the next day, I immediately called to see how Daddy had fared overnight and if Mother's cold was better. To my distress, there was no answer. "Ken," I told my husband, "I'm worried. Where could they be? Do you suppose Daddy has taken a turn for the worse and they're at the hospital? Or maybe Mother's cold became worse."

I sensed that Ken was concerned too as he tried to reach them several times. There was no answer. We left several urgent messages.

After three hours had passed, we decided to call the hospital. They hadn't admitted my father or my mother. Then we tried to call my brother, aunts, uncles, and cousins. No one was home. "They're at the emergency room with my parents," I told Ken as my anxiety heightened. I canceled my plans for the morning and sat by the phone and waited and prayed.

At last I received a call in the afternoon from Mother. "Where have you been?" I demanded.

She laughed.

"I'm sorry we worried you," she said, "but you know your father. He awoke early and insisted on taking a walk in garden. He spotted some tiny black bugs on his roses and we've been spraying the bushes."

"How on earth could he be spraying roses?" I asked. "Isn't his arm in a cast up to his shoulder?"

"Don't worry," Mother said. "I sprayed, he supervised."

Relieved, I marveled at their partnership. I told Ken, "They are certainly good role models for God's plan for marriage. Mother was Daddy's arm."

"Isn't that what's marriage is all about?" Ken reminded me. "Teamwork—especially in sickness and in health." I hugged Ken and thanked God for his beautiful design.

SUSAN WALES

In true marriage lies
Nor equal, or unequal
Each fulfills
Defect in each other, and always thought in thought,
Purpose in purpose, will in will, they grow
The single pure and perfect animal,
The two-cell'd beating with one full stroke, Life.
ALFRED, LORD TENNYSON

As Long As We Both Shall Live

Thy love is such I can no way repay,
The heavens reward thee manifold I pray.
Then while we live, in love so persever,
That when we live no more, we may live ever.

ANNE BRADSTREET

THERE IS AN ABSOLUTENESS TO THE WEDDING VOWS. BEFORE YOUR FRIENDS, FAMILY, AND GOD, YOU PLEDGE THAT AS LONG AS YOU DRAW BREATH, AS LONG AS YOUR HEART BEATS WITHIN YOU, YOU WILL BE THERE, WHOLLY AND TRUE, FOR YOUR BELOVED.

GOD DOESN'T TAKE YOUR VOWS LIGHTLY. THEY ARE SACRED—HOLY—TRANSCENDING THE MORTAL EARTHLY PLANE ON WHICH YOU LIVE YOUR LIFE. THE WITNESSES AND CONGREGATION GATHERED AT YOUR WEDDING HOLD YOU ACCOUNTABLE AND FAITHFUL TO THE PROMISES YOU MAKE. WHAT GOD JOINS TOGETHER, NO ONE TEARS APART WITHOUT BEING FULLY ACCOUNTABLE TO HIM.

LIFELONG MARRIAGE WAS GOD'S PLAN FROM THE TIME OF CREATION SO HE DESIGNED YOU, BODY, SOUL, AND SPIRIT, TO

BE MOST FULFILLED WITH ONE PARTNER UNTIL DEATH. THERE IS NO SECOND-BEST OPTION IN GOD'S BOOK. SO BE BOLD AS YOU PREPARE TO LOVE UNTIL DEATH DO YOU PART. AS YOU LIVE WHAT THIS MEANS, YOU WILL FIND THE MOST SATISFYING PLACE IN GOD'S GREAT UNIVERSE. YOU WILL FIND PEACE OF HEART AND DYNAMIC LOVE THAT LASTS.

YOU FIND A STATE OF GRACE THE MOMENT YOU REPEAT, "...AS LONG AS WE BOTH SHALL LIVE."

ANNIVERSARIES

Courage is grace under pressure.
ERNEST HEMINGWAY

aul and I loved any excuse to celebrate. We marked birthdays, anniversaries, family reunions, and all of the national holidays with good food, good company, and warm togetherness. Our life had a foundation of joy.

I met Paul, a junior in college in my hometown, when I was just eighteen. He was a returning veteran who'd never expected to go to college; I was a freshman just out of high school. Our courtship was as romantic as a storybook fairy tale. I felt proud that such a man saw something special in me.

After we became engaged, we spent a year apart. Eight hundred miles away, Paul earned a master's degree while I toiled on at the local newspaper where I'd worked summers and weekends. I wrote a twice-weekly column and postponed my dreams of finishing college. It was the first of many sacrifices Paul and I both made in our forty-three years together.

But along with the sacrifices, there was love—enduring, faithful, unselfish—on both our parts. That love, on his part, encompassed kindness—the first quality of his I fell in love with. He never went to sleep without saying, "I love you." I returned his love by establishing a happy home and supporting him in everything he did, no matter what trials we faced.

The years brought six children and many changes, but we built on our foundation of joy with family parties for every occasion. We always celebrated the Fourth of July by finding a spot where we could view for free the city's beautiful and exciting display of fireworks. We would pop several bags of popcorn, fill a gallon jug with iced tea, and make an event of the evening.

On New Year's Eve, we always had a party for our friends. Paul showed his festive spirit by starting a conga line through the house just before midnight.

For Paul's birthday I always made a white cake with peanut butter and marshmallow frosting, an invention of his Aunt Helen's. Because his birthday fell in April, near Easter, the children and I decorated his cake with jelly beans spelling *DAD*.

Eventually our family nest emptied. Paul and I continued to celebrate special days and events, and the children joined us whenever they could. Then illness numbered our days together. Bedfast, Paul asked me one July 5, over and over, what day it was.

I had hung a calendar near his bed, but I'm not sure he ever really saw it. Sadness engulfed me as I realized that he was losing his grip on time. Of course, neither of us knew he had only a week more to live.

When he anxiously and tearfully repeated the date, I asked why he was concerned. He said, "You know why. This is the first year we haven't done something for the Fourth of July."

I knew.

After I lost Paul, celebrations took on a different flavor, but I kept them. Our foundation was firm and our joy was worth maintaining. This year, our daughter and son-in-law invited me to take part in the Independence Day celebration in their hometown, Sterling-Rock Falls, Illinois. The love and consideration they showed me helped me miss Paul less.

I've started a new tradition at Christmastime. So that I can celebrate with loved ones instead of alone, I leave my hometown and head West for visits with our son in San Francisco, our daughter and her husband in Huntington Beach, and a friend in San Diego.

Paul's birthday is still an important event, but I no longer bake an elaborate cake. Nowadays I buy jelly beans to put on top of graham crackers spread with peanut butter for a little private ceremony of my own.

I often get together with our friends. When invited out with couples with whom Paul and I once shared bridge games and evenings together, I make sure I stay interested, that I add to the laughter and not remind them of my loss; they are well aware of the loss of someone whose wry and witty humor was always part of the fun.

And I remember Paul daily in a little ritual. I complete a puzzle— "find six differences between pictures"—published among the classified ads in the newspaper that he worked every day. When I succeed I say, "We did it again, honey," with a real sense of accomplishment.

The celebrations keep Paul present to me. I see him in glorious sunrises and in the phases of the moon. I talk to him among the stars. I imagine him embraced by the saving arms of Jesus and helping Jesus welcome our deceased friends as newcomers to heaven. I know he's the first to throw a party for every familiar face, and I know that one day, Paul and I will celebrate our love again, on our first anniversary in heaven.

HELEN TROISI ARNEY

A LETTER FROM
MY HEART

☙

'Tis the last rose of summer
Left blooming alone
All her lovely companions
Are faded and gone.

THOMAS MOORE

Saying that final good-bye is the hardest thing a couple ever has to do, but some partners find creative ways to ease the transition for one another. Maynard Smith is one of those. He wanted his wife, Helen, to let the joy of their lives together overwhelm the pain of their parting, so he thoughtfully wove loving words into a secret letter. After his death, his secretary told Helen of the letter tucked quietly away in a safety deposit box.

When Helen read the letter, Maynard's wish was fulfilled. His touching tribute to his wife and their marriage brought comfort, thankfulness, and release—all the ingredients of a healthy and timely good-bye. Here are the words Maynard wrote from his heart.

Dearest Helen,

I'm writing this while in good health and am happy with no real worries in this world. This seems like a strange time for the thoughts I'm about to express, but what could really be a better time? I know that at some future date I am going to depart this world and I would hate it if I did not have a chance to say to you the things I feel so strongly.

To begin with, I could not have used better judgment than when I asked you to share my life with me and let me share in yours. There has never been a minute when I felt otherwise. You have been all that anyone could expect or hope for in a mate. I have never doubted your love or loyalty. I have said to others and I want to say it to you now: You are truly the finest human being I have known in my life. God did not make many, if any, like you and I have never forgotten to be grateful for my good fortune. I love you as a wife, a mother, and as a friend with a tenderness that can't be described. You have given your very best and that was always good enough—perfect in fact. You caught all the passes, made the third-down plays, and crossed the goal line when called upon.

HM may not completely appreciate her mother now and this is natural, but some day, she will realize what a fortunate daughter she has been to have a mother like you. I really don't know how to write a farewell letter to you and I suppose there is no adequate way, but I had to try as feeble as this effort is. I know as I write this that I am not able to express what I feel so deeply. Words can't do it justice. Just know in your heart, as I know, that your role in life has been one of perfection and you should never feel any regrets about anything.

Don't be sad. God could not have been better to me. I have had a great life, good fortune…my wife, my daughter, my profession, my friends, and my associates. What more could anyone ask? I have tried to be true and honorable in my life so you would be proud of me. I'm sure I could have done better and should have, but after all I was human and thus unable to be all that I would have liked to have been.

You know that I have never doubted that there is a God and a hereafter. I firmly believe this is not the end. I believe there is a place where I am going that is better than the one I am leaving.

I look forward to seeing my mother, my father, and my friends who have preceded me. And my dearest, I will be looking forward to spending an eternity with you in another land when your life is over.

Remember, you have no reason to grieve. Make a new life. Marry if you find someone that can make you happy and you can make him happy. Life and death are as natural as any other fact of life. Accept it. Living alone is no good and I want you to be happy. Just don't be as happy with anyone as I think you were with me! I could say something cute here and you know what it would be, but this is not the time.

I love you in life and I will love you in death just as truly and tenderly as the day I married you.

Me

HELEN SMITH

THE WAY WE WERE

_&_

Hitch your wagon to a star;
keep your seat and there you are.

ANONYMOUS

he Way We Were" is more than a heartfelt ballad by Barbra Streisand. For George and me it is a theme song for a joyful part of our life story.

When our story began we existed in separate worlds. We had both been involved in unhappy marriages and disappointed in love. I was working as principal of a school for juvenile delinquents in Alabama. George and his partner owned a successful insurance agency in Georgia.

A dear friend who was a center of influence in my life kept encouraging me to try another business. Finally, I decided to take the plunge and became an insurance sales agent in Alabama. It was very rare in those days for a female to work in that field.

After my first year in the business, I attended my first national business conference in Georgia. The head of my Alabama agency called our sister agency in Georgia. He happened to speak to George and said, "Why don't you go to the conference and meet my new female agent?"

George had already planned to welcome all of the attendees to Georgia and to extend an invitation to visit his office. Since George and his partner had one of the top-ten agencies in the country, all of the attendees wanted to visit them.

I will never forget our first meeting. It was break time, and I had left the conference room for some fresh air. A dashing young man in a three-piece suit came up to me, holding out his hand to shake mine. He said, "You must be the new female agent from Alabama!" He kept talking and holding my hand. I don't remember what he said because I was very uncomfortable. He was too charming, too self-assured, and too much into my personal space. I finally retrieved my hand from his grip and returned to the meeting. George returned to his office.

As it turns out, my hard work and perseverance over the last year had paid off; I had written more premium-dollar contracts than any other first-year person in the nation, so I was to be honored at this conference. Since I was also the first woman to win the award, the company had to change the title from New Man of the Year to New Agent of the Year.

After the awards were given and the conference was over, the company had hired an orchestra for dancing. It seemed that everyone except me had a partner and was heading for the dance floor. I was sitting alone at a table when George came up and asked me to dance. This time, for some reason, I did not feel crowded or put off. Both of us loved dancing and we had a wonderful, crazy evening. We danced to every song that the orchestra played. George had a great sense of humor and projected a genuine love of life. It's amazing how well we got to know each other while he was twirling me around the dance floor!

Our courtship continued and Streisand's "The Way We Were" provided the soundtrack for a love that continued to grow. We were married a year later.

We enjoyed almost twenty-two years before George died of cancer. Now when I listen to our song the words make me cry. I was blessed with the perfect husband and "cherish the memories" and the man who helped create them.

MARILYN MURDOCK

THE GUIDE

❧

Love consists of this:
To be able to find joy in another's.
MARIA RANIER RILKE

e'd been married less than a year when my husband, Jerry, and I moved to Atlanta with great anticipation. I had finally gotten my big break in publishing. And Jerry, in an enormous show of support, had quit his job just so I could reach for my brass ring.

The day the movers delivered our furniture in Atlanta couldn't have gone any smoother. They were quick and careful and also understanding of our stress. In fact, one of the men kept taking time out to throw the ball for my Shetland sheepdog, Gypsy, who was being completely ignored in all the hustle and bustle.

At the end of the day we sat on the back deck and looked up at the heavens. Somehow the stars in Atlanta seemed brighter and happier to me than anywhere else I'd ever lived. I still had a week to get our nest completely built before I started my job, and Jerry had received a good job lead. We were truly feeling blessed.

The next day was Saturday, and we got to meet some of our new neighbors. On the west side was a sweet elderly couple, Art and Maggie, who laughed a lot and spoke of world travels together over their forty-seven years of marriage. They were a warm pair, and Art had a keen sense of humor: "I only married Maggie to get her to stop begging me to marry her." Maggie simply giggled like a schoolgirl and shook her head. We also met the couple who lived behind us—coincidentally they had a dog just like ours. Moving to an unfamiliar place is always such a gamble, but this time it seemed to be turning out just right.

Again that evening, Jerry and I found ourselves on our back deck, stargazing. It was becoming our nightly routine. We began imagining our future selves. Would we be like Maggie and Art, still laughing together after nearly five decades of marriage? We wondered how many times Art had told his funny "stop the begging" line. More so, we pondered how many times Maggie had laughed and pretended it was the first time she had ever heard it. They were truly friends, a sometimes rare and wonderful element in a lifelong union.

With all our good fortune, imagine how far from cloud nine I fell when we awoke on Monday morning to the sound of our lovely dog coughing and thrashing on the floor, having some sort of seizure. We rushed her to a vet but were grieved to learn that we needed to put her to sleep right away. Unbeknownst to us, she had had a brain tumor, probably for years, that finally destroyed her life. We were heartsick.

That night I sat in my new living room unable to stop the tears. I knew it was probably childish. After all, Gypsy was just a dog, right? I tried to look through the window at those stars that seemed so brilliant the night before, but they all blurred together like snow. Then my eye caught something odd. A dark, slow-moving car was creeping into our driveway. Something was very wrong.

It was a hearse. The driver, in a black suit and cap, got out of the car and walked up to ring our bell. Jerry answered, and I could hear their voices, but I couldn't make out any words. After what seemed like hours, Jerry sat beside me and said the driver needed to park in our driveway because there was no room in our elderly neighbors' drive. I looked around and for the first time noticed that there were ten or fifteen cars parked along our street, along with a fire truck and ambulance. Jerry went on to explain that apparently Art had passed away peacefully during a nap on the couch. And by the family's request, a hearse instead of the usual ambulance had been requested to move the body.

Of course we let the driver park in our driveway. Jerry immediately went next door to see if there was anything we could do. I should have gone too, but I just sat frozen on the couch, feeling hurt and helpless. Frustrated, I threw a dog ball hard into the next room, but it only started the tears again when Gypsy didn't bring it back.

I carried so much shame that week, knowing I'd failed my new neighbor in her time of need. Guilt consumed me when I saw Maggie over the fence, although she seemed to be doing fine and was surrounded by loved ones. She even kept her normal routine of babying her day lilies and rose beds. But I still couldn't say anything. I was still distraught over Gypsy's death, and my throat seemed paralyzed.

Not too many days later, the funeral was over and all of Maggie's relatives went home. I was flattening one of our last packing boxes and stacking it outside with the others when I saw Maggie tending her garden. She had her back to me but I could hear her humming a sad tune.

I knew I needed to apologize for not visiting her. As I worked on what to say, Maggie turned around and said, "Dee Ann, come here for a minute."

My heart jumped into my throat as I walked toward our adjoining fence. Before I could stammer out a word, Maggie grabbed my hand and looked at me with her soft brown eyes. With the most tender voice she said, "I want to give you something—something to think about."

She wants to give me something? I thought.

Maggie squeezed my hand and said, "Dee Ann, I know you've been troubled these last days. Sometimes God's plans for us don't seem to make any sense at all. And I must admit I've had some choice words with him myself, but only because I miss Arty so very much." She straightened her back and lifted her chin, trying to swallow her tears. "But, young lady, I want you to try to have an open mind about what I want to tell you."

I was confused. *Is this grieving widow trying to comfort me?*

Maggie continued, "Arty was an old man, Dee Ann. He couldn't see very well anymore and that really bothered him. He didn't mind losing part of his hearing and he rarely complained about his arthritis. But not being able to work in his summer garden and not being able to read his

Bible were things he could never adjust to."

I felt like I needed to jump in and say something reassuring, but her eyes locked with mine and I thought better of it.

After a moment of silence, Maggie patted my hand and smiled. "Did you ever think that maybe, just maybe, God needed a little dog to help guide Art into the gates of heaven?"

To this day Maggie and I remain dear friends. I will forever be grateful for the sense of closure she gave me and for how she didn't judge my pain, never thinking her sorrow should have been more of a priority than mine. But most of all, I'll always remember Maggie holding my hand, comforting me at a time when she needed it most.

DEE ANN GRAND

DELAYED DELIVERY

If I could have thought thou couldst have died
I might not weep for thee;
But I forgot, when by thy side
That thou couldst mortal be;
Yet there was round thee such a dawn
Of light never seen before,
As fancy never could have drawn,
And never can restore!

CHARLES WOLFE

Stella had known that Dave wouldn't live to see Christmas. When the doctors had diagnosed her husband's terminal cancer last January, her world had shattered. But through the ensuing months Dave had managed to put his affairs in order, to show her everything she needed to learn about managing the house, everything except how to live without him. Now the loneliness weighed upon her like lethargy, stealing her energy, her ability to find joy in life, even in Christmas.

She had turned down an invitation to spend the holiday with old friends in Florida. Somehow that had seemed worse than staying home alone. Not only would she miss her husband of forty-eight years, but she would miss the snow and the familiarity of home. They had been a childless couple and in the last decade had lost several friends and even family. But it had all been bearable with Dave by her side. Bearable until now.

A snowstorm was brewing outside the window as Stella prepared a bowl of soup. She ate slowly, moving the radio knob with one hand, stopping at the sound of a familiar Christmas carol. The sudden, joyful chorus only served to deepen her loneliness. With shaky fingers she lowered the volume to a muted background.

She was surprised by the slap of damp envelopes on the floor as the mailman dropped them through the door slot. She left her soup to retrieve them. Moving to the living room, she sat on the piano bench and opened them. They were mostly Christmas cards and her eyes smiled at the traditional scenes and the loving messages inside. Carefully, her arthritic fingers arranged them among the others clustered on the piano top. In her entire house they were the only seasonal decoration. The holiday was days away and she just didn't have the heart to put up the tree or bring out the stable that Dave had lovingly built.

Suddenly engulfed by the finality of her aloneness, Stella buried her lined face in her hands, lowering her elbows to the piano keys in an abrasive discord and let the tears come. How would she get through Christmas and the dismal winter months beyond?

The ring of the doorbell startled her. Who could be calling on such a stormy day? The doorbell rang a second time. Wiping her eyes, she pulled herself up off the bench to answer it.

On her front porch, buffeted by waves of wind and snow stood a young man, his hatless head barely visible above the large carton in his arms. She peered beyond him to the driveway, but there was nothing about the small car to give a clue to his identity.

"Mrs. Thornhope?"

Stella nodded.

"I have a package for you."

Curiosity won over caution. She pushed the door open enough for the stranger to shoulder it and stepped back into the foyer to make room. He brought with him the frozen breath of the storm. Smiling, he carefully placed his burden down, then handed her the envelope that he pulled from an inner jacket pocket. Suddenly, a muffled yelp came from the box. Stella actually jumped. The man laughed and bent to straighten up the cardboard flaps wide enough for her to peek inside.

It was a dog! A yellow Labrador puppy, to be exact. The man lifted its squirming body up into his arms and explained, "This is for you, ma'am. He's six weeks old and housebroken." The young pup wiggled in happiness at being released from captivity and lapped ecstatic kisses on the young man's chin. "We were supposed to deliver him on Christmas Eve," he continued with some difficulty, trying to raise his chin out of reach, "but the staff at the kennel wanted tomorrow off. Hope you don't mind an early present."

When Stella made no move to take the animal from him, he placed him on the floor. "But who...?" she stammered.

The young man tapped the envelope in her fingers. "The letter pretty much explains everything. The dog was purchased last July while his mother was still pregnant. It was meant to be a Christmas gift. I have some other things in the car. I'll get them."

Before she could protest, he disappeared back into the snowstorm. He returned carrying another big box with a leash, dog food, and a book entitled *Caring for Your Labrador Retriever.* All this time the puppy had sat quietly at her feet, panting happily as his brown eyes watched her.

The stranger was turning to go. "But who...who bought it?"

Pausing in the doorway, his words all but snatched away by the wind, he replied, "Your husband, ma'am." And then he was gone.

It was all in the letter. Forgetting the puppy entirely at the sight of his familiar handwriting, Stella walked to her armchair by the window. Unaware that the little dog had followed her, she forced tear-filled eyes to read her husband's words. He had written it three weeks before his death and had left it with the kennel owners to be delivered with the puppy as his last gift to her. It was full of love and admonishments to be strong. He vowed that he was waiting for the day when she would join him. Until then, this dog would keep her company.

Remembering the little creature for the first time she was surprised to find him patiently looking up at her. Stella put the pages aside and reached for the bundle of golden fur. She had thought he would be heavier, but he was only the size and weight of a sofa pillow. And so soft and warm. She cradled him in her arms and he licked her jaw, then snuggled into the hollow of her neck. Her tears began again.

Finally Stella lowered him to her lap where he regarded her solemnly. She wiped vaguely at her cheeks, then mustered a smile.

"Well, little guy, I guess it's you and me." Her gaze shifted sideways to the window. Dusk had fallen and the storm seemed to have spent the worst of its fury. Through fluffy flakes that were drifting down at a gentler pace, she saw the cheery Christmas lights that edged the roof lines of her neighbors' homes. The strains of "Joy to the World" floated in from the kitchen.

Stella's grief and loneliness subsided and a new sensation of peace came over her like a loving embrace. Rising from her chair, she spoke to the little dog whose ears perked up at the sound of her voice. "You know, fella, there's a box in the basement with a tree in it and lights I think you'd like. And I think I can find that old stable too. What d'ya say we go hunt for it?"

The puppy barked in agreement, as if he understood every word.

CATHY MILLER

THE GOOD-BYE KISS

To know of someone here and
there whom we accord with,
who is living on with us, even in silence—
this makes our earthly fall a peopled garden.

WILHELM MEISTER'S APPRENTICESHIP
(1786–1830)

I am so aware in life that God is interested in details in our lives that are important to us. My father was seventy-nine years old, he had congestive heart disease, and his life was coming to an end. He knew it and all the people who loved him knew it. As he prepared for his next life there were conditions that were important to him that God was merciful and sensitive to. It was such a testimony that God is not only interested in how we live, but in how we die.

In death, it was important to my father that he leave here from his farm, in his bedroom, surrounded by his family.

My father was a very special man, loved and respected by all that knew him. He was orphaned by age nine and it seemed that everyone that he loved and knew had died before he was twelve years old. In spite of this, he grew up with a vision to have a wife and family. He worked as a tenant farmer until he was able to purchase his own farm. God was his father; he provided and instructed him in how to prosper.

He and my mother worked hard and accomplished a marriage of fifty-two years. Near the end of his life, God moved me back to Georgia from Texas, so that I could spend time with him during the last days of his life. In the year and a half that I had with him, God prepared us to say good-bye.

During his illness, God surrounded my father with all who loved him. As he convalesced, there was a steady stream of loved ones that came to visit him and tell him how much they loved him.

In spite of his weakness, he wanted to visit with everyone—and he would get really irritated if we tried to protect him. He would wake every morning and get ready for his company, no matter how weak he was.

His final wish was that he would die at home, surrounded by his family and friends. The day came and my mother called me to say that it was time to come home. He woke when I arrived and then went into a coma later that day. As my mother stood over him, stroking his head and comforting him, he regained consciousness, puckered up, and with all the strength he had in him, pulled her to him and kissed her, with the longest and most passionate kiss ever.

It was their good-bye kiss.

KAY JONES

TRAVELIN' MAN

⌖

Paradise itself were dim
And joyless, if not shared with him!
THOMAS MOORE

Throughout our marriage, my husband, Art, has traveled. In the first twenty years of our marriage, he left early Monday morning and returned late Friday evening by car or plane. As a young bride, I would cry when Art would leave and count the hours until he returned. When he was late returning home, I would pace the floor imagining all sorts of terrible things that could have happened to him. I'm embarrassed to admit that on more than one occasion, I called the hospital or the police station to make sure he wasn't in a car accident. The very thought of living without Art was too painful to comprehend.

When Art would return home from his weekly trip, I would run into his open arms…just like the movies. Art always brought me—and later the children—a little memento from each trip. Soap from the hotel, a book of matches from a well-known restaurant, or a pen that advertised, "See Rock City." After thirty years you can imagine the collection I amassed in our attic!

After our fourth child was born, our lives were perfectly normal—until Art would leave town. It seemed that something bad always happened when he was gone. He was in Seattle when Sally broke her arm, and when Eddie was bitten by the dog he was in New York. I recall that Art was in Kansas City when Jeffery got caught smoking in the boys' bathroom at school, and when Eric flunked his math test, Art was in Miami. You tell me the name of a city and I can tell you what traumatic event occurred in our family!

Now that our children are grown and have left home and Art has been promoted several times, he doesn't travel as often. It's funny, but I almost miss his time away—at least for short periods. My eyes light up when he tells me he is scheduled to go out of town. No longer a young wife and mother, I look forward to my time alone. I stash a pile of books away that I can devour while he's away. I eat frozen dinners that I prepare in the microwave or go out with my girlfriends for pizza. Yes, now when Art travels, I cherish the time we have apart and I have a glorious time. And I don't worry about his safety. My faith and trust in God has also grown through the years.

And when Art returns from one of his infrequent trips, it's like a honeymoon all over again. It's true what they say: Absence makes the heart grow fonder! My heart beats faster as I anticipate his arrival while I drive to airport to pick up my date! I always plan a romantic dinner for two, or we go out to a favorite restaurant and share what's gone on in our lives when we are apart. It's all very exciting and keeps the romance alive in our lives. Isn't it funny how we change with age? Instead of praying for him to come home, I now pray for him to travel!

But one memorable day, I wanted Art home more desperately than at any time when we were young. Like so many times before, that Monday morning I had driven my husband to the airport, pecked his cheek, waved good-bye, and drove away. I uttered the same little prayer I've been praying for thirty years—"Please God, bring Art safely back to me"—as I watched him disappear into a tiny speck in my rearview mirror.

I glanced at the clock and realized that I was going to be late for school! You see, when Art and I first married, we hadn't planned for me get pregnant right away, but it happened. We had promised one another that when the time came for the baby to go to first grade, I would go back to college, but that time never came...only more babies! When the kids left home, I went back to college and I would be graduating in just two weeks. Art had surprised me on our drive to the airport this morning when he told me that he had planned a trip to Hawaii for just the two of us to celebrate my graduation. "And if we love it," he'd said, "I'll retire and we might just move there—life is so short!" I nodded in agreement. I had dreams of being an interior designer and I could be a designer in Hawaii just as well as I could in Chicago.

When I returned home from school that afternoon, I was still dreaming of Hawaii as I picked up the remote and began to channel surf until I settled on my favorite talk show. As I listened intently, the program was suddenly interrupted by a news bulletin. My whole world went black and the room began to spin as the tears began flowing. Because I'd been in class, I hadn't heard the earlier news bulletins, but there had been a plane crash. It was the airline Art was flying on, near the city where his meeting was scheduled.

I immediately fell to my knees and begged God to spare Art, but then the news bulletin announced, "There are no survivors." I reached for the cordless phone—not taking my eyes off the television. I tried to get through to the 800 number that was flashing across my television screen, but the lines were busy. I called out for God to please help me and give me strength. Just minutes ago, I was dreaming about Hawaii, and now my dear husband was gone! I fell to the floor, this time face down.

The doorbell rang and there stood my precious neighbor, Ann Johnson. "Was Art on that plane?" Ann asked sympathetically. We had talked over the fence to Ann and her husband, Charlie, before we left for the airport this morning, so word had spread quickly through the neighborhood. When Ann looked at my ashen, tear-streaked face, she didn't have to ask me any more questions. She hugged me and pulled me down beside her on the sofa and then said a sweet prayer asking God to sustain us through this dark hour. The next thing I knew our pastor was at the door. Carol from across the street was at my backdoor, bringing a casserole. We were all on the sofa with our eyes glued to the television when another person walked through the back door.

"What's happening?" It was a familiar voice, the most familiar I had ever known. It was the voice of my dear husband.

"Arrrrrrt? What…are you doing…here?" called out our pastor, who looked as though he'd seen a ghost. The rest of us were speechless.

"I lived here the last time I checked," he said matter-of-factly. Suddenly concerned, Art asked, "Did someone die?"

"Yeah, you," I blurted as I embraced my puzzled husband and cried. There were tears of joy mixed with relief.

"Would someone please tell me what's going on?" he pleaded.

"Didn't I put you on that airplane this morning?" I asked, still trembling.

"Yes," he explained, "but my business partner paged me. Our meeting was canceled, so I took a cab over to our office by the airport where I've been working most of the day. I didn't phone because one of the guys agreed to drop me by the house on his way to a sales call. What on earth is going on?"

Everyone spoke at once, explaining to Art that the plane on which he had reservations had crashed leaving no survivors. He was stunned and grateful—very grateful—that his meeting had been canceled and that he had missed that flight.

As Art and I sat down to dinner later that night, we prayed for the family and friends of the plane crash victims. We were awed that his canceled meeting had saved his life.

"I was ready to meet my Maker," Art assured me. "But I'm glad it wasn't my time."

I knew without a doubt that God once again heard the same old prayer that I'd been praying for thirty years and spared my husband's life. I suddenly thought of all the other wives, mothers, husbands, and family members who had uttered a prayer for their loved ones that morning, and I was even more grateful that my husband's time had not come.

I was never more happy to have Art home as I was that night.

SYLVIA TAYLOR, AS TOLD TO SUSAN WALES

THE RED CARNATIONS

The music in my heart I bore
Long after it was heard no more.
WILLIAM WORDSWORTH

When Coretta Scott agreed to marry the charismatic Martin Luther King Jr., she knew that she would have to share the great leader with the world. The late civil rights leader was the recipient of the Nobel Peace Price in the '60s for his work in human rights. He was also considered the torchbearer in the Civil Rights movement, and organized peaceful marches and protests throughout the country. Perhaps it was because Coretta Scott King knew God had called them that she was able to bear the separation and loneliness of her husband's travels.

Coretta Scott King describes her husband's thoughtfulness and love for her in her book, *My Life with Martin Luther King Jr.*

The strain of Martin's responsibilities was growing more intense. At the suggestion of his doctor, he decided to go away for a few days' rest. Then, on March 12, just before he was to leave, he called me on the telephone from his office and asked, "Did you get the flowers?"

I told him that none had come, and Martin explained that when he was downtown shopping for some much-needed clothing for himself, he had gone next door to the florist and purchased some flowers for me. The proprietor had promised to deliver them right away. I was touched by this gesture of love. By the time he had come home to pick up his bag to leave for the airport, the flowers had arrived.

They were beautiful red carnations, but when I touched them I realized they were artificial. In all the years we had been together Martin had never sent me artificial flowers. It seemed so unlike him. I kissed him and thanked him. I said, "They are beautiful and they're artificial."

"Yes," Martin said. "I wanted to give you something that you could always keep."

They were the last flowers I ever got from Martin. Somehow in some strange way, he seemed to have known how long they would have to last here.

Less than a month later, Martin Luther King Jr. left for the sanitation workers' strike in Memphis. The couple kissed good-bye like they had so many times before. In a few weeks he was planning to lead the Poor People's March in Washington.

This trip was not without risks, however Coretta and Martin both knew that his life was always in jeopardy but they could not deny the work that God had given them to do. It was not surprising that the jet that carried Martin and his delegation to Memphis had to be thoroughly checked prior to takeoff. A death threat followed Martin wherever he went.

When he arrived in Memphis, Martin called Coretta to tell her he loved her as he always did when he was away.

The next afternoon, April 4, 1968, on the hotel balcony, a gunshot shattered the lives, the hopes, and the dreams of Martin Luther King Jr. and his wife Coretta, as well as black men, women, and children throughout the world. A few hours later she received the news of her husband's death.

Once Coretta Scott King had walked the road to freedom with her husband, and now she walked alone. With God's strength she flew to Memphis and led the march in her husband's place, giving comfort and hope to all his followers. Later this beautiful and courageous widow stood in for her husband at the Poor People's March in Washington, D.C., where 3,000 marchers were expected and 50,000 came to show their support.

Today, the red carnations are a reminder of her husband's love. You see, Martin unknowingly sent this bouquet that would have to last a lifetime. Neither he nor Coretta knew what was going to happen that day in Memphis. *God knew.*

Editor's note: Mrs. King established the Martin Luther King Jr. Center for Social Change in Atlanta in her husband's memory.